'Guy Harrison has produced a fascinating book ranging and genuinely new facets of psycho-spiritu compelling blend of personal research and inter-disciplinary reflection puts flesh and feeling on the bones of rigorous analysis. A truly holistic achievement which prom   radical thinking'

— *Revd. Canon Dr M   al and*
pastoral theological educator, forme   and
Lead Chaplain at   Hospitals

'This book will be required reading for the rapidly growing number of health care practitioners and trainees who want to know more about the contribution psychologically-informed spiritual care can make to psychological health in the UK. Accessible and engaging, it provides an excellent overview of the development of psycho-spiritual care in the context of holistic health. Harrison and his colleagues invite the reader on an important journey, grounded in innovative research and illustrated with fascinating case vignettes, which gives a voice to the lived experience of patients and health care staff alike.'

— *Professor Simon du Plock, Head of the Faculty of Post-Qualification and Professional Doctorate, Metanoia Institute & Middlesex University*

'This easy-to-read book draws on more than two decades of experience of working with patients and carers. The result is a compelling book that provides important insights into the nature of care and caring. Highly recommended for all who are interested in contributing to a holistic care environment.'

— *Professor Debra Jackson PhD FACN, Director of the Oxford Institute of Nursing, Midwifery & Allied Health Research (OxINMAHR)*

of related interest

Spiritual Care in Common Terms
How Chaplains Can Effectively Describe the Spiritual
Needs of Patients in Medical Records
Gordon J. Hilsman, D.Min.
Foreword by James H. Gunn
ISBN 978 1 78592 724 9
eISBN 978 1 78450 369 7

Journeying with Psyche and Soul
Spiritual Accompaniment and Counselling in Dialogue
Edited by Peter Madsen Gubi
ISBN 978 1 78592 025 7
eISBN 978 1 78450 271 3

Hope and Grace
Spiritual Experiences in Severe Distress, Illness and Dying
Dr Monika Renz
Translated by Mark Kyburz
ISBN 978 1 78592 030 1
eISBN 978 1 78450 277 5

Spiritual Care in Practice
Case Studies in Healthcare Chaplaincy
Edited by George Fitchett and Steve Nolan
Foreword by Christina Puchalski
ISBN 978 1 84905 976 3
eISBN 978 0 85700 876 3

**Assessing and Communicating the Spiritual
Needs of Children in Hospital**
A New Guide for Healthcare Professionals and Chaplains
Alister Bull
ISBN 978 1 84905 637 3
eISBN 978 1 78450 116 7

Positive Psychology Approaches to Dementia
Edited by Chris Clarke and Emma Wolverson
Foreword by Christine Bryden
ISBN 978 1 84905 610 6
eISBN 978 1 78450 077 1

Spiritual Care with Sick Children and Young People
A handbook for chaplains, paediatric health professionals,
arts therapists and youth workers
Paul Nash, Kathryn Darby and Sally Nash
ISBN 978 1 84905 389 1
eISBN 978 1 78450 063 4

Psycho-spiritual Care
in Health Care Practice

EDITED BY GUY HARRISON

Jessica Kingsley *Publishers*
London and Philadelphia

Tami Spry's poem on autoethography on pages 47–48 is published with kind permission of Sage Publications Ltd.

First published in 2017
by Jessica Kingsley Publishers
73 Collier Street
London N1 9BE, UK
and
400 Market Street, Suite 400
Philadelphia, PA 19106, USA

www.jkp.com

Library of Congress Cataloging in Publication Data
Title: Psycho-spiritual care in health care practice / edited by Guy Harrison.
Description: London ; Philadelphia : Jessica Kingsley Publishers, 2017. |
    Includes bibliographical references.
Identifiers: LCCN 2016055927| ISBN 9781785920394 (alk. paper) | ISBN
    9781784502928 (ebook)
Subjects: | MESH: Spiritual Therapies | Psychotherapy--methods | Pastoral Care
Classification: LCC RZ401 | NLM WM 427 | DDC 615.8/52--
dc23 LC record available at https://lccn.loc.gov/2016055927

British Library Cataloguing in Publication Data
A CIP catalogue record for this book is available from the British Library

ISBN 978 1 78592 039 4
eISBN 978 1 78450 292 8

Printed and bound in Great Britain

Contents

Acknowledgements

I would like to thank the following:

- Christine Stevens and the staff at Metanoia Institute for their insight, practical wisdom and for the support and encouragement they gave me throughout my doctoral studies. Also Flippa Watkeys and Ros Alstead for their unstinting support through the process, not least by granting much-needed study leave.

- My chaplaincy colleagues Charlotte Collins, Anne Douglas and Jean Fletcher and the many other colleagues, patients and staff with whom I have shared conversations and who have enriched my understanding and experience of spiritual and pastoral care and counselling and psychotherapy.

- Rachel Freeth, Mel Bowden, Bob Heath, Kate Butcher, Steve Nolan, Judy Davies, Isabel Clarke, Sean O'Mahony, Gavin Garman, Emma Louis and William West who made the symposium held in March 2016 such a rich and meaningful occasion and without whom this book would not have been possible.

- Victoria Slater, without whose constant support, patience and encouragement I could not have completed this book.

List of Contributors

Melanie Bowden is a consultant psychiatrist and psychotherapist for an NHS psychological service. She also has an interest in supervision, training and educating and how to help individuals and teams communicate and be supported to work well. She teaches and develops courses in communication both here and abroad with a multi-cultural emphasis. As a committed Christian, Melanie has an interest in how faith and spirituality link to clinical work and to supporting clinicians.

Kate Butcher is a registered nurse with extensive experience of community nursing and practice development across Oxfordshire. Currently she is Education Lead at Sobell House Hospice, Oxford, and also still practises clinically. In 2016 Kate achieved an MSc in Clinical Leadership for Cancer, Palliative and End of Life Care.

Isabel Clarke is a consultant clinical psychologist with over 20 years' experience working as a therapist in the NHS with people with complex problems. Her books, *Psychosis and Spirituality: Consolidating the New Paradigm* (Wiley, 2010) and *Madness, Mystery and the Survival of God* (O-Books, 2008), explore the themes of spirituality, mental health and being human.

Judy Davies is a Methodist minister who has worked for over 20 years as a health care chaplain in hospital and hospice settings, specializing in palliative care. She served as President of the Association of Hospice and Palliative Care Chaplains from 2012 to 2015 and is currently chaplain at the Sue Ryder Duchess of Kent Hospice in Reading.

Rachel Freeth is a psychiatrist working in an NHS community team in Herefordshire. She also works as a Person-Centred counsellor for a counselling charity in Gloucestershire. In both roles she bridges the worlds of psychiatry and counselling, and the contrasting worlds of psychiatry and the Person-Centred approach. She is author of *Humanising Psychiatry and Mental Healthcare: The Challenge of the Person-Centred Approach* (CRC Press, 2007), and has also written a number of articles and chapters on subjects relating to counselling and mental health care.

Gavin Garman is deputy director of nursing in a mental health Trust in the southwest of England with a doctorate in psychology. He has 20 years' professional experience in psychiatry (largely in forensic services) and has contributed to a number of human rights projects in Eastern Europe. He follows the Buddhist teachings developed by Vietnamese monk Thich Nhat Hanh. He lives and works by the sea in Devon.

Guy Harrison is an Anglican priest who has worked as a senior chaplain in palliative care, acute care and mental health care contexts for 20 years and was appointed to his current role as Head of Spiritual and Pastoral Care in 2012. He is a registered BACP (accredited) psychotherapist and a trained supervisor and mediator. In 2016 he also became Director of the newly established Oxford Centre for Spirituality and Wellbeing. In 2016 he was awarded a doctorate in psychotherapy (DPsych) which he undertook in order to develop and integrate his knowledge and experience.

Bob Heath was the resident music therapist at Sobell House Hospice in Oxford for over ten years. He has worked extensively in palliative and bereavement care both as a clinician and a lecturer/teacher and also has many years' experience working in dementia care and special educational settings. He has published work in various books and journals and continues to practise as a therapist in end-of-life care and in community mental health settings. Bob has presented his work at a wide range of events, including the Hay Literature Festival and Medicine Unboxed, and continues to offer and develop a range of training courses for therapists and health care practitioners.

Emma Louis has worked in health care chaplaincy for 16 years and is currently Head of Diversity and Spirituality at Black Country Partnership NHS Foundation Trust in the West Midlands. Emma has a particular interest in using mindfulness in her work in the mental health and learning disability setting, as well as putting it into practice as a key element of her own spiritual journey. Emma practises with a mindfulness group in the tradition of Zen Master Thich Nhat Hanh and has formally developed her mindfulness teacher training skills to enable her to teach mindfulness-based cognitive therapy (MBCT) and other approaches in the NHS.

Steve Nolan has been chaplain at Princess Alice Hospice, Esher, UK, since 2004. He holds a PhD from the University of Manchester and is dual qualified as a BACP accredited counsellor/psychotherapist. He has published widely on chaplaincy and spiritual care issues, including several articles discussing psycho-spirituality, as well as writing and co-editing *Spiritual Care at the End of Life: The Chaplain as a 'Hopeful Presence'*

(Jessica Kingsley Publishers, 2012), *A–Z of Spirituality* (with Margaret Holloway; Palgrave, 2014) and (*Spiritual Care in Practice: Case Studies in Healthcare Chaplaincy* (with George Fitchett; Jessica Kingsley Publishers, 2015). He holds a Visiting Research Fellowship at the University of Winchester.

Sean O'Mahony is currently a mental health social worker and deputy team manager for the Oxfordshire Early Intervention Service, part of Oxford Health NHS Trust. He has worked in the NHS for the past nine years, and prior to that worked in the voluntary sector. His previous background includes philosophy, social research and the social sciences. He has an ongoing interest in the dynamic interface between clinical care, subjective experiences of psychosis and spirituality, and the philosophical questions that arise from that interface.

William West is a Visiting Professor in Counselling at the University of Chester and Honorary Reader in Counselling Studies at the University of Manchester. He is most noted for his interest in spirituality and for his work with doctorate and PhD students. He has written widely on topics around his areas of interest, such as *Psychotherapy & Spirituality: Crossing the Line between Therapy and Religion* (Sage, 2000) and *Spiritual Issues in Therapy: Relating Experience to Practice* (Palgrave, 2004). He has edited a number of books that bring together his own writings with those of like-minded contributors. Examples include *Exploring Therapy, Spirituality and Healing* (Palgrave, 2011) and *Therapy, Culture and Spirituality: Developing Therapeutic Practice* (with Greg Nolan; Palgrave, 2014).

Introduction

When you talk about God or religion, they think you really are ill.

I need help so that I can begin to put my life back together again…to know how to live when much of the time it's like I'm frozen with fear…

To speak of my life I need to put it in a context in which I can find some sort of meaning, a way of understanding how I've got to where I am now.

I need someone to listen to me, to take my beliefs seriously…

These quotations represent the voices of patients. They express in different ways the need to make sense of what is happening in their lives and to have their spiritual needs taken seriously and attended to as part of the care they receive. This call for understanding challenges practitioners to find ways to integrate spiritual care into a truly holistic approach to the provision of health care. This book seeks to contribute to the development of such an understanding, so that this challenge can be met. The evidence from organizations such as the Mental Health Foundation (1997, 2000, 2002, 2006) and the Royal Colleges of Nursing (2011) and Royal College of Psychiatrists (2010), and from the report *One Chance to get It Right* (Leadership Alliance for the Care of Dying People 2014) indicates that while there is a developing interest in applying spiritual understandings to the provision of health care, in practice there is an urgent need to address effectively the spiritual needs of patients and carers. My recent doctoral research and my experience of more than 20 years' professional practice in hospice, acute and mental health contexts together with the reflections of my colleagues tell me that the voices of the patients represented above are by no means unique. It is clear that there is a significant gap between theory and practice.

An increasing amount of research on spiritual care[1] is being generated within both health care and counselling and psychotherapy related academia (e.g. Mearns and Cooper 2005; McSherry 2006; Cook, Powell and Sims 2009; Koenig 2009; Holloway and Moss 2010; Jenkins 2011; Nolan 2011; Pargament 2011). A number of organizations and special interest groups have also sprung up in recent years. Examples include the British Association for the Study of Spirituality (BASS), which held its first conference in 2010 and which publishes the *Journal for the Study of Spirituality*, and the launch in 1999 of the Royal College of Psychiatrists (RCPsych) Special Interest Group on Spirituality. Nevertheless, it is my contention that in health care contexts we are still some way away from the tipping point that is the understanding that spirituality is as worthy of study, research and development as any other health care or psychology-related discipline. This book offers a contribution to the development of this understanding.

The book is for anyone who works in health-related care who, like me, sees that there is this continuing gap between theory and practice and who seeks to bring psychologically informed spiritual care in the form of psycho-spiritual care into dialogue with both psycho-social care and medical care. It speaks to contemporary explanations of how we provide psycho-spiritual care in highly pressurized and increasingly under-resourced contexts. It is rooted in practice and seeks to engage with practitioners from all health-related disciplines in challenging the status quo and developing Person-Centred[2] approaches to care that incorporate all aspects of human flourishing.

The provision of psycho-social care in health care practice is long established, though as Barnard (1984) indicates, it has tended to encompass indiscriminately everything that is not bio-medical in origin. Those of us who work in health care, whether that be on an acute ward in a general hospital, a community health care team, hospice or mental health unit, know how much more nuanced and complex the provision of a truly holistic approach to care is in practice. We also know, because patients tell us, that spiritual need is often neglected, misunderstood, pathologized or even ignored. This is not to discount the experience of many health care staff who often do understand their role in the assessment of spiritual need

---

1. In this context spiritual care can be understood as care that responds to people's need to find meaning, purpose, relationship and hope and may include transcendent understandings of the Divine or of ultimate meaning. See Chapter 1, section 'Spiritual care and counselling and psychotherapy in health care' for a fuller discussion of this concept of care.

2. Throughout the text the use of 'Person-Centred' with upper-case letters refers to the particular psychotherapeutic approach pioneered by Carl Rogers.

and the provision of spiritual care but do not feel sufficiently resourced or confident enough to be able to respond. The experience of staff is too often one of a lack of training, awareness, confidence or time or a mixture of all four. As one practitioner said, 'I absolutely believe in the need for spiritual care. I just don't have the time or wherewithal to deliver it…and I feel guilty for not doing so.'

Although the term 'psycho-spiritual care' has been used (cf. Barnard 1984; Assagioli 1993; Nolan 2006; Harrison 2016) to suggest that spiritual care has a direct link with emotional and physical care, the question remains as to how health care staff can step closer to understanding and meeting the psycho-spiritual needs of patients and carers. If one accepts that within all traditions of faith and within humanistic and existential understandings of human flourishing there lies a deep strand of psycho-spiritual concern for wellbeing, then it should be possible to find ways of adopting psycho-spiritual approaches to care. This book is intended to help to bridge the divide, or as a participant in a peer review of my research put it, the 'chasm', that lies at the heart of health care practice. In too many instances, spiritual care has been confined to the margins or solely to the remit of the health care chaplain who, for a variety of reasons that have been widely discussed elsewhere (cf. Orchard 2001; Mowatt 2008; Swift 2014), may also occupy a marginal or liminal place in an organization, be under-resourced or sometimes ill equipped. The purpose of this book is therefore to generate insight into the relationship between spiritual care and therapeutic practice within multi-disciplinary contexts in order to contribute to both the knowledge base and the development of practice.

The structure and approach of the book

The book is in two parts. Part 1, The Development of Psycho-spiritual Care: Research and Practice, represents aspects of the autoethnographic[3] research that I undertook on the relationship between spiritual and pastoral care[4] and counselling and psychotherapy in my own practice as Head of Spiritual and Pastoral Care in a medium-sized British mental and community health National Health Service (NHS) Foundation Trust. In this role as a person who is trained to provide spiritual and pastoral care and is also a trained psychotherapist, the motivation for doing the research

---

3. A research methodology that seeks to describe and systematically analyse personal experience in order to understand cultural experience (Ellis 2004).

4. This includes more general approaches to pastoral care as being concerned for the wellbeing of a person or care provided within a faith tradition.

was to clarify how these two dimensions of my training and development are related in my practice. The insights gained from research into the elements of my own practice could then inform understandings of how to develop psychologically informed spiritual care in practice more generally. Part 2, Aspects of Psycho-spiritual Care in Health Care Practice, is the fruit of a symposium, which developed from my doctoral studies, that was held in March 2016 and was facilitated by Professor William West, Visiting Professor in Counselling at the University of Chester. It features an introduction by Professor West, and contributions from symposium members comprising five experts in their field, most of whom have published work in their area of practice, together with responses from five leading practitioners.

In Part 1, Chapter 1 is an overview of the contemporary role of a health care chaplain. It discusses existential, Person-Centred and theological perspectives on care and outlines the development of the relationship between spiritual and pastoral care and counselling and psychotherapy.

Chapter 2 describes an autoethnographic narrative case study approach to research and the implications of the findings for psycho-spiritual care in health care practice. It is presented as an example of an autoethnographic research methodology that is guided by a desire to construct an account of personal and professional practice rather than following a predetermined theoretical stance. It describes a form of inductive qualitative research that begins with detailed observations and moves towards more abstract ideas that seek to construct and interpret meaning. This methodological approach, while comparatively unusual, is gaining followers within the academy as it gives an alternative source of ideas for the development of a framework for practice and for further research.

Chapter 3 is an exploration of one of my main research themes: liminality and healing. This theme explores the idea that liminal spaces, betwixt and between places of transition, waiting and not knowing, while being sometimes chaotic, are also spaces that contain the seeds of healing, wholeness and recovery. The chapter describes how the adoption of Person-Centred therapeutic responses, as first postulated by Carl Rogers (1951), enables cathartic 'I–Thou' (Buber 1958) moments of profound healing or growth.

Chapter 4 focuses on the development of psycho-spiritual care as an aspect of holistic health and summarizes my research evidence which indicates that there is much work to be done in providing a truly integrated and therefore holistic approach to care. The chapter further explores the apparent gap in practice and evidences how the close relationship between spiritual and pastoral care and psychotherapy can build a bridge, thereby holding the potential to make a significant difference to patient care.

Chapters 2, 3 and 4 use field stories of my practice that are presented using the lens of a researcher-practitioner interpretation of what took place. A reflexive approach is adopted in order to convey as faithful an account as possible of the elements of each encounter. The reflective nature of the writing is both iterative and creative in its approach. In places, I have presented patient voices in poetic form. One of the advantages of using a poetic form in research is that it can present evocative insights into the lived experience of clients or patients in ways that ordinary academic prose cannot (Furman, Lietz and Langer 2006). The goal of generating and presenting research data in this way is to inspire an empathic reaction such that the reader may develop a deeper understanding of the subject of the data.

In this kind of qualitative research, ethical requirements as they relate to patient confidentiality and data protection are of paramount importance. For this reason, it is important to note at this point that each patient narrative is based on my work as a whole and cannot be attributable to any one individual. I have presented each story in the words of, for example, Claire or Steve in order to give the narrative both coherence and integrity. All the names I use are purely fictional.

The research findings articulated in Part 1 demonstrate that within the complexities of my role as a person who is head of spiritual and pastoral care and also a trained and experienced psychotherapist, it is possible to bring together psychological, spiritual and pastoral insights into practice in ways that are integrative and holistic.

Part 2 of the book, which presents the work done at the 2016 symposium, brings together health care practitioners from different disciplines who are also therapists or whose training and experience incorporate psychological understanding. The uniting factor is the fact that all the authors who presented papers at the symposium and the practitioners who have responded to those papers did so because of a desire to integrate spiritual care within their practice or because they supported psycho-spiritual approaches to patient care. Each author has chosen to incorporate the responses to their paper in different ways.

Both parts of the book illustrate how the potential development of psycho-spiritual care within health care practice is dependent upon the ability of skilled practitioners to find allies and develop partnerships within the predominant medical model of health care. The experience of health care chaplains and others is that for patients, questions of value and meaning occur when they find themselves in acute pain and/or distress. For some this crisis of meaning or aspect of pain may be described as spiritual distress which can be simply described as a loss of meaning or purpose in life that may include the loss of worth, identity, self-esteem, or may feature regret or unresolved guilt. This distress is often associated with a crisis or major change that challenges a person's values, beliefs or relationships with self, others and 'God' or ultimate reality. This may or may not include a religious dimension. This book explores the various ways in which this distress may be attended to that avoid the potential pathological bias of bio-medical or psycho-social understandings of illness and disease. It offers the proposition that the integration of contemporary spirituality with pastoral and psychological insights (including the application of aspects of the Person-Centred modality of counselling and psychotherapy) can act as a resource for the development of what I describe in the conclusion as Radical Presence.[5]

In the conclusion, I emphasize that there is much work to be done in order to attend to a person's spirituality within multi-disciplinary approaches to patient care. While spirituality may remain peripheral to many health professionals (Swinton 2000), it is of central importance to a significant number of people who are struggling with the pain and confusion of mental or physical illness. Consequently, there are significant implications for the development of research, training and support for all staff who are required to provide holistic/integrated forms of patient care.

In Chapter 2 and in the Conclusion, I outline one example of how this might be addressed via the launch of the Oxford Centre for Spirituality and Wellbeing (OCSW). The vision of OCSW is 'to generate practice-based evidence of the benefits of an integrated approach to care through research which will underpin the development of training for staff so that they are equipped and supported in the provision of spiritual care' (OCSW 2016).

Who this book is for?

This book is for all those who:

- like Puchalski, 'believe that spirituality, broadly defined, is increasingly recognized as an essential element of care' (2012, p.197)

- want to further their knowledge and understanding of psycho-spiritual care from the perspective of practice

---

5. I would like to thank Christine Stevens at the Metanoia Institute, who was my DPsych academic advisor, for the suggestion of this term as a way of integrating the various elements of psycho-spiritual care.

- are interested in a reflexive qualitative research approach that starts with the researcher-practitioner voice and is informed by patient, carer and staff experience rather than with theory alone

- believe that adopting psychologically informed spiritual care as psycho-spiritual care enables patients, carers and staff to find hope amidst despair; to find meaning and purpose when experiencing pain and/or suffering; and to develop resilience against the ongoing effects of uncertainty, loss and stress

- want to know more about how the Person-Centred approach can inform psycho-spiritual care

- believe that psycho-spiritual care forms the glue that binds the mind-spirit aspects of medical care

- accept the premise that healing and wholeness derive from a therapeutic relationship that involves being attentive to *all* dimensions of care for patients, carers and staff and that integral to that relationship is the ability to listen and respond with empathy and compassion

- hope that psychologically informed spiritual care may become the foundation for whole-person care.

Finally, I want to stress that while I write as a health care chaplain who is also a therapist, practitioners do not have to be either of these in order to develop the understanding and practice of psycho-spiritual care. This book is for all health care professionals and for counsellors or psychotherapists who work in the general field of health care practice. It will also be of interest to those in training, whether that be in health care, including nursing, medicine, therapy or chaplaincy, or counselling and psychotherapy.

References

Assagioli, R. (1993) *Psychosynthesis.* London: Penguin.

Barnard, D. (1984) Illness as a crisis of meaning: Psycho-spiritual agendas in health care. *Pastoral Psychology,* 33(2), 74–82.

Buber, M. (1958) *I and Thou* (2nd revised edition). Translated by R. Gregor Smith. New York: Charles Scribner's.

Cook, C., Powell, A. and Sims, A. (eds) (2009) *Spirituality and Psychiatry.* London: RCPsych Publications.

Ellis, C. (2004) *The Ethnographic I: A Methodological Novel about Autoethnography.* Walnut Creek, CA: Alta Mira Press.

Furman, R., Lietz, C. and Langer, C. (2006) The research poem in international social work: Innovations in qualitative methodology. *International Journal of Qualitative Methods,* 5(3), 1–8.

Harrison, G. (2016) *The relationship between counselling and psychotherapy and spiritual and pastoral care in the role of a healthcare chaplain: An autoethnographic narrative case study evaluation.* Unpublished DPsych final project. Metanoia Institute and Middlesex University.

Holloway, M. and Moss, B. (2010) *Spirituality and Social Work.* London: Palgrave Macmillan.

Jenkins, C. (2011) Priest? Therapist? Both? Learning from research and experience. *Thresholds: Counselling with Spirit,* Spring, 19–22.

Koenig, H. (2009) Research on religion, spirituality, and mental health: A review. *Canadian Journal of Psychiatry,* 54(5), 283–291.

Leadership Alliance for the Care of Dying People (2014) *One Chance to Get It Right: Improving People's Experience of Care in the Last Few Days and Hours of Life.* Publications Gateway Reference 01509. Available at www.gov.uk/government/uploads/system/uploads/attachment_data/file/323188/One_chance_to_get_it_right.pdf, accessed on 10 December 2016.

McSherry, W. (2006) *Making Sense of Spirituality in Nursing and Health Care Practice: An Interactive Approach.* London: Jessica Kingsley Publishers.

Mearns, D. and Cooper, M. (2005) *Working at Relational Depth in Counselling and Psychotherapy.* London: Sage.

Mental Health Foundation (1997) *Knowing Our Own Minds.* London: Mental Health Foundation.

Mental Health Foundation (2000) *Strategies for Living.* London: Mental Health Foundation.

Mental Health Foundation (2002) *Taken Seriously – The Somerset Spirituality Project.* London: Mental Health Foundation.

Mental Health Foundation (2006) *The Impact of Spirituality on Mental Health.* London: Mental Health Foundation.

Mowatt, H. (2008) *The Potential for Efficacy of Healthcare Chaplaincy and Spiritual Care Provision in the NHS (UK): A scoping review of recent research.* Aberdeen: NHS Yorkshire and Humber.

Nolan, S. (2006) Psychospiritual care: A paradigm (shift) of care for the spirit in a nonreligious context. *Journal of Health Care Chaplaincy,* 7(1), 12–22.

Orchard, H. (ed.) (2001) *Spirituality in Health Care Contexts.* London: Jessica Kingsley Publishers.

Oxford Centre for Spirituality and Wellbeing (2016) Oxford Centre for Spirituality & Well-Being. Available at www.oxinahr.com/our-centres-and-groups/oxford-centre-for-spirituality-well-being-ocsw, accessed on 11 December 2016.

Pargament, K. (2011) *Spiritually Integrated Psychotherapy: Understanding and Addressing the Sacred.* New York: Guilford Press.

Puchalski, C. (2012) Restorative Medicine. In M. Cobb, M. Puchalski and B. Rumbold (eds) *Oxford Textbook of Spirituality in Healthcare.* Oxford: Oxford University Press.

Rogers, C. (1951) *Client-Centered Therapy.* London: Constable.

Royal College of Nursing (2011) *Spirituality in Nursing Care: A Pocket Guide.* London: Royal College of Nursing.

Royal College of Psychiatrists (2010) *Spirituality and Mental Health.* London: Royal College of Psychiatrists.

Swift, C. (2014) *Hospital Chaplaincy in the Twenty-first Century: The Crisis of Spiritual Care in the NHS* (2nd edition). Farnham: Ashgate.

Swinton, J. (2000) *Spirituality and Mental Health Care.* London: Jessica Kingsley Publishers.

PART 1

The Development of Psycho-spiritual Care

Research and Practice

Guy Harrison

1

The Practice of
Psycho-spiritual Care

Not everyone has encountered or heard of the work of health care chaplaincy, sometimes also known as spiritual and pastoral care, so this first chapter begins with a brief summary of the context of health care chaplaincy in the UK together with an overview of the contemporary role of the chaplain and their potential contribution to the understanding and development of psycho-spiritual care. It goes on to discuss existential, Person-Centred and theological perspectives on care and outlines the relationship between pastoral care and counselling and communities of faith. The chapter also explores the development of the relationship between spiritual care and counselling and psychotherapy as they relate particularly to the role of the health care chaplain.

The role of the health care chaplain

The genesis of the health care chaplain's role gives some indication of the present context in which chaplains are appointed. It also contributes to an understanding of the health care chaplains' contemporary contribution to the potential development of psycho-spiritual care. For this reason, what follows is a brief account of the context.

According to Swift (2014), the appointment of clergy to work in hospitals in England is a practice that has been happening for several hundred years. Initially, this was due to the religious character of the medieval monasteries from which they sprang. Within the religious context of the life of a medieval hospital the chaplain was a key figure who would lead daily worship, dispense religious advice and often, in the context of repentance and prayer for forgiveness, pronounce absolution prior to death. By so doing, the chaplain as priest would act as guarantor of God's salvation for the poor and the weak. Hospitals were institutions that extended the

Church's influence in providing the poor with shelter, food and general care. As Swift points out, the Church was demonstrating a 'practical social endeavour alongside similar enterprises in education and the distribution of alms' (2014, p.13). However, following the Reformation, the role of the chaplain changed dramatically. Rather than simply exercising a purely religious role, chaplains became beholden to both the state, in the form of the monarch as head of the Church of England, and the institution in the form of the hospital governors. Swift indicates that this dual accountability meant an emphasis was placed upon upholding moral conduct and moral instruction rather than daily worship and administration of the sacraments.

Further dramatic change came in the Victorian era with the development of workhouses and asylums. Prior to the nineteenth century, the mentally ill were judged to be morally contaminated and their problems were judged to be spiritual in origin and therefore untreatable (Bartlett and Wright 1999). In effect the 'mad' were left to roam the streets begging for food and shelter. In theory, the newly built Victorian asylums, often magnificently built with extensive grounds, became places of sanctuary and care. In practice, according to Finnane (1985), they often became warehouses for society's outcasts at a time when cures for both mental and physical illness were far fewer than the Victorian medical establishment had initially hoped. Each institution had a chaplain who was accountable to the hospital's Master for the moral and religious welfare of the patients and the staff. They effectively adapted a parochial model to that of the hospital community. This meant conducting marriages, baptisms and funerals and dispensing religious and moral advice as well as ensuring all within the institution regularly attended Sunday services.

Swift (2014) states that at the founding of the NHS in 1948 there were approximately 28 chaplains, all of whom came from and were expected to return to, usually Church of England, parish ministry. With the advent of the 1948 reform, assurance was given that each hospital would have a chaplain and a chapel funded out of the overall hospital budget. Writing in 1966, Norman Autton, who has been described as the father of modern health care chaplaincy in the UK, described the chaplain's role within the comparatively new NHS as one who comes with 'spiritual instruments to instil faith, implant courage and create meaningful relationships and open the way for restoration of the body' (1966, p.6). Perhaps most significantly, Swift quotes Autton as stating that the role of the chaplain 'must be as meaningful as medicine itself. His [sic] position must be not less professional than that of other members of staff, and his science and skill not less marked than those of the surgeon' (2014, p.45).

The founding of the NHS meant that chaplains could now 'relate to a shared body of knowledge, practice and professional standards' (Swift 2014, p.51). More recently this focus on a more professional approach has paved the way for a significant increase in the development of, and tentative research into, health care chaplaincy. The growing body of research and approaches to professional development includes most notably: the Orchard report on hospital chaplaincy (Orchard 2000); the South Yorkshire NHS Workforce Development Confederation national strategy, 'Caring for the Spirit', published in 2003; Department of Health guidance (NHS Chaplaincy Guidelines 2015); and the publication of recent books by, for example, Nolan (2011) and Swift (2014) and a plethora of articles published, for example, in the *Journal of Health Care Chaplaincy*. Alongside the published material has been the development of professional associations and of ecumenical and multi-faith perspectives. The overall effect has been a significant expansion in the numbers and the professional development and resourcing of chaplaincy in the past few years. At the time of writing, the College of Health Care Chaplains registrar and the Church of England Hospital/Health Care Chaplaincy administrator give the current number of employed chaplains as 407 working full time and 374 working part time.

According to Orchard (2000), today's health care chaplains would on the whole see themselves as 'spiritual care professionals' whose tasks include:

- responding to the religious, spiritual and existential needs of patients, carers and staff

- providing general emotional support to patients, carers and staff

- acting as advocates and mediators

- providing education, training and personal and professional development

- giving advice on ethical issues and more generally on implementing values-based health care.

James Woodward argues that, 'chaplains might be described as liminal people. They are *in-between*; and the freedom, or potential freedom, this position imparts gives them the possibility of relating to and interpreting reality in all kinds of creative ways' (1998, p.268). This freedom enables the chaplains to seek ways in which they can collaborate with other health care professionals in imparting a holistic understanding of whole-person health which, it is hoped, contributes towards a wider vision of greater wellbeing[1] for all in society. This holistic approach is evidenced in my job description, the broad outline of which includes the following:

- develop the provision of Spiritual and Pastoral care to all patients, staff and carers across the Trust;

- provide direction, strategic vision and professional leadership for the service;

- manage the Trust's Spiritual and Pastoral Care and Equality and Diversity services' resources in collaboration with Heads of Service;

- work with other lead Allied Health Professionals and other professional leads to promote spiritual care for patients, carers and the Trust;

- take a Trust-wide role in supporting the development of staff wellbeing and psychological support, promotion of organizational values, promotion and monitoring of equalities and human rights, mediation and management of bereavement services;

- provide a direct Spiritual Care service to patients and staff with complex needs;

- increase awareness and understanding of the needs of people suffering mental ill health with representatives of local faith communities.

As evidence of the need to incorporate training and experience in spiritual and pastoral care and counselling or psychotherapy at a 'high level', the person specification includes in the essential criteria the following:

- training in counselling or psychotherapy;

- recognized qualification in pastoral, spiritual and religious care;

- a high level of psychologically informed knowledge in the complex relationship between human spiritual-religious and mental-emotional development.

While there is clear acknowledgement of the need for a high level of training in 'psychologically informed knowledge', there is no attempt to define what is meant by this statement or by the term 'therapeutic spiritual counselling'. Given that the above is a description of my responsibilities, together with a list of specifications for the role, it is perhaps not surprising. However, it is precisely this lack of clarity that forms the basis

1. I define wellbeing as a state of physical, mental and spiritual health such that each person can realize his or her potential, live a fruitful life and make a contribution to his or her community.

for my exploration of the dialogic relationship between counselling and psychotherapy and spiritual and pastoral care and how this impacts on and is encapsulated in my role as head of spiritual and pastoral care. What follows is a delineation of the main parameters of the contextual background relevant to the discussion of this relationship in order to locate it within a broader spiritual, pastoral and psychological frame of reference. This will provide an initial mapping of the main theoretical perspectives with which this discussion is in dialogue.

I will begin with a consideration of the nature of care before locating it within a critical dialogic approach to understanding and defining both counselling and psychotherapy and spiritual and pastoral care as they relate to the worlds of faith, health care and chaplaincy. Whilst acknowledging the influence of other theoretical positions, for example existential, Jungian and psychodynamic approaches, I will be focusing on my practice as a Person-Centred therapist and the extent to which Person-Centred theory may be integrated into the practice of spiritual care in health care.

The nature of care: Existential, Person-Centred and theological perspectives

The term 'caring' is used to describe a wide range of personal involvement, from love to friendship, from caring for the garden to caring about work and to caring for and about patients. According to Benner and Wrubel:

> Caring is essential if the person is to live in a differentiated world where some things really matter, while others are less important or not important at all. Caring is a word for being connected and having things matter, it works well because it fuses thought, feeling and action – knowing and being. (1989, p.1)

Here, then, is an emphasis on the use of connectedness and the importance of 'being' alongside 'doing'. Caring is by its very nature relational. However, it may be argued that:

> Relational care runs counter to the current cultural mores of society which can lead people to become individualistic in pursuit of wealth, status and independence, to such an extent that the quest to be in charge of one's own life may mean controlling all the options, including feelings. Consequently, this becomes a negative freedom in which individuals become so disconnected from each other that they potentially lose the freedom to choose and act, and thereby the ability to care and be cared for. (Harrison 1998, p.4)

If this is true it means that health care staff are sometimes working counter-culturally, with all the concomitant problems of living and working in a society that has the potential to become more fragmented and therefore less caring.

Caring sets up a relationship or a set of relationships that enable something or someone to matter. Caring thereby creates personal concern. However, because caring is about what matters to a person, the emphasis is also on what counts as being painful and what available options there are for coping. Caring therefore potentially puts a person in a place of vulnerability. For example, a patient on an acute mental health ward, in a stroke unit or in a hospice may be dependent upon staff for many of the most basic functions of life. As a consequence, issues around relationships and existential questions of meaning and purpose become very stressful for them. If, however, staff and carers exercise a person-centred care that seeks to empower a person, it becomes possible for the patient to discover appropriate and acceptable coping strategies.

Within most aspects of health care, it is members of the multi-disciplinary team who provide often intimate care in the midst of pain, loss, fear, anxiety and transition to recovery or death and dying. The carer may become the interpreter or possibly the advocate for the patient of matters that at first diagnosis are only half understood or half heard when first communicated, thus, 'These and other features of the dynamic of care offer a potent and powerful means for creativity or dysfunction, for growth or disabling isolation' (Harrison 1998, p.8). It may therefore be argued that the nature of the care that is offered emphasizes sensitivity in becoming a fellow traveller, a companion on someone else's journey, with the aim of enabling dignity and integrity without invading privacy and that it helps without seeking to dominate or create dependency. Thus the carer who is empathic, even when presented with an ambiguous or closed response, may be described as embodying loving care.

Whether or not we wish to use the term 'loving care', according to Mayeroff (1971), cited in Orchard (2001), care is 'a process, a way of relating to someone that involves development' (p.66). Mayeroff identified eight essential components of care which can be paraphrased as:

- an understanding of the other's need as the basis of care involving explicit and implicit knowledge

- adopting an alternating rhythm of interaction with others and personal reflection on the outcomes of the interaction

- the capacity for a form of patience that is not only passive waiting but which enables 'others to grow in their own time and style'

- rigorous honesty that is open and able to confront self and others

- trusting relationships that respect the independence of others, allowing them to develop in their own way

- having the humility to listen and learn from others whilst at the same time acknowledging one's own limitations

- hopeful commitment to the other person

- the courage to sometimes take risks rooted in trust in the ability of both carer and cared-for to grow.

(Mayeroff 1971, cited in Orchard 2001)

Counselling and psychotherapy, in its various forms, is an expression of what is involved in this care. Traditionally, it contrasts with patient care in that it seeks to care more fully for persons. Mair describes this type of caring as an arena that highlights issues to do with 'knowing; involving both ontology (ways of being) and epistemology (aspects of knowledge)' (1989, p.16). It is a form of caring in which we come to know ourselves and others.

Carl Rogers first posited the notion of client-centred therapy, now widely referred to as Person-Centred therapy. Rogers (1967) suggests that this caring has a number of characteristics, including the ability to be trustworthy. For Rogers, cultivating trustworthiness means being 'real' or congruent. Being congruent with oneself and, as and when appropriate, with a client, means being integrated as a person in that moment. Closely related is the ability to be sufficiently expressive as a person such that what I am will be communicated unambiguously, 'If I am reasonably congruent, if no feelings relevant to the relationship are hidden either to me or the other person, then I can be almost sure that the relationship will be a helpful one' (1967, p.51). Therefore, it will be a caring one. The theory goes that if I care enough for myself and I can be sufficiently aware of and accepting of my own feelings then there is a strong likelihood that I will be able to care for a client. A further characteristic of a caring relationship is the ability to express a positive attitude to another person that is warm, caring and respectful. This approach is counter to some other forms of therapy such as the psychodynamic approach that demands a certain distance, a 'blank screen', but is one that, it may be argued, is characteristic of Person-Centred spiritual and pastoral care. According to Rogers, working in this way also means being strong enough to be separate from the other person I am caring for. In other words, it requires the adoption of a stance that enables the therapist to be strong enough to stand in their own separateness and allow the other person to be what they are (however honest or deceitful) in ways that enable the therapist to contain the anger, distress, fear, depression or need for dependence or love.

The Person-Centred therapist expresses care by entering as fully as possible into the world of the clients' feelings and personal meanings without judgement and with empathy. This kind of empathy is accompanied by acceptance, known in the Rogerian tradition as unconditional positive regard. In addition, the development of a relationship that is free of judgement and evaluation enables the client to recognize that the locus of evaluation lies within themselves. This kind of relationship is ultimately about confirming the other or, as Buber puts it (as cited by Rogers):

> accepting the whole potentiality of the other…I can recognise in him [*sic*], know in him, the person he has been…created to become…I confirm him in myself, and then in him, in relation to this potentiality that…can now be developed, can evolve. (Rogers 1967, p.55)

This Person-Centred approach to care is summed up by Mearns and Thorne (1999) as a form of loving care, or at least treating people in a loving way.

Traditions of care exist in all the major faith traditions, though the Western tradition of care is rooted in Judeo-Christian theological understandings. For example, the following text from the New Testament is over the entrance areas of many older or former hospital and health care establishments:

> For I was an hungred, and ye gave me meat: I was thirsty, and ye gave me drink: I was a stranger, and ye took me in: Naked, and ye clothed me: I was sick, and ye visited me: I was in prison, and ye came unto me. (Matthew 25.35–36, King James Version)

Christian concepts of care emphasize the infinite capacity of God to care. Jewish acts of caring are obligatory and meritorious in both Jewish law and ethics. Visiting the sick, called in Hebrew *bikur cholim*, is a religious obligation, a mitzvah. The Talmud (rabbinic commentary on the Torah and Jewish law) teaches that when Jews care for the sick, they take away a small piece of illness. Consequently, when Jews offer this care they are acting as God's agents in the world.

Muslim understandings of care have their foundation in one of the sayings of the Prophet Mohammed, who indicated that mutual love and mercy is similar to a living body: if one part feels pain, the whole suffers. Visiting and caring for the sick becomes the clearest sign of such mutual love, mercy and empathy. Hinduism also has at its core an understanding of worship being through charity and faithful activity in the care of, and service to, other people, while the Buddhist concept of care is encapsulated in the saying of the Buddha that 'He [sic] who attends on the sick attends on me.'

Within my own Christian tradition, God's loving care is found in the person of Jesus Christ who embraced the prodigal son (Luke 15.11–32) and touched the leper (Matthew 8.1–4). In first-century Palestine, this was radical behaviour because in Jewish law, teaching such people made the person 'unclean'. It is certainly the case that:

> risk taking, rule breaking and boundary-stretching behaviour are characteristic of the good news of genuinely Christian altruistic caring, expressed within a gift relationship in which the motive for care is not related to any expectations of reward. (Orchard 2001, p.67)

However, twentieth-century Christian theologians have struggled with trying to reconcile a God of love with the concept of suffering as experienced, for example, in the horrors of two world wars and the Holocaust. Various theodicies (theodicy meaning 'the justifying of God's ways') of suffering have been suggested in order to respond to the widespread question of 'how can a God of loving care allow suffering?' Some theologians, for example Whitehead (1929) and Williams (1964), have resolved this question by describing God as love who unconditionally involves God's self in human suffering. Others, for example Soelle (1975), understand God as co-sufferer who demands our solidarity, while according to Moltmann (1974), God's suffering becomes the source of strength and hope in humanity's struggle against pain and suffering. Such understandings seek to inspire and give expression to hope that may be denied or suppressed by people facing illness, disability or their own mortality. It is this hope that undergirds the loving care expressed within communities of faith.

In order to further understand the notion of psycho-spiritual care as it may be applied to the role of a health care chaplain I now turn to a consideration of how these communities have sought to express this loving care in the form of pastoral care and counselling and psychotherapy.

Pastoral care and counselling and psychotherapy and the community of faith

Foskett (2001) makes the point that the support of individuals and groups through pastoral conversation has existed throughout the Christian tradition and prior to this within the Wisdom tradition of Judaism.

However, within other major world faiths there is not the same formally defined role and function of the pastor. For example, within Islam, traditionally the guidance of the community of believers is set within the framework of the all-encompassing law. Thus, Muslims who are appointed to be health care chaplains essentially interpret Sharia (Islamic law) in the light of difficulties of faith, moral dilemmas or life crises. Equally, within Hinduism the emphasis is on spiritual enlightenment and not on Western psychological concepts. Similarly, in Buddhism the emphasis is on searching for wisdom or ultimate truth rather than pastoral care or counselling. However, it is important to note at this point that within health care chaplaincy there are an increasing number of chaplains from different faiths and beliefs who are adopting less of a teaching or guiding role and more of a pastoral role. For example, one of my former colleagues, Imam Bhatti, not only visits Muslim patients but also works generically. In other words, as well as responding to specific requests from Muslim patients he will also see patients of all faiths and beliefs. In this capacity, he perceives his role as offering pastoral care. Nevertheless, amongst a wide network of chaplaincy colleagues, I am not aware of any Muslim, Hindu, Sikh or Buddhist health care chaplains who are also counsellors or psychotherapists. For these reasons and because I am a practitioner-researcher whose work and ministry is from within the Christian tradition, my discussion is set within a Christian context.

There are of course diverse understandings of pastoral care. For example, the term 'pastoral care' in this country until comparatively recently has been used in education to distinguish the caring and welfare role of staff from their teaching function. However, according to Browning (1977), Campbell (1986) and Willows and Swinton (2000) any definition of pastoral care within a faith context has at its core a way of understanding relatedness to the Divine and those things that may enhance or detract from that relatedness. In a classic definition, the well-known psychologist William James defines religion as being 'the acts and feelings of individual men [sic] in their solitude, as far as they apprehend themselves to stand in whatever they may consider the divine' (1936, p.32). For the purpose of this discussion I define pastoral care as theologically informed care that is concerned with the wellbeing of individuals and communities. According to Clebsch and Jaekle (1967), it is usually offered by representative persons of faith (not necessarily ordained clergy) and is concerned to respond to human distress wherever it is found, especially when that distress leads to a loss of hope in the transforming nature of love.

It is argued (e.g. Bridger and Atkinson 2007) that pastoral care is distinct from counselling and psychotherapy in that it deals with what may be described as 'ultimate meanings and concerns' involving 'healing, sustaining, reconciling and guiding' (Clebsch and Jaekle 1967, p.12). However, historically counselling and psychotherapy within the life of communities of faith (especially within the Judaeo-Christian tradition) have been an expression of its ministry of pastoral care. The historian Holifield (1983) has identified four post-Reformation traditions of pastoral care which he traces down the centuries from the sixteenth century to the 1960s. These are Roman Catholic, Lutheran, Anglican and Reformed. In the 1960s a separate group of specially trained 'pastoral counsellors' emerged, who trained with organizations such as the Bridge Foundation (formerly known as Clinical Theology), the Extension Studies Unit at St John's Theological College Nottingham, the London School of Theology, and the Westminster Pastoral Foundation. The Westminster Pastoral Foundation has subsequently shortened its name to WPF, which could be seen as a move away from its former pastoral emphasis. A further group has emerged within health care chaplaincy, especially but by no means exclusively mental health chaplains, and among a small number of parish clergy and other chaplains such as school or prison chaplains. This group consist of clergy who, often as a result of their pastoral practice, have perceived a need for more training and so have chosen to train in counselling or psychotherapy. Such training has, with the exception of, for example, St John's College Nottingham and the London School of Theology, taken place within 'secular' institutions and across the spectrum of therapeutic modalities with an emphasis on the humanistic, typically Person-Centred, transpersonal or psychodynamic.

In the UK, it is only in the past 60 years or so that pastoral counselling as an activity influenced by psychological thinking and practice has grown. In the United States, with the exception of some evangelical Christian groups, from the 1920s until comparatively recently there has been a wholesale movement towards adopting psychotherapy and counselling as the preferred paradigm for pastoral care. This is often in the form of clinical pastoral education (CPE), which was developed by Boisen, Keller and Cabot in the 1930s and adopted by the newly formed Institute of Pastoral Care in 1967 (Duff 3003, p.35; cf. section 'Counselling and psychotherapy and spiritual and pastoral care in the practice of a health care chaplain' below). In the 1980s, Arnold (1982) and others sought to counter this trend and explore and/or incorporate a more overtly Christian emphasis. Wise (1980) seeks to bring the two concepts of pastoral care and therapy together. He compares theology with psychological theory and roots his conclusion exclusively within Christian theology and practice. In a similar way, Lynch (1999) locates pastoral counselling within a religious institution or organization. Nevertheless, training in pastoral counselling or pastoral therapy retains its emphasis on psychological insight and as such is an essential component of health care chaplaincy training in the United States, where CPE is mandatory.

In the UK definitions vary from those that see pastoral counselling as professional counselling in religious settings to those that understand pastoral counselling as embodying a certain kind of relational attitude that may be found in a range of different settings. For example, Taylor (1983) explores the relationship between therapy and pastoral care within the Christian tradition, and Bridger and Atkinson (2007) are keen to preserve a distinctively Christian model. In contrast, Foskett (1984), writing as a leading mental health chaplain in the NHS and a British Association of Counselling and Psychotherapy (BACP) Fellow, views pastoral counselling as an extension of pastoral care. He understands the relationship between the two as being intrinsic. In practice, therefore, the pastoral counsellor moves between basic understandings of what makes us human, and spiritual and theological exploration. However, in the UK this stance is also not without its critics. The relationship between pastoral care and psychological theory is sometimes criticized and the perceived hegemony of secular counselling theories and methods is rejected. Alongside Bridger and Atkinson, who are deeply concerned about what they term the threat to 'Christian counselling' from humanistic psychology, stands Pattison (2000). Pattison is concerned about the professional 'captivity' of pastoral care as it relates to counselling and psychotherapy. Equally, Campbell (1986) is concerned that much recent pastoral care literature is so enamoured of psychodynamic insights and counselling methodologies that it only refers to theology in a functional way.

It is of note that with the exception of Pattison much of the writing illustrated above is from the 1980s. It is hard to know why there isn't any recent writing, other than the possibility that much of the thinking on pastoral care is applied to what is now known as the wider discipline of practical theology. Indicative of this change from a focus on pastoral care to practical theology is the change of name of what used to be known as *Contact: The Interdisciplinary Journal of Pastoral Studies* to *Practical Theology*. *Contact* welcomed articles that 'contributed to the understanding of the theory and practice of care and promoting human well-being' (cover page of each edition, 1994). *Practical Theology* has a wider remit, drawing on 'contributions from counselling, social work, psychology, sociology, ethics, as well as pastoral and practical theology' (cover page of each edition, 2014). Given the title, it is not surprising that my reading of the journal over the past few years suggests that the majority of articles are on practical rather than necessarily pastoral theology.

Some work has been done on comparing and contrasting the differences between pastoral care and pastoral counselling. For example, Jacobs (1984) describes how the pastoral counsellor's studies in psychology and theology complement and inform each other. His description of the pastoral carer is of someone who has a more informal, less task-orientated approach of listening and responding to people. However, Jacobs is also clear that the pastor should also utilize the insights, skills and knowledge of human personality and development. In this sense, pastoral care may involve meeting people at home or in hospital in order to understand issues that are similarly talked about in counselling but in a less structured context. For Foskett (1984) the distinctions seem to be even more subtle. He quotes Derek Blows, one of the founders of the Association for Pastoral Care and Counselling (now known as BACP Spirituality) and a former chief executive of the Westminster Pastoral Foundation, who states:

> The pastor needs help with the intellectual, imaginative and emotional assumptions which structure his perceptions of the human situation around him… He [sic] will need to know about human growth and development as it is described by the behavioural sciences and something of how this growth can be helped and hindered. He will need, finally, to be able to relate what he learns to his understanding of the Christian tradition in such a way that both are challenged and illuminated by each other. (1984, p.106)

For Foskett, then, the insights and practices of counselling need to be adapted for the work of pastoral care.

Lyall (1994) describes the differences in terms of practice. In pastoral care it is the pastor who makes the first approach, responding to perceived need as part of their ministry, while in pastoral counselling it is the parishioner or client who will take the initiative, following which the pastoral counsellor will negotiate an explicit contract. Lyall uses the example of how in a pastoral care relationship the pastor will hesitate before addressing the psychodynamic concept of resistance, while a more explicit pastoral counselling contract allows this to happen. In practice, however, Lyall accepts that pastoral care can easily develop into pastoral counselling. More recently, Jenkins (2011) suggests a more integrative approach. He speaks of being the priest, imam or rabbi *and* therapist that the client needs. In this view, sitting alongside the therapeutic role is the traditional pastoral/priestly role of being 'in loco Dei' (2011, p.21), thus embodying what God has to offer free of expectations of both 'priest' and therapist.

He describes this 'grace building on nature' as the 'human work to do' in order to open oneself to 'God's work'.

On the issue of whether or not it is possible to integrate pastoral or spiritual approaches into counselling and psychotherapy, a comparatively new approach has been suggested by Richards, Hardman and Berrett. In a paper on theistic counselling and psychotherapy which they ground in a world view of the theistic religions of Judaism, Christianity and Islam, they invite pastoral counsellors to join in the approach of considering how the client and counsellors' faith in 'God's loving and healing influence' (2007, p.86) may help them to seek and encounter what they describe as 'effective healing strategies' (2007, p.87). Their hope is that 'efforts to add a theistic spiritual dimension *within* psychological theory and practice will further enhance the synergy between pastoral counsellors, clergy and mental health professionals' (2007, p.87). In this way, a more collaborative stance might be fostered whereby psychological and spiritual insights into healing and therapeutic change might be shared.

It is clear that, as with any discussion of the relationship between pastoral care and counselling and the community of faith, this is a complex area with several different interpretations. In order to be able to widen the focus and begin to relate the discussion to health care practice, I now turn to discussing the relationship between spiritual care and counselling and psychotherapy within the literature on health care.

Spiritual care and counselling and psychotherapy in health care

A literature review using the ATLAS online data base reveals that there is an increasing amount written about the relationship between spiritual care and counselling and psychotherapy, for example, Richards and Bergin (1997), West (2000), Lines (2007) and Thorne (2012). However, there is very little written in the field of spiritual care and psychotherapy in the context of health care. It is equally clear that both in the literature and in practice, the concepts of spiritual care and pastoral care are often used interchangeably. I therefore intend to develop an understanding of both as they relate to my practice as a health care chaplain who is also a psychotherapist. However, in order to give some context to the discussion, it is first necessary to map out the terrain of counselling and psychotherapy within the field of health care more generally, and specifically in relation to spiritual care.

As indicated in the previous section, in practice pastoral care and/or religious care and spiritual care may overlap. The same is true when they are considered in health care contexts. In the United States in particular, both concepts of care sometimes take on similar meanings. Pargament's recent book (2011) is a good example. The title is *Spiritually Integrated Psychotherapy: Understanding and Addressing the Sacred.* In this and other writing (e.g. 1997 and 2013), he defines spirituality as a sacred domain and rejects what he defines as the increasing polarization of spirituality and religion within health care. The psychiatrist Harold Koenig, an equally prolific American writer on spiritual and pastoral care in health care and co-editor with King and Carson of the revised *Handbook of Religion and Health* (2012), also rejects this distinction.

Similarly, in the UK some writers place the two concepts in alignment. Thus Ross, referring to spiritual care in a health care context, defines spirituality as attending to:

> that element within the individual from which originates: meaning, purpose and fulfilment of life; a will to live; belief and faith in self, other and God and which is essential to the attainment of an optimum state of health, well-being or quality of life. (1997, p.27)

Alternatively, again from the United States but cited extensively in the UK when referring to end-of-life spiritual care in a hospice, the National Hospice Organization of the United States defines spirituality as:

> The dynamic process of religion, that is concerned with binding together, tying up, and tying fast. On the intrapersonal level, hospice endeavours to support the integration of the human personality in the face of physical deterioration... The interpersonal dimension seeks to promote the development and continuance of significant human relationships... And finally, in regard to the eschatological dimension of human life affirms each person's search for ultimate meaning by respecting and responding to each individual's personal truth. (1982, p.5)

This is also the case with any number of similar definitions given by writers from the worlds of mental health care such as Gilbert, Kaur and Parkes (2010), of end-of-life care such as Kearney (1996) or of counselling and psychotherapy such as Moore and Purton (2006) and West (2011).

However, in a similar way to that in which some writers distinguish between spiritual care and pastoral care, distinctions may also be made between spiritual and religious. This suggests that spirituality is not tied to religious belief or tradition. For example, the National Mental Health and Spirituality Forum's *Report on the Place of Spirituality in Mental Health* states that, 'religion is the way people organize their way of relating to what they hold to be sacred and transcendent whereas "spirituality" is something that arises from within us…a person's own sense of their place in the universe and how they relate to it' (2011, p.4). In an oft-quoted definition from Murray and Zentner spirituality is perceived thus:

> In every human being there seems to be a spiritual dimension, a quality that goes beyond religious affiliation, that strives for inspiration, reverence, awe, meaning and purpose, even in those who do not believe in God. The spiritual dimension tries to be in harmony with the universe, strives for answers about the infinite, and comes essentially into focus in times of emotional stress, physical (and mental) illness, loss, bereavement and death. (1989, p.259)

Alternatively, Holloway and Moss cite Grainger (1998) as someone who 'suggests that religion should be understood as a way of thinking and living, not simply adherence to a set of handed down beliefs and traditions – in other words the opposite to organized religion' (2010, p.4). Such an understanding could equally be applied to the world of counselling and psychotherapy and the client who is faced with a number of existential challenges in their life.

In a Royal College of Psychiatrists leaflet on spirituality and mental health it is suggested that spirituality involves experiences of a deep-seated sense of meaning and purpose in life, a sense of belonging, a sense of connection of the deeply personal with the universal, and acceptance, integration and a sense of wholeness (2010, p.1). In this sense, it is argued that spirituality and therefore spiritual need is part of human experience and becomes more important at times of distress, stress, bereavement and loss and the approach of death. If all health care is about relieving pain and suffering then holistic care seeks to care for the whole person, including the spiritual dimension. Kearney (1996), writing as a former medical director of a hospice, speaks about 'soul pain', which he suggests can be recognized by words such as 'suffering', 'anguished' or 'tortured'. He suggests that the physical aspects of personhood are intimately connected with the psyche. In a previous research project, I cite Coates (1995) and suggest the following:

> Coates helps to explain the significance when he describes a number of manifestations of spiritual pain, the first of which is crisis. This is the part where the systems of belief and value which have influenced a person until that time are seriously weakened and questioned. Significantly he points out that this crisis is likely to be encountered whether or not a person is explicitly religious. In fact, I would want to argue that the person who has found comfort and understanding in faith, and in

particular the Christian faith, often finds such a crisis harder to cope with and may well turn away from a position of confidence into a position of despair or anguish and a feeling that some divine error has been perpetrated. On the other hand, patients who have not articulated a system of belief will often speak in terms of God or a power who has intervened and caused this chaos. (Harrison 1998, pp.37–38)

In other words, it is clear that for some patients faith has a number of negative connotations.

Within the past 20 years or so there has been a phenomenal rise in interest in the link between spirituality and health care. Within the area of mental health this link has been recognized by the American Psychiatric Association (1990) and more recently the UK General Medical Council (2008), who have adopted best practice guidelines. The Royal College of Psychiatrists (2011) and the Royal College of Nursing (2011) have also recently issued guidance to their members for good practice in spiritual care. There are also at least eight peer-reviewed journals dedicated to publishing papers on health and religion and/or spirituality. These include the *Journal for the Study of Spirituality*, *Journal of Religion and Health*, *Mental Health, Religion and Culture*, and the *Journal of Religion, Spirituality and Health*.

A number of spiritual care assessment tools have also been developed. For example, the World Health Organization has developed a quality-of-life measure with a subscale that measures spirituality, religion and spiritual beliefs, while the HOPES questionnaire as published by the Mental Health Foundation (2006) seeks to ascertain:

- a patient's source of hope or help (H)
- whether or not they are a member of an organized (O) religion
- whether they have important personal (P) or spiritual beliefs
- what the effects (E) of these beliefs may be for the patient during their illness
- what support (S) the patient would welcome.

Koenig, McCullough and Larson (2001) brought together and critiqued 1200 separate studies that explored the interaction between religion and health and which show a positive correlation between religious faith and wellbeing. These include:

- Religiousness is associated with less coronary heart disease, hypertension, stroke, cancer and lower overall mortality, together with fewer negative health behaviours such as smoking and substance abuse.

- Affiliation to a religious community is consistently related to lower mortality and longer survival.

- Those who use religion as a source of coping adapt better, experience less anxiety and are more hopeful.

- Most studies show a positive correlation between religious involvement, wellbeing, happiness and life satisfaction; hope and optimism; purpose and meaning in life; higher self-esteem; adaptation to bereavement; lower rates of depression and faster rates of recovery from depression; lower rates of suicide; less anxiety; and lower rates of drug and alcohol abuse.

(Koenig et al. 2001, pp.514–544)

While not insignificant, Koenig's results should, however, be treated with some caution as the majority of studies are based in the United States, the findings of which are not necessarily transferable to all cultures or settings. Nevertheless, research in the UK seems to bear out some of these findings. For example, research with mental health patients undertaken by Sproston and Nazroo (2002) indicates that those not reporting any particular religious faith often wish to discuss spiritual support. In a survey conducted by the Mental Health Foundation (1997) over half the patients explicitly said that they had a spiritual belief that is important to them. However, contemporary scientific understandings do not fit very easily with spirituality and Culliford (2002) points out that psychiatry has traditionally excluded spiritual understandings, other than as a form of pathology or pathological response. As Swinton suggests, 'while spirituality remains a peripheral issue for many mental health professionals it is in fact of central importance to many people who are struggling with the pain and confusion of mental health problems' (2000, p.7). Similarly, McSherry states that:

> At the heart of holistic health, and arguably good health care practice, is spirituality – a concept that through its long history and association with health care has never witnessed and enjoyed such popularity as it does today... Yet despite this growing popularity research still suggests that many people working within health care...are not aware of this dimension within themselves, their patients, clients or the communities they service. (2006, pp.14–15)

Ross, writing from a nursing perspective, indicates that:

> Research shows that patients considered their spiritual needs of importance. Nurses held a similar view but felt the need for further

education to help them give spiritual care. The nursing literature suggests that spiritual care is part of the nurse's role and guidelines for nurse education state that it should be taught to nurses. It is not clear, however, if or how the subject is taught. (1996, p.38)

Within counselling and psychotherapy several definitions of spiritual care are advanced, all of which appear to have relevance to health care contexts but are taken purely from the world of individual or group therapy. For example, Rowan (1993), a key figure in humanistic and transpersonal therapeutic practice, suggests that spirituality is rooted in human experience rather than theology, deals with meaning making, faces suffering and the causes of suffering, refers to 'soul' or 'higher self', involves relationship with others and the universe and is often expressed within prayer, meditation, yoga, tai chi and mindfulness. Alternatively, the term 'spiritual crisis' is often referred to and is described in the literature on transpersonal psychology (e.g. Grof and Grof 1989) as 'a turbulent period of spiritual opening and transformation, where a process of spiritual emergence or awakening becomes unmanageable for the individual' (Spiritual Crisis Network 2014). This terminology is increasingly used within some strands of psychological care in mental health care when referring to patients experiencing a psychotic breakdown.

However, the current predominant NHS therapy of choice is cognitive behavioural therapy (CBT). Generally, CBT makes no reference to patients' spirituality. For example, the NHS Choices website describes CBT as being 'based on the concept that your thoughts, feelings, physical sensations and actions are interconnected, and that negative thoughts and feelings can trap you in a vicious cycle' (NHS Choices 2014). More recently, the NHS has seen a rapid rise in the use of what has been termed mindfulness-based cognitive therapy (MBCT) and its cousin mindfulness-based stress reduction (MBSR). MBCT utilizes the science behind CBT and combines it with contemporary forms of mindfulness meditation which are based on Buddhist and other ancient practices found within various faith traditions, including Christianity, Islam and Hinduism. MBCT has become the treatment of choice for the prevention of recurrent depression and anxiety-related disorders. MBSR is used for a variety of conditions but is primarily a tool for stress reduction. While all the above have roots in spiritual teachings, as they are applied in the NHS they are strictly non-religious. Dialectical-based therapy (DBT) is also derived from CBT and is widely used by occupational therapists and others in mental health services. It was originally developed to help treat patients with borderline personality disorder and focuses on trauma and post-traumatic stress responses. As an approach, it emphasizes the psycho-social (not spiritual) aspect of treatment and practitioners also teach mindfulness skills.

A widespread feature of mental health services since 2008 is the government-backed Improving Access to Psychological Therapies (IAPT) programme, which provides short-term evidence-based CBT, dynamic interpersonal therapy (DIT) for the treatment of anxiety and depression, and interpersonal psychotherapy (IPT), also for the treatment of depression, and, when appropriate, eye movement desensitization and reprocessing (EMDR) for the treatment of trauma and increasingly for phobias, anxiety and depression.

Other psychological approaches to care within the NHS include a significant number of child and adolescent psychotherapists who utilize a family systems approach to counselling and psychotherapy, a small number of psychoanalytically trained psychotherapists and an even smaller number of psychiatrists who are also psychotherapists.

Family systems therapy does not work with specific issues, spiritual or otherwise. During family systems therapy, family members act out their roles in such a way that the therapist and other family members are able to see the cause and effect of certain behaviours. The family can then work to understand how their actions affect each other. With the possible exception of palliative care, where existential and spiritual issues are often freely discussed, psychoanalytical literature in health care generally does not pay specific attention to spiritual issues. While there has been strong support for religion among some key psychoanalytic figures, for example Jung (1933) and Maslow (1968), over the decades since Freud, many writers have echoed his conceptualization of religious behaviours as sublimations of sexuality or aggression. Examples of this are Ellis (1980) and Rempel (1997). It has also been postulated (e.g. Wallace 1983) that psychoanalysis owes its rise to the dying off and subsequent redundancy and therefore irrelevance of communities of faith and belief.

In light of the brief survey above, whichever modality we refer to in terms of health care provision it may be concluded that, apart from the spiritual crisis network, which is still comparatively small, there is minimal reference to spirituality within counselling and psychotherapy in health care.

Having explored the field of health care in relation to spiritual care and the limited links with counselling and psychotherapy I now turn to a consideration of the links between *both* spiritual and pastoral care and their relationship to counselling and psychotherapy within the role of the health care chaplain. By so doing I will begin to further define psycho-spiritual care in health care practice.

Counselling and psychotherapy and spiritual and pastoral care in the practice of a health care chaplain

Swinton, writing as an academic and former mental health chaplain, states that:

> Within the area of mental health care, it is very rare for matters of spirituality and religion to be taken seriously within the therapeutic process, that is, as something which has the potential to positively affect the outcome of the therapeutic process as opposed to a manifestation of psychopathology. Whilst many might acknowledge spirituality as subjectively important, in the sense of being an experience or outlook which may in some way be helpful to particular individuals, few would wish to pursue the implications of a person's spirituality within the therapeutic care plan. (1997, p.118)

While this is undoubtedly true, there are a small number of chaplains who are also therapists who would argue the case, from the perspective of multi-disciplinary practice, for spirituality and faith to be taken seriously as a form of therapeutic care. Head, referring to her work with older adults with mental health needs, says, 'The notion of *relationality* and the communication of *presence* are the most vital aspects of spiritual care giving as they relate to the maintaining of personhood' (2006, p.14, emphasis in original).

Nolan (2011) also writes from the perspective of practice. As a hospice chaplain, he introduces a number of concepts from the world of counselling and psychotherapy. These include the idea of the hospice chaplain as 'evocative presence' and the idea 'that when chaplains stay with a negative transference, they demonstrate their preparedness to be in human contact with a person who is dying no matter what'. He identifies this as 'the point at which the relationship between the dying person and the chaplain can turn into something that has the potential to be creatively therapeutic' (p.16).

Writing as a former mental health chaplain who was for many years based at the Maudsley Hospital in South London, Sutherland (2006) seeks to bridge the gap between psychiatry and spirituality. He does this by outlining a view of transpersonal psychology that takes account of Ken Wilber's (2000) four quadrants of consciousness. These are:

1. the spiritual

2. the scientific observational

3. culture-myth shared systems of meaning

4. social structures.

Sutherland suggests that chaplains, while inhabiting the spiritual quadrant in their work, hold the tension between all four. His argument is that 'all spiritual practices, whether incorporated into conventional religious systems, or esoteric, are designed to relax the boundaries around the self-centre so that more energy from the spiritual ground can safely be incorporated within an expansion of self-centre' (2006, p.3). Self-centre he defines as a psychological entity that derives from a person's soul or spirit and states that for chaplains it is imperative that they understand that when the 'soul fails to incarnate and fully inhabit the self-centre it always remains half open to the spiritual ground. It becomes mad in order to express the excruciating suffering of having no way back and yet no way forward either' (p.6). As a view of 'madness', transpersonal theory suggests that 'soul suffering' is a necessary process of soul making. Sutherland's approach to transpersonal theory suggests that the role of the mental health professional is to somehow help a patient interpret and resolve their psychopathology. In this regard the chaplain's role would therefore appear to be central. However, this radical approach to patient care has not been translated into practice within the NHS and with the present predominance of psycho-pharmaceutical care it seems doubtful that it will. Nevertheless, this is clearly an important attempt to bridge the gap between psychiatry and spirituality.

Apart from contributions from Nolan, Head and Sutherland, I am unaware of any other health care chaplains writing today who write or research from a context of training and experience in counselling and psychotherapy.

Other health care practitioners who state their interest in spiritual and pastoral care do not explore the relationship between therapeutic practice and spiritual and pastoral care. For example, in the book *Spirituality and Psychiatry,* Cook, Powell and Sims (2009) do not refer to the concept of spiritual and pastoral care as therapeutic practice. Cox, Campbell and Fulford (2007) take account of personal relationships, spirituality, ethics and theology. However, the concept of relating spiritual and pastoral care to therapy is not explored. Similarly, in a seminal book (though now somewhat dated) entitled *Being There: Pastoral Care in Time of Illness*, Speck (1988) gives a detailed account of pastoral practice within health care but does not refer to counselling or psychotherapy.

Unlike the UK, in the US the relationship between counselling and psychotherapy and spiritual and pastoral care has been formalized. Training is delivered to clergy (mandatory for health care chaplains) in the form of clinical pastoral education, which integrates pastoral and spiritual and psychological approaches to care. CPE is the primary method of training hospital and hospice chaplains in the United States, Australia, Ireland, Canada and New Zealand. It uses the real-life ministry encounters of students to develop pastoral care. However, CPE is not recognized or generally practised in the UK.

Given the dearth of literature on the subject, the lack of any formalized CPE in this country and the consequent need for further research, it may therefore be argued that the most obvious place to explore the relationship between therapy and spiritual and pastoral care is within the NHS, where chaplains who may also be therapists, such as myself, are employed as part of the multi-disciplinary team providing spiritual and pastoral care.

I have come to realize that as a health care chaplain, my training and experience in spiritual and pastoral care cannot be separated from my training and experience in counselling and psychotherapy. I have argued above that health care chaplains who are trained as therapists will, to a greater or lesser extent, bring the whole of their training and experience to bear on their interactions with patients, carers and staff. As previously indicated, my job description presupposes a high level of training in 'psychologically informed knowledge'. Yet as I stated earlier, there is no attempt to define what is meant by this. This lack of clarity is the basis for my exploration of the relationship between counselling and psychotherapy and spiritual and pastoral care. The issue of how health care chaplains might bring together theological and psychological insights into their practice is crucial, if they are going to work in ways that are integrative and holistic.

References

American Psychiatric Association (1990) Guidelines regarding possible conflict between psychiatrists' religious commitment and psychiatric practice. *American Journal of Psychiatry*, 147(4), 542.

Arnold, W.V. (1982) *Introduction to Pastoral Care*. Philadelphia, PA: Westminster Press.

Autton, N. (1966) *The Hospital Ministry*. London: Church Information Office.

Bartlett, P. and Wright, D. (1999) *Outside the Walls of the Asylum: The History of Care in the Community 1750–2000*. London: Athlone Press.

Benner, P. and Wrubel, J. (1989) *The Primacy of Caring: Stress and Coping in Health and Illness*. Boston, MA: Addison-Wesley.

Bridger, F. and Atkinson, D. (2007) *Counselling in Context: Developing a Theological Framework*. Pasadena, CA: Fuller Seminary Press.

Browning, D. (1977) Pastoral care and models of training in counselling. *Contact: The Interdisciplinary Journal of Pastoral Studies*, 57, 12–19.

Campbell, A.V. (1986) *Rediscovering Pastoral Care*. London: DLT.

Clebsch, W.A. and Jaekle, C.R. (1967) *Pastoral Care in Historical Perspective*. New York: Harper.

Coates, S. (1995) Spiritual components in palliative care. *European Journal of Palliative Care,* 2(1) (Spring), 37–39.

Contact (1994) *The Interdisciplinary Journal of Pastoral Studies.* Lightwater: Contact Pastoral Trust.

Cook, C., Powell, A. and Sims, A. (eds) (2009) *Spirituality and Psychiatry.* London: RCPsych Publications.

Cox, J., Campbell, A.V. and Fulford, K.W.M. (eds) (2007) *Medicine of the Person: Faith, Science and Values in Health Care Provision.* London: Jessica Kingsley Publishers.

Culliford, L. (2002) *Spiritual Care and Psychiatric Treatment: An Introduction.* London: Royal College of Psychiatrists.

Duff, V. (2003) Clinical pastoral education (CPE): A reflection. *Scottish Journal of Healthcare Chaplaincy,* 6(2), 35–38.

Ellis, A. (1980) Psychotherapy and atheistic values: A response to A.E. Bergin's 'psychotherapy and religious values'. *Journal of Counselling and Clinical Psychology,* 48(5), 635–639.

Finnane, M. (1985) Asylums, families and the state. *History Workshop Journal,* 20(1), 134–148.

Foskett, J. (1984) *Meaning in Madness: The Pastor and the Mentally Ill.* London: SPCK.

Foskett, J. (2001) Can pastoral counselling recover its roots in madness? *British Journal of Guidance and Counselling,* 29(4), 403–413.

General Medical Council (2008) *Personal Beliefs and Medical Practice.* London: General Medical Council.

Gilbert, P., Kaur, N. and Parkes, M. (2010) Let's get spiritual. *Mental Health Today,* October, 28–33.

Grainger, R. (1998) *The Social Symbolism of Grief and Mourning.* London: Jessica Kingsley Publishers.

Grof, C. and Grof, S. (1989) *Spiritual Emergency: When Personal Transformation Becomes a Crisis.* Los Angeles: Tarcher.

Harrison, G. (1998) *Hospice Spiritual Care and Suffering: An Examination of the Role of the Hospice Multi-disciplinary Team in Providing Spiritual Care and an Assessment of the Implications for Constructing a Practical Theodicy of Suffering.* Unpublished MTh dissertation. Westminster College, Oxford.

Head, J. (2006) A rich tapestry: Emergent themes in spirituality in the care of older adults with mental health needs. *Spirituality and Psychiatry Special Interest Group Newsletter,* 21, 1–18.

Holifield, E.B. (1983) *A History of Pastoral Care in America: From Salvation to Self-Realization.* Nashville, TN: Abingdon Press.

Holloway, M. and Moss, B. (2010) *Spirituality and Social Work.* London: Palgrave Macmillan.

Jacobs, M. (1984) *Still Small Voice.* London: SPCK.

James, W. (1936) *The Varieties of Religious Experience: A Study in Human Nature.* New York: Modern Library.

Jenkins, C. (2011) Priest? Therapist? Both? Learning from research and experience. *Thresholds: Counselling with Spirit,* Spring, 19–22.

Jung, C. (1933) *Modern Man in Search of a Soul.* San Diego, CA: Harcourt Brace.

Kearney, M. (1996) *Mortally Wounded: Stories of Soul Pain, Death and Healing.* Dublin: Marino.

Koenig, H., McCullough, M. and Larson, D. (eds) (2001) *Handbook of Religion and Health.* New York: Oxford University Press.

Koenig, H., King, D. and Carson, V. (eds) (2012) *Handbook of Religion and Health* (2nd edition). New York: Oxford University Press.

Lines, D. (2007) *Spirituality in Counselling and Psychotherapy*. London: Sage.

Lyall, D. (1994) *Counselling in the Pastoral and Spiritual Context*. Buckingham: Open University Press.

Lynch, G. (ed.) (1999) *Clinical Counselling in Pastoral Settings*. London: Routledge.

Mair, M. (1989) *Between Psychology and Psychotherapy: A Poetics of Experience*. London: Routledge.

Maslow, A. (1968) *Toward a Psychology of Being* (2nd edition). New York: Van Nostrund.

McSherry, W. (2006) *Making Sense of Spirituality in Nursing and Health Care Practice: An Interactive Approach*. London: Jessica Kingsley Publishers.

Mearns, D. and Thorne, B. (1999) *Person-Centred Counselling in Action* (2nd edition). London: Sage.

Mental Health Foundation (1997) *Knowing Our Own Minds*. London: Mental Health Foundation.

Mental Health Foundation (2006) *The Impact of Spirituality on Mental Health*. London: Mental Health Foundation.

Moltmann, J. (1974) *The Crucified God*. London: SCM.

Moore, J. and Purton, C. (eds) (2006) *Spirituality and Counselling: Experiential and Theoretical Perspectives*. Ross-on-Wye: PCCS Books.

Murray, R.B. and Zentner, J.P. (1989) *Nursing Concepts for Health Promotion*. London: Prentice Hall.

National Hospice Organisation (1982) *Standards of a Hospice Programme*. Arlington, VA: McLean.

National Mental Health and Spirituality Forum (2011) *Report on the Place of Spirituality in Mental Health*. London: National Mental Health and Spirituality Forum.

NHS Chaplaincy Guidelines (2015) *Promoting Excellence in Pastoral, Spiritual and Religious Care*. London: Department of Health.

NHS Choices (2014) Cognitive Behavioural Therapy (CBT). Available at www.nhs.uk/ Conditions/Cognitive-behavioural-therapy, accessed on 11 December 2016.

Nolan, S. (2011) *Spiritual Care at the End of Life: The Chaplain as a Hopeful Presence*. London: Jessica Kingsley Publishers.

Orchard, H. (2000) *Hospital Chaplaincy: Modern, Dependable?* Sheffield: Lincoln Theological Institute for the Study of Religion and Society.

Orchard, H. (ed.) (2001) *Spirituality in Health Care Contexts*. London: Jessica Kingsley Publishers.

Pargament, K. (1997) *The Psychology of Religion and Coping: Theory, Research, Practice*. New York: Guilford Press.

Pargament, K. (2011) *Spiritually Integrated Psychotherapy: Understanding and Addressing the Sacred*. New York: Guilford Press.

Pargament, K. (ed.) (2013) *APA Handbook of Psychology, Religion, and Spirituality*. Washington, DC: American Psychological Association.

Pattison, S. (2000) *A Critique of Pastoral Care*. London: SCM.

Rempel, M. (1997) Understanding Freud's philosophy of religion. *Canadian Journal of Psychoanalysis*, 5(2), 215–242.

Richards, P., Hardman, R. and Berrett, M. (2007) Theistic counselling and psychotherapy: Conceptual framework and application to counselling practice. *Counselling and Spirituality*, 26(2), 79–102.

Richards, S. and Bergin, A. (1997) *A Spiritual Strategy for Counselling and Psychotherapy*. Washington, DC: American Psychological Association.

Rogers, C. (1967) *On Becoming a Person: A Therapist's View of Psychotherapy.* London: Constable.

Ross, L. (1996) Teaching spiritual care to nurses. *Nurse Education Today,* 16(1), 38–43.

Ross, L. (1997) *Nurses' Perception of Health Care.* Aldershot: Avebury.

Rowan, J. (1993) *The Transpersonal: Psychotherapy and Counselling.* London: Routledge.

Royal College of Nursing (2011) *Spirituality in Nursing Care: A Pocket Guide.* London: Royal College of Nursing.

Royal College of Psychiatrists (2010) *Spirituality and Mental Health.* London: Royal College of Psychiatrists.

Royal College of Psychiatrists (2011) *Recommendations for Psychiatrists on Spirituality and Religion.* Position Statement PS03/2011. London: Royal College of Psychiatrists. Available at www.rcpsych.ac.uk/pdf/PS03_2013.pdf, accessed on 9 December 2016.

Soelle, D. (1975) *Suffering.* London: DLT.

South Yorkshire NHS Workforce Development Confederation (2003) *Caring for the Spirit: A Strategy for the Chaplaincy and Spiritual Health Care Workforce.* Sheffield: South Yorkshire Strategic Health Authority.

Speck, P. (1988) *Being There: Pastoral Care in Time of Illness.* London: SPCK.

Spiritual Crisis Network (2014) *Stanislav Grof's Description.* Available at http://spiritualcrisisnetwork.uk/what-is-sc/stanislav-grofs-description, accessed on 20 January 2017.

Sproston, K. and Nazroo, J. (eds) (2002) *Ethnic Minority Psychiatric Illness Rates in the Community (EMPERIC) Quantitative Report.* London: Department of Health.

Sutherland, M. (2006) Transpersonal psychology – bridging the gap between psychiatry and spirituality. Unpublished workshop notes at Chaplaincy Study Day, 27 November, Musgrove Park Hospital, Taunton.

Swift, C. (2014) *Hospital Chaplaincy in the Twenty-first Century: The Crisis of Spiritual Care in the NHS* (2nd edition). Farnham: Ashgate.

Swinton, J. (1997) Resurrecting the person: Redefining mental illness – a spiritual perspective. *Psychiatric Care,* 4(3), 118–121.

Swinton, J. (2000) *Spirituality and Mental Health Care.* London: Jessica Kingsley Publishers.

Taylor, M. (1983) *Learning to Care: Christian Reflection on Pastoral Practice.* London: SPCK.

Thorne, B. (2012) *Counselling and Spiritual Accompaniment: Bridging Faith and Person-Centred Therapy.* Chichester: Wiley-Blackwell.

Wallace, E. (1983) Reflections on the relationship between psychoanalysis and Christianity. *Pastoral Psychology,* 31, 215–233.

West, W. (2000) *Psychotherapy and Spirituality: Crossing the Line between Therapy and Religion.* London: Sage.

West, W. (ed.) (2011) *Exploring Therapy, Spirituality and Healing.* Basingstoke: Palgrave Macmillan.

Whitehead, A.N. (1929) *Process and Reality: An Essay in Cosmology.* New York: Macmillan.

Wilber, K. (2000) *Integral Psychology: Consciousness, Spirit, Psychology, Therapy.* Boston, MA: Shambhala Publications.

Williams, D.D. (1964) *Christianity and Naturalism.* London: Nislet.

Willows, D. and Swinton, J. (eds) (2000) *Spiritual Dimensions of Pastoral Care: Practical Theology in a Multidisciplinary Context.* London: Jessica Kingsley Publishers.

Wise, C.A. (1980) *Pastoral Psychotherapy: Theory and Practice.* New York: Jason Aronson.

Woodward, J. (1998) *A study of the role of the acute health care chaplain in England.* Unpublished PhD thesis. Open University.

2

An Autoethnographic Narrative Case Study Approach to Research

In this chapter I describe the autoethnographic narrative case study approach that I used in my research based on my practice as a health care chaplain who is also a trained psychotherapist. I go on to consider the implications of this research for the development of psycho-spiritual care in health care practice. My rationale for including here the autoethnographic methodological approach, one that until very recently was comparatively unknown, is that within qualitative approaches to research it illustrates a way of understanding my role in terms of the meanings I bring to it. According to McLeod, 'The starting point for qualitative research is conversations and stories and interpretations of object, images and rituals that tell stories or are meaningful in some way' (2011, p.3). Autoethnography is increasingly adopted whenever researchers wish to move from the prevalent scientist-practitioner discourse (McIlveen 2007) in order to connect the personal with the cultural by giving voice to personal experience in order to extend understanding and develop practice.

According to Spry autoethnography is:

Body and verse.
It is self and other and one and many.
It is ensemble, a capella, and accompaniment.
Autoethnography is place and space and time.
It is personal, political and palpable.
It is art and craft. It is jazz and blues.
It is messy, bloody, and unruly.
It is agency, rendition, and dialogue.
It is danger, trouble, and pain.
It is critical, reflexive, performative, and often forgiving.

…

It is sceptical and restorative.
It is an interpreted body
of evidence.
It is personally accountable.
It is wholly none of these, but fragments of each.
It is a performance of possibilities.

(Spry 2011, p.497)

Locating a study within qualitative research

Qualitative research is a way of seeking to understand how the social, personal and relational world of the various research participants is constructed and applied. It seeks to understand the often complex and multi-layered perspectives of all who take part in the research. Qualitative approaches are engaged with exploring, describing and interpreting experience. Rather than attempt to test a preconceived hypothesis, qualitative researchers seek to understand experience from the participant's frame of reference or world view. My choice of research methodology was guided by my desire to construct an account of my practice rather than being guided by a predetermined theoretical stance. It was therefore inductive qualitative research, which begins with detailed observations and moves towards more abstract notions and ideas. According to Bager-Charleson, 'inductive reasoning is typically characterized by unbiased observations; it starts with an open mind and a deliberate attempt to suspend explanatory models or theories' (2014, p.4). This runs counter to any assumption that research is deductive, starting with a theory or a particular hypothesis which is then tested out.

Cresswell (2007) indicates that Denzin and Lincoln's (2011) most recent definition of qualitative research emphasizes not only its capacity to describe, construct and interpret meaning but also the capacity to transform the world. This definition is in accord with my desire to inform and elucidate an alternative source of ideas for the development of a framework for practice and for further research into psycho-spiritual care.

Key to all qualitative research is the descriptive process. This is the detailed account of a particular element of social reality that is being investigated. Only when this reality has been described is it possible to analyse or interpret it in the context of its wider meaning and significance. For this reason, the first element of any qualitative research is usually phenomenology, a description of the lived world of experience. The second element in qualitative research is hermeneutics, 'the process of understanding the meaning of a particular phenomenon' (McLeod 2011, p.21). Both elements were basic to my research approach. Referring to Seamon (2000), Finlay states that:

> Phenomenologists seek to capture lived experience – to connect directly and immediately with the world as we experience it. The focus is on our personal or shared meanings, as distinct from the objective physical world explored by science: The aim is to clarify taken-for-granted human situations and events that are known in everyday life but typically unnoticed and unquestioned. (Finlay 2011, p.15)

Heidegger (1962) used the concept of 'everydayness' to argue that both phenomenology and hermeneutics should be seen as being integral aspects of any study of human experience. Heidegger's aim was to develop an appreciation of the 'essence' of everyday life and everyday understanding. Van Manen (1990) developed this concept into a research approach which he terms 'hermeneutic phenomenological reflection'. This form of reflection has increasingly been adopted and adapted by researchers in counselling and psychotherapy. Van Manen argues that there are four fundamental 'existentials' by which human beings experience the world. These are lived space, lived body, lived time and lived other. Utilizing these four existentials in my research I endeavoured to:

- Enquire into the ways in which I experience my day-to-day work of meaning making, in my relationship with patients, clients, staff and the organization. This is my lived space.

- Understand how, when I encounter the world of another person, we first of all meet through our physical presence. This is my lived body, a place of potential revelation and concealment.

- Explore the connections with personal life history (my own and those I encounter) – past, present and future. This is my lived time.

- Assess the interpersonal connections with those I meet in my day-to-day work which have the potential for being transcended into what Buber (1958) describes as an I–Thou encounter. This is the lived other.

According to Finlay, the aim of hermeneutic phenomenology is 'to evoke lived experience through the explicit involvement of interpretation. Lived experience is thematized through language and understood by being refracted through a variety of lenses – philosophical, theoretical, literary and reflexive' (2011, p.110).

In my analysis, I therefore used an interpretive hermeneutic. In this research tradition, 'the intent is not to develop a procedure for understanding, but to clarify the conditions that can lead to understanding' (Holroyd 2007, p.1). This engagement in the experience of understanding is an ongoing discovery that is quite different from an objectified method of gaining knowledge. By adopting this approach to research I brought as much of myself as I could (body, mind and spirit) into the research. My role as interpreter was therefore conditioned by my personal and professional frame of reference as both practitioner and researcher. My research findings were also mediated by my own personal circumstances and background as a chaplain and therapist whose role is head of spiritual and pastoral care in an NHS mental and community health care Trust. To help me in maintaining and understanding this constant interplay my writing was reflexive. By adopting a reflexive approach to my autoethnographic writing, I was seeking to understand how I construct meaning in and through the lived experience of my practice.

The assumption that as human beings we are constantly seeking to interpret, to make meaning out of experience, is influenced by the conviction that forms the basis of Gadamer's hermeneutics, 'that understanding is not just one of the various possible *behaviours* of the subject, but the mode of being of There-being itself' (1979, p.xviii, emphasis in original). The world views, values and pre-existing theories of the researcher therefore inevitably influence and shape the research, and the research process in turn influences the researcher. A reflexive approach seeks to make this reciprocal relationship explicit. The researcher becomes the primary research tool enabling the dialogically extrapolated meanings of any particular issue or conversation to be explored and interpreted. Researcher reflexivity so constructed may therefore be understood as 'the capacity of the researcher to acknowledge how their own experiences and contexts (which might be fluid and changing) inform the process and outcomes of inquiry' (Etherington 2004, pp.31–32). By using reflexivity in my research I was attempting to close the gap between what I thought I knew as researcher and practitioner and what was known by those I met in my daily interactions with patients, carers and staff. Reflexivity also helps with processing the often difficult and deeply moving stories of pain and suffering. Most especially in this context, reflexivity has supported my understandings of myself as endeavouring to be completely attentive to the other, offering an unconditional and empathic presence. This attitude is described by Doane (2008) as reflexive presence.

As du Plock (2010) states, 'reflexivity enables therapists to ground their research in subjective experience and naïve inquiry with confidence' (p.134).

Choosing autoethnography

I chose autoethnography as my methodological approach primarily because my aim was to produce research that is grounded in personal experience and alerts readers to the culture- and values-laden institutional context in which I exercised my role as researcher. As Ellis (2004) says, 'Autoethnography is an approach to research and writing that seeks to describe and systematically analyse (*graphy*) personal experience (*auto*) in order to understand cultural experience (*ethno*)' (p.1).

In a counselling and psychotherapy context McLeod suggests that as a research approach 'ethnography is uniquely capable of capturing the quality and characteristics of the "lived interactions" between therapists and client' (2001, p.68). As a developing field within counselling and psychotherapy research autoethnography particularly appeals to therapists who are trained in humanistic approaches and who use congruence and/or self-disclosure as a way of assisting clients to tell their particular story. It therefore fits into my own Person-Centred modality of training and practice.

Probably one of the foremost proponents of autoethnography is Kim Etherington (2000, 2004). Etherington states that autoethnography 'has provided a methodology that legitimizes and encourages the inclusion of the researcher's self and culture, as an ethical and politically sound approach' (2004, p.141). According to Rossman and Sallis, 'this takes into consideration the complex interplay of our own personal biography, power and status, interactions with participants, and written word' (1998, p.67). In relation to autoethnography, Riessman and Speedy have also stated that 'approaching texts as narrative, whether written or conversational, has a great deal to offer the practicing professions, showing how knowledge is constructed in everyday worlds through ordinary communicative action' (2007, p.431).

Angus and McLeod (2004) argue that the concept of narrative is so fundamental to human psychological and social life and carries with it such a rich set of meanings that it provides a genuine meeting point between theoretical schools of therapy that have previously stood apart from each other. In other words, according to McLeod (2003), it becomes a powerful discovery-orientated approach to research which may be informed by 'indwelling' (Moustakas 1990) on all aspects of practice.

As I stated in the Introduction, the focus of my research was an evaluation of my practice as head of spiritual and pastoral care within an NHS health Trust. Within this role, I sought to combine my training and experience in Person-Centred therapy with my training and experience in spiritual and pastoral care. It was a personal story researched through an in-depth, single-narrative case study of practice, set within an autoethnographical frame.

My rationale for choosing this methodological approach reflects the fact that while numerous studies of spiritual care exist and the relationship with counselling and psychotherapy is often referred to, they bear little resemblance to the role I inhabit. None of the published research captures the experience of caring for patients and how contextual influences shape and constrain such care. This lack of integration provided the impetus to research my own experience.

One criticism of the autoethnographic approach is to suggest that by focusing on myself in this way I ran the risk of shaping the production of the data in such a fashion that I could be said to be producing what I expected to find. In order to address this risk the approach had reflexivity as a central component. As previously indicated, reflexivity is a way of making transparent my values and beliefs as they affect my interpretations and as they consequently influence the research process and its outcomes. As Finlay states, 'Reflexive revelations in the research context probably have greatest value when one's own experiences shed light on others' experience, i.e. when the account goes *beyond* the personal' (2011, p.15, emphasis in original).

In addition, McLeod (2010) suggests that by employing the qualitative research tradition of narrative inquiry the researcher 'emphasises the role of storytelling and narrative as a distinctive way of knowing' (p.27). McLeod also suggests that narrative case studies 'serve as an invaluable heuristic source of ideas for the development of theory and research' (p.27).

The goal of autoethnography is to produce analytically accessible texts that affect the researcher, practitioner and reader in ways that enable positive and creative change. By applying an autoethnographic approach as both researcher and practitioner I sought to construct an intimate and sometimes visceral critical understanding of my identity in relation to my day-to-day experience as a chaplain who is also trained as a therapist. I also sought to develop my awareness of the influences and roles in my work with patients, staff and carers with a view to influencing the development of an integrated approach to my work; in other words, an approach that focuses on the development of a model of psycho-spiritual care that is inclusive of counselling and psychotherapy and spiritual and pastoral care.

I also chose to use the term 'narrative case study'. Narrative is the means by which I interact with patients, carers and staff. Narrative also conveys my experience of care. Narrative has been defined as:

> A story that tells a sequence of events that is significant for the narrator and his or her audience. A narrative as a story has a plot, a beginning and an end. It has an internal logic that makes sense to the narrator. A narrator relates events in a temporal, causal sequence: every narrative describes a sequence of events that have happened. (Denzin 1989, p.37)

This is a helpful framework in which I can place the narrative of my 'lived world' of experience as head of spiritual and pastoral care. The challenge of my reflexive writing and subsequent analysis was to make clear to the reader something of the meaning, purpose and values within the narrative that seek to influence me and inform the development of the theory and practice of psychologically informed spiritual and pastoral care. In order to facilitate this, I sometimes utilized a simple poetic form with the aim of constructing a narrative that conveys the essential essence of a conversation. Ricoeur describes something of this process when he defines narrative as 'containing images and metaphors, symbols of the narrator's lived experience, literary devices which provide poetic language strategies to articulate lived experience' (1981, p.26). Narrative is also relational. The stories I tell are told at particular times to particular people for particular reasons. In this sense narratives relate what people mean to each other; the relational nature of the storytelling establishes a relationship and the possibility of connectedness to others' experience.

Because autoethnographic findings relate to unique situations, the question of generalization and the usability of the findings in different situations needs to be addressed. The primary aim of autoethnography is not to produce an analytic account but an evocative narrative that expresses the essence of what it is like to be in a given situation. The intention is to enable the reader, as far as they are able, to enter into the experience for themselves and to construct their own understandings and interpretations of the material that is produced. As stated previously, my aim was to 'produce research that is grounded in personal experience and alerts readers to the cultural and values laden institutional context in which as researcher I exercise my role' (Harrison 2014, p.136).

The act of doing, sharing and reading autoethnography aims to transform researchers and readers alike. Autoethnography is a form of idiographic knowledge which presumes that what is discovered is a set of unique, non-replicable experiences that hold meaning and value. As an approach it helps to give authority to the practitioner-researcher voice. It enables further understanding of the cultural context and the interpersonal influences that shape a given situation. It can also provide an alternative source of ideas for the development of theory and further research. Slater (2013), referring to case study, points out that:

> The issue of generalisation crystallises the rich potential of the paradox at the heart of case study: the more in-depth the exploration of the particular, the greater the potential both for the discovery of something unique and the recognition of a universal 'truth'... It is through the study of the unique case that we come to understand the universal. (2013, p.49)

The same can be said to be true of autoethnography.

Because of the personal nature of the material, in any research of this kind the ethical considerations need careful attention. In the next section of this chapter, I therefore consider the ethical implications of researching my practice and the need for a robust approach to ensuring accountability and transparency as a researcher-practitioner.

The ethical implications of researching my practice and the use of reflexivity within practitioner research

The use of an autoethnographic methodology meant that I adopted a form of practitioner-research described by Rolfe as 'research that is undertaken by the practitioner into herself and her own practice' (1998, p.675). Such an undertaking raised a number of ethical concerns, not least of which was the issue of whether the reader was sufficiently cognizant of the underlying influences and values that may affect what I portrayed in each data set. To counteract the potential criticism that I was insufficiently aware of such influences and values it was important to include my researcher perspective by way of a reflexive approach to writing. As Altheide and Johnson state when describing the 'arts and practices of interpretation, evaluation and representation', the researcher has 'an ethical obligation to make public their claims, to show the reader, audiences, or consumer why they should be trusted as faithful accounts of some phenomenon' (2011, p.584). Reflexive writing appropriately addresses this ethical concern by 'making transparent the values and beliefs we hold that almost certainly influence the research process and its outcomes' (Etherington 2007, p.601).

As an extended narrative of my practice over a six-month period, the research sought to be as honest, open minded and questioning of my experience and involvement as possible. Citing Alvesson and Skohlberg, Etherington states, 'interpreting one's own interpretations, looking for one's own perspectives, and turning a self-critical eye onto one's own authority as interpreter and author enhances the trustworthiness of the findings and outcomes of research' (2004, p.32).

Hudson Jones (1998), cited by Bolton, further evidences the efficacy of the above approach when she describes how narratives of practice are used to teach 'narrative ethics, offering richer ethical discourse for all' (2010, p.60).

Personal integrity is a key ethical hallmark of practitioner research. Recognizing and respecting the dignity of self and others is clearly a vital component of all research, as is taking responsibility for the choices that are made in the subsequent interpretation and analysis of the research. My aim throughout was to make my values as explicit as possible. It was vital to me to be able to portray my experiences as near to reality as possible, as respectful, honest, visceral, complex, mundane, powerful and sometimes exhausting as they were!

In this research project I was both researcher and participant. Since my practice as a health care chaplain is based on interactions with patients, carers, students, staff and colleagues, I have a duty to uphold their dignity, rights, safety and wellbeing.

An excellent example of how it is possible to develop practitioner research, whilst maintaining an ethical stance that upholds patient dignity and wellbeing, is that of Duke (2007). Duke's PhD research is grounded in autobiographical observation and reflection on her day-to-day interactions with patients and staff as a lecturer-practitioner in palliative care. In a similar way, my work was premised on the basis that the only participant in the research was myself as practitioner–researcher. My participation in the research was in the context of the interactions I had with patients and staff in my practice as head of spiritual and pastoral care. The perspectives, reflections on or construction of these interactions were set within my research practice. In this sense, I privileged my own voice. Other voices were present through my various interactions; however, their voices were re-presented through my reflections. In order to preserve the integrity of the conversations I had with patients and staff and in order to avoid any misrepresentations, I carefully recorded, analysed and portrayed the experience in ways that I hope respect the original intention of the interaction. On several occasions, I used the words, phrases and images that were similar to those described by the person themselves. However, they were only ever presented in the context of snapshots of much longer conversations or as an aid to distilling the essence of a particular encounter. The use of poetic form was especially useful in this latter regard. It is important to reiterate at this point that the analysis and evaluation of each narrative was based on my work as a whole and cannot be attributable to any one individual. No additional information, for example demographics, was collected. Names of people and places within the narrative were anonymized.

The research process has brought insights from the theory and practice of counselling and psychotherapy and spiritual and pastoral care into critical dialogue with an analysis of the empirical data and insights from my own phronesis. As a result, this process has generated new insight into the relationship between counselling and psychotherapy and spiritual and pastoral care. This new insight has a number of significant implications for the development of psycho-spiritual care.

The implications for developing psycho-spiritual care in health care practice

My research, the attendant literature and subsequent feedback strongly suggest that the work of the chaplain who is also a therapist is a form of boundary dwelling. As part of a holistic approach to patient care this 'dwelling place' is one that needs spiritual awareness; pastoral knowledge in the form of understandings of immanence, transcendence and the nature of suffering; and a high degree of psychological insight and training which for some will be in the form of counselling and psychotherapy. For those who inhabit such boundaries, they are often painful and fearful places as well as being places of transition.

In person-centred terms, such *in-between*, liminal places are places where chaplains, patients and staff may collaborate in creative ways, sharing deep fears and hopes and offering empathic care. As I shall explore in more detail in the following chapter, liminal places are also risky places, places of birth, death and re-birth where transitions are sometimes mediated by ritual, whether sacramental or symbolic or a mixture of both. They are places where chaplains and others may 'live the questions of suffering… places of sudden encounter and exchange, which can be surprising, or shocking; where suddenly there is a meeting or encounter *in* Love and *in* Truth' (Robinson 1995, p.5). What Robinson calls Love may be defined theologically as agape, which I understand to mean unconditional love and which correlates with what Person-Centred therapists term 'unconditional positive regard' and empathy which is understood to be the necessary condition for healing to occur. These liminal places are places where it is important to stay present, where for the person of faith God is experienced as being somewhere in the chaos, the messiness of life or the life-limiting zombie-like state that some patients are left in by medication. They are also places where the principles of the Recovery Approach (cf. Chapter 3), which seeks to place the patient at the centre of care, are at the forefront of an inclusive, holistic approach to care that includes the spiritual aspects of personhood and of human flourishing.

Liminal places are also places that demand a quality of 'being' rather than 'doing'. My research suggests that it is ultimately the chaplain's 'being' and the quality of the chaplain's presence that are most essential to, and held in common by, spiritual care, pastoral care and counselling and psychotherapy. 'Being' is understood as a combination of curiosity, openness, non-judgement, empathy and present moment awareness, which in Zen Buddhism is called 'beginner's mind'. According to Gordon-Graham, 'beginner's mind is a mind that is open, fresh, curious, present here and now, natural, free and uncluttered' (2014, p.24). It is a form of unconditional presence that is open to lived and felt experience.

In his controversial book *The Divided Self* (1965) Laing also talks about the importance of love. He argues that psychopathology needs to be contextualized within the perspective of a phenomenology of love and human relatedness. My research supports Laing's view that by enabling a process of journeying inward, we may discover our relatedness to the outer world and find the possibility of love in that relatedness which is healing. Following Buber (1958), this is the 'I–Thou' relational approach that offers the potential for profound healing and growth rather than the contrasting 'I–It' style of relating with its potential for objectification. In Buber's work, the word 'I–It' denotes the world of experience in which things and people are experienced as objects. In contrast the word 'I–Thou' spoken with the whole of one's being establishes the world of relationship. As Buber says, 'as experience, the world belongs to the primary word I–It. The primary word I–Thou establishes the world of relation' (1958, p.18). However, as Denham-Vaughan (2010) points out, 'I–Thou' 'cannot be directly willed or aimed for'. It is 'in the necessary oscillation between the two (I–It and I–Thou) that we glimpse the dialectic of will and grace emerging and liminal space existent between the dialogic partners' (p.38).

My research evidence, a peer review of aspects of that evidence and feedback from workshops, advisors and critical friends strongly suggest that while there is an increasing interest in applying spiritual understandings to practice, in reality there still remains a gap or 'chasm' between theory and practice. I have used the term 'psycho-spiritual care' to suggest that spiritual care has a direct link with emotional and physical care. However, the question remains as to how health care staff can step closer to understanding and meeting spiritual needs. If we believe that within all traditions of faith as well as humanistic and existential understandings of human flourishing, there lies a deep strand of psycho-spiritual care then it should be possible to find ways of adopting psycho-spiritual approaches to care.

One possible way of developing psycho-spiritual care in mental health care is to use the Recovery Approach as a way of responding to spiritual questions of meaning and purpose. This approach suggests that recovery is a process of growthful self-change. For example, Deegan (2001), writing as a former service user and a clinical psychologist, describes how she 'experienced recovery as a transformative process in which the old self is gradually let go and a new sense of self emerges' (p.1). According to Ellingham (2013), this is essentially a psychotherapeutic process which is in harmony with Roger's core conditions and the reorganization of the self-structure, 'a holistic attitude towards the individual, one that is liberated from psychiatric diagnosis, is a feature of both Recovery and Rogerian thinking' (p.32).

At the heart of the research lay the question of whether as a chaplain, I am a pastoral and spiritual carer or a therapist or both of these. In response, the findings suggest that developing a psycho-spiritual approach enables the chaplain who is also a therapist to integrate their training and experience in both disciplines in order to respond to whatever need is being presented in each therapeutic encounter. For some patients, this will mean emphasizing the spiritual or pastoral, for others appropriately employing the skills and training of counselling and psychotherapy; for many it will be enough to be present for that person in whatever way they need me to be at that point in time.

However, the development of psycho-spiritual care within a multi-disciplinary team will be dependent upon the ability of the chaplain who has trained as a therapist and others who share this integrative approach to find allies and develop partnerships within the still predominant medical model of health care. One way of doing this is to continually emphasize the issues of meaning that are associated with illness, in order to avoid the potential pathological bias of bio-medical or psycho-social understandings of illness and disease. To reiterate, it is the experience of chaplains that for patients, as with all of us on the continuum of wellbeing, questions of value and meaning occur when they find themselves in acute pain and/or distress. For some this crisis may be described as spiritual distress. The chaplains' specialist role is then to respond to both patient need and the need to support nursing, medical and allied health care staff who may lack the confidence or skill or may be ambivalent about embracing a compassionate care that is inclusive of spirituality.

My research reinforced the fact that staff support is a key element of the role of head of spiritual and pastoral care, as it is of chaplaincy generally. My data sets included several significant encounters with staff who also experienced crisis or profound change in their lives, sometimes caused or exacerbated by working for an ever-demanding NHS. In my research analysis, I termed staff support and patient care a form of hospitality, a welcoming presence that can sometimes appear lacking in a very busy and potentially self-absorbed institution. This is a hospitality that is unconditional, that opens up the possibility of new ways of being with people within a caring organization that enables the 'guest' and 'host' to realize their potential for mutual growth and development. Over the years, I have heard several chaplains say that patients 'teach them how to live'. This reciprocity is at the heart of hospitality.

The findings also suggest that as a manager within a health care Trust, the role of a head of spiritual and pastoral care is to help the organization take seriously its responsibility to explore ways in which vulnerable patients and staff make sense of life and co-create health and wellbeing. As a chaplain who is also a therapist and 'senior leader', this will mean helping a health care organization develop its spiritual and emotional intelligence. Emotional intelligence may be defined as the capacity of individuals to recognize their own and other people's emotions and to use emotional information to guide their thinking and responses to others. De Board (1978) suggests that high levels of personal effectiveness are dependent upon high levels of organizational psychological development. As spiritual and emotional intelligence along with developing understandings of psycho-spiritual approaches to wellbeing are incorporated into daily practice, both organizational and personal wellbeing will flourish.

In order to take forward this agenda and in response to the findings of my research the Oxford Centre for Spirituality and Wellbeing (OCSW) was founded and began its work in May 2016. The work of OCSW is in line with the national agenda for the development of spiritual care in health care as enshrined in national guidance on patient care. This includes *NHS Chaplaincy Guidelines* (Department of Health 2015); *From Values to Action: The Chief Nursing Officer's Review of Mental Health Nursing* (Department of Health 2006); *Quality Standards for End of Life Care* (NICE 2011); CQC standards; *One Chance to Get it Right* (Leadership Alliance for the Care of Dying People 2014). Spiritual care is also the subject of an increasing amount of writing and research in academic and nursing literature, for example: *Knowing Our Own Minds* (Mental Health Foundation 1997); *Spirituality in Nursing Care: A Pocket Guide* (Royal College of Nursing 2011); *Spirituality and Mental Health* (Royal College of Psychiatrists 2010); Kearney (1996); Ross (1997); McSherry (2006); Clarke (2010); Holloway and Moss (2010); West (2011). Its importance is also attested to by the comments of patients in the introduction. Each of the guidelines mentioned above incorporate spiritual health care into their recommendations: guidance from England and Wales' Chief Nursing Officer on Mental Health, *From Values to Action*, enshrines people's spiritual and religious needs as an aspect of life to be addressed by mental health nurses (Department of Health 2006); *CQC standards* measure how Trusts provide services that are fair, sensitive and responsive to the individual religious and spiritual needs of the whole population; *Quality Standards for End of Life Care* (NICE 2011), contains the statement: 'People approaching the end of life are offered spiritual and/or religious support appropriate to their needs and preferences' (2011, p.2).

In summary, the national agenda emphasizes the following:

- the importance of addressing peoples' spiritual and religious beliefs

- ensuring patient choice in this area

- that a personal sense of meaning and identity can keep people healthy

- that spiritual care can make a significant contribution to wellbeing and recovery.

However, while departments of chaplaincy and spiritual care work to enable the spiritual and religious needs of patients and staff to be understood and met, the reality is that it is in day-to-day caring relationships that this dimension of care is realized. It is therefore to the development of psycho-spiritual care in health care practice that OCSW will address its work.

The Oxford Centre for Spirituality and Wellbeing (OCSW)

OCSW is a centre within the Oxford Institute of Nursing, Midwifery and Allied Health Research (OxINMAHR). This is an Oxford Brookes University-led partnership that brings together the major organizations that contribute to health in Oxfordshire, including Oxford Brookes University, Oxford University Hospitals NHS Foundation Trust, Oxford Health NHS Foundation Trust, Health Education England Thames Valley and the University of Oxford.

The work of OCSW is predicated on the need to develop and disseminate an integrated and holistic model of care. Its vision is 'to generate practise-based evidence of the benefits of an integrated approach to care through research that will underpin the development of training for staff so that they are equipped and supported in the provision of spiritual care' (OxINMAHR 2016).

The Centre aims to realize this vision using an interlinking tripartite working model as set out below.

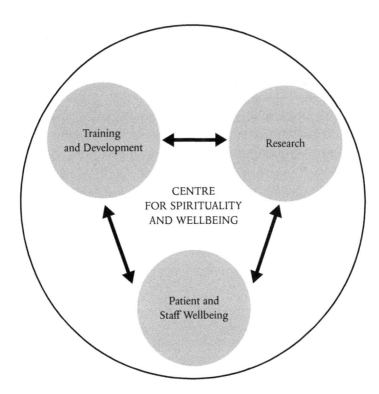

Figure 2.1 Model for the Oxford Centre for Spirituality and Wellbeing

In this model, each sphere is connected to and influences the others. It is based on the following pathways of mutual influence:

- the evidence from practice research will resource better staff training and development

- patient wellbeing will be enhanced by both the research and staff training and development

- the capacity and ability of staff to deliver spiritual care will be impacted by the improved self-understanding, awareness and confidence which are a result of good training and support and are essential to staff wellbeing.

The work of the Centre is in the early stages and I will say more about the development of OCSW in the Conclusion to this book.

I began Chapter 1 with an overview of the historical context of health care chaplaincy before going on to consider present-day understandings of the health care chaplain. I discussed existential, Person-Centred and theological perceptions of care, how communities of faith have expressed *pastoral* care and counselling and psychotherapy, and how the relationship between *spiritual* care and counselling and psychotherapy has developed over the past 30 years. I also sought to elucidate the links between spiritual and pastoral care and their relationship to counselling and psychotherapy within the role of the health care chaplain. This discussion only serves to highlight the need for further research into practice.

In Chapter 2 I have introduced autoethnography as a methodological approach to research which describes and analyses personal experience in order to understand a wider cultural context and experience. I have discussed the implications of the research findings for developing psycho-spiritual care in health care practice as they relate to the work of the health care chaplain and as they relate to the integration of psychologically informed spiritual care per se. Finally, I have outlined a practical illustration of how the development of psycho-spiritual care might be achieved in the form of the development of a centre for spirituality and wellbeing.

The next two chapters go on to elucidate two of the themes from the research, that of liminality and healing, and the development of psycho-spiritual care as an aspect of holistic health. These findings give credence to the view that there is an urgent need to integrate the theory and practice of psychologically informed spiritual care.

References

Altheide, D. and Johnson, J. (2011) Reflections on Interpretive Adequacy in Qualitative Research. In N. Denzin and Y. Lincoln (eds) *The Sage Handbook of Qualitative Research.* Thousand Oaks, CA: Sage.

Angus, L. and McLeod, J. (eds) (2004) *The Handbook of Narrative and Psychotherapy Practice, Theory and Research.* London: Sage.

Bager-Charleson, S. (2014) *Doing Practice-Based Research in Therapy: A Reflexive Approach.* London: Sage.

Bolton, G. (2010) *Reflective Practice: Writing and Professional Development* (3rd edition). London: Sage.

Buber, M. (1958) *I and Thou* (2nd revised edition). Translated by R. Gregor Smith. New York: Charles Scribner's.

Clarke, I. (ed.) (2010) *Psychosis and Spirituality: Consolidating the New Paradigm* (2nd edition). Chichester: Wiley-Blackwell.

Cresswell, J. (2007) *Qualitative Inquiry and Research Design.* London: Sage.

de Board, R. (1978) *The Psychoanalysis of Organisations: A Psychoanalytical Approach to Behaviour in Groups and Organizations.* London: Tavistock/Routledge.

Deegan, P. (2001) Recovery as a Self-Directed Process of Healing and Transformation. In C. Brown (ed.) *Recovery and Wellness.* New York: Haworth Press.

Denham-Vaughan, S. (2010) The liminal space and twelve action practices for gracious living. *British Gestalt Journal,* 19(2), 34–45.

Denzin, N. (1989) *Interpretive Interactionism.* London: Sage.

Denzin, N. and Lincoln, Y. (eds) (2011) *Handbook of Qualitative Research* (4th edition). London: Sage.

Department of Health (2006) *From Values to Action: The Chief Nursing Officer's Review of Mental Health Nursing.* London: Department of Health.

Department of Health (2015) *NHS Chaplaincy Guidelines: Promoting Excellence in Spiritual Care.* London: Department of Health.

Doane, G. (2008) Reflexivity as Presence: A Journey of Self-Inquiry. In L. Finlay and B. Gough (eds) *Reflexivity: A Practical Guide for Researchers in Health and Social Sciences.* Oxford: Blackwell Publishing.

Duke, S. (2007) *A narrative case study evaluation of the role of the nurse consultant in palliative care.* Unpublished PhD thesis. University of Southampton.

du Plock, S. (2010) The Vulnerable Researcher: Harnessing Reflexivity for Practice-Based Qualitative Inquiry. In S. Bager-Charleson, *Reflective Practice in Counselling and Psychotherapy.* Exeter: Learning Matters .

Ellingham, I. (2013) Counselling and recovery. *Therapy Today*, 24(6), 30.

Ellis, C. (2004) *The Ethnographic I: A Methodological Novel about Autoethnography.* Walnut Creek, CA: Alta Mira Press.

Etherington, K. (2000) *Narrative Approaches to Working with Adult Male Survivors of Child Sexual Abuse.* London: Jessica Kingsley Publishers.

Etherington, K. (2004) *Becoming a Reflexive Researcher: Using Our Selves in Research.* London: Jessica Kingsley Publishers.

Etherington, K. (2007) Ethical research in reflexive relationships. *Qualitative Inquiry*, 13, 599–616.

Finlay, L. (2011) *Phenomenology for Therapists: Researching the Lived World.* Chichester: Wiley-Blackwell.

Gadamer, H.G. (1979) *Truth and Method.* London: Sheed & Ward.

Gordon-Graham, C. (2014) Beginner's mind. *Therapy Today*, 25(5), 22–25.

Harrison, G. (2014) Case Study: An Introduction to Autoethnography. In S. Bager-Charleson, *Doing Practice-Based Research in Therapy: A Reflexive Approach.* London: Sage.

Heidegger, M. (1962) *Being and Time.* Translated by J. Macquarrie and E. Robinson. London: SCM Press.

Holloway, M. and Moss, B. (2010) *Spirituality and Social Work.* London: Palgrave Macmillan.

Holroyd, A. (2007) Interpretive hermeneutic phenomenology: Clarifying understanding. *Indo-Pacific Journal of Phenomenology*, 7(2), 1–12.

Hudson Jones, A. (1998) Narrative in medical ethics. *Western Journal of Medicine*, 171(1), 50–52.

Kearney, M. (1996) *Mortally Wounded: Stories of Soul Pain, Death and Healing.* Dublin: Marino.

Laing, R.D. (1965) *The Divided Self: An Existential Study in Sanity and Madness.* London: Penguin Books.

Leadership Alliance for the Care of Dying People (2014) *One Chance to Get It Right: Improving People's Experience of Care in the Last Few Days and Hours of Life.* Publications Gateway Reference 01509. Available at www.gov.uk/government/uploads/system/uploads/attachment_data/file/323188/One_chance_to_get_it_right.pdf, accessed on 10 December 2016.

McIlveen, P. (2007) The Genuine scientist-practitioner in vocational psychology: An autoethnography. *Qualitative Research in Psychology*, 4(4), 295–311.

McLeod, J. (2001) *Qualitative Research in Counselling and Psychotherapy* (1st edition). London: Sage.

McLeod, J. (2003) *Doing Counselling Research* (2nd edition). London: Sage.

McLeod, J. (2010) *Case Study Research in Counselling and Psychotherapy*. London: Sage.

McLeod, J. (2011) *Qualitative Research in Counselling and Psychotherapy* (2nd edition). London: Sage.

McSherry, W. (2006) *Making Sense of Spirituality in Nursing and Health Care Practice: An Interactive Approach*. London: Jessica Kingsley Publishers.

Mental Health Foundation (1997) *Knowing Our Own Minds*. London: Mental Health Foundation.

Moustakas, C. (1990) *Heuristic Research: Design, Methodology and Applications*. Thousand Oaks, CA: Sage.

National Institute for Clinical Excellence (NICE) (2011) *Quality Standards for End of Life Care*. London: NICE.

Oxford Institute of Nursing, Midwifery and Allied Health Research (OxINMAHR) (2016) Oxford Centre for Spirituality & Well-being (OCSW) Available at www.oxinahr.com/our-centres-and-groups/oxford-centre-for-spirituality-well-being-ocsw, accessed on 12 December 2016.

Ricoeur, P. (1981) Narrative Time. In W. Mitchell (ed.) *On Narrative*. Chicago, IL: University of Chicago Press.

Riessman, K.C. and Speedy, J. (2007) Narrative Inquiry in the Psychotherapy Professions: A Critical Review. In D.J. Clandinin (ed.) *Handbook of Narrative Inquiry: Mapping a Methodology*. London: Sage.

Robinson, W. (1995) *The Lost Traveller's Dream: Developing a Theology for Working with Mental Illness*. Oxford Christian Institute for Counselling, Occasional Paper 1. Oxford: OCIC.

Rolfe, G. (1998) The theory–practice gap in nursing: From research-based practice to practitioner-based research. *Journal of Advanced Nursing*, 28(3), 672–679.

Ross, L. (1997) *Nurses' Perception of Health Care*. Aldershot: Avebury.

Rossman, G.B. and Sallis, S.F. (1998) *Learning from the Field: An Introduction to Qualitative Research*. Thousand Oaks, CA: Sage.

Royal College of Nursing (2011) *Spirituality in Nursing Care: A Pocket Guide*. London: Royal College of Nursing.

Royal College of Psychiatrists (2010) *Spirituality and Mental Health*. London: Royal College of Psychiatrists.

Seamon, D. (2000) A Way of Seeing People and Place: Phenomenology in Environment-Behaviour Research. In S. Wapner, J. Demick, C.T. Yamamoto and H. Minami (eds) *Theoretical Perspectives in Environment-Behaviour Research*. New York: Plenum.

Slater, V. (2013) *The fresh significance of chaplaincy for the mission and ministry of the Church in England: Three case studies in community contexts*. Unpublished PhD thesis. Anglia Ruskin University.

Spry, T. (2011) Performative Autoethnography: Critical Embodiments and Possibilities. In N. Denzin and Y. Lincoln (eds) *The Sage Handbook of Qualitative Research*. Thousand Oaks, CA: Sage.

van Manen, M. (1990) *Researching Lived Experience: Human Science for an Action Sensitive Pedagogy*. Albany, NY: State University of New York Press.

West, W. (ed.) (2011) *Exploring Therapy, Spirituality and Healing*. Basingstoke: Palgrave Macmillan.

3

Liminality and Healing

The word 'liminal' is derived from the Latin *limen,* meaning 'threshold'. It is defined as a place of transition, waiting and not knowing. The psychotherapist Denham-Vaughan describes liminality in the following terms: 'When behind you lies all that is known, you stand on the threshold of the unknown to which the process of change leads you' (2010, p.35). In a seminal study of small-scale societies, the anthropologist Arnold van Gennep (1960) was one of the first scholars to describe liminality. He distinguished three phases of transition. These he described as separation, liminality (or margin) and aggregation (when a person is reintegrated into the structure of society). He suggested that a person who is in a liminal phase is outside and between the structures of society. For both van Gennep and Denham-Vaughan this liminal space, margin, or moment in time is characterized by a willingness to let go of the familiar in order to be open to the possibility of a new and emerging reality. It lies at the moment of both 'being and becoming' and is often interpreted by those who describe themselves as experiencing spiritual awareness as the coming together of immanence and transcendence. For example, George Macleod, the founder of the Iona Community, as quoted by Ferguson (2001), described the liminal place of pilgrimage that is the island of Iona as being like a piece of 'tissue paper' between earth and heaven.

The reflections contained within this chapter indicate that for many patients and staff a liminal place, a threshold between one thing and another and therefore a place of possibility, is also often a terrifying place. For example, for Kelly (see below) this was the place in which she was searching painfully for her real self. However, research experience points to the fact that while a liminal space is a marginal and sometimes chaotic one, it is also one that contains the seeds of healing, wholeness and recovery. I define healing as a form of 'wholeness' that incorporates physical, emotional and spiritual dimensions. The concept of 'recovery' as it has been applied to mental health care is closely related to healing.

Recovery is defined by Anthony as 'a way of living a satisfying, hopeful, and contributing life even with the limitations caused by illness. Recovery involves the development of new meaning and purpose in one's life as one grows beyond the catastrophic effects of mental illness' (1993, p.15). I understand these questions of 'meaning and purpose' to be spiritual questions to which a health care chaplain's focus is directed. Such questions may be tentatively expressed, partially hidden and often only understood in retrospect. They are often a mix of existential and spiritual understandings on the part of both patient and chaplain, which can only ever be truly explored in relationship.

In this chapter I also want to illustrate what appears to be one of the paradoxes of working in a 'caring' organization such as an NHS trust; this is that patients like Kelly are sometimes made into what psychiatrist Di Nicola (2010) describes as zombie-like people. This zombie-like state appears to be a state of seemingly semi-permanent stasis of mourning between life and death. I suggest that this state occurs when we don't listen to patients like Sian, or when we convince them they have the wrong questions, assumptions or goals. In an institutional context that may seek to modify or control behaviour, questions of meaning may be re-directed into questions of behaviour. For example, a clinical psychologist working with a patient with an eating disorder focuses on the present by weighing their patient and adopting behavioural strategies in order that the patient might put on weight. Given limited resources and following NICE (National Institute for Health and Care Excellence) guidance, this is undoubtedly the best short-term strategy. However, it is seemingly pursued to the exclusion of the possibility of exploring the traumas of the past, traumas that are often bound up with the present, and traumas that patients tentatively explore with myself and my colleagues. This positivist approach, often exemplified by the dominance of cognitive behavioural therapy (CBT), considers a patient's cognitive 'distortions' and thought patterns and, in Kelly's case as a forensic patient, her index offence, in order that they be removed. Fonagy seems to give credence to this view when he states that:

> Increased neuroscientific knowledge will help us to help the brains of our patients to devise and make use of sometimes complex and sometimes simple strategies to cope with weaknesses in their brain function, whether…caused by genetic vulnerability, development assault or a unique combination of the two. (2004, p.358)

However, this approach can lead to patients who do not have a voice, who lack the narrative resources or the expressive capacities to articulate their predicament, being treated like zombies, albeit unintentionally. Further evidence of this happening in an otherwise caring environment was uncovered in the Francis Report (2013) into the failings at Mid-Staffordshire NHS Foundation Trust. According to Francis, 'The most basic standards of care were not observed and fundamental rights to dignity were not respected' (Robert Francis, press statement, 6 February 2013). The report made 290 recommendations covering a broad range of issues relating to patient care and safety in the NHS and called for a 'fundamental change' in culture whereby patients are put first.

This chapter illustrates how one of my roles is to seek to enable patients and staff to find their own voice instead of living in a life-limiting zombie-like state. Enabling patients and staff in this way opens up the potential for healing and wholeness. This chapter therefore takes the form of a series of personal reflections, each of which illustrates how at the heart of the practice of a health care chaplain who is both spiritual and pastoral carer and who is trained in psychotherapy lies this often challenging but highly rewarding relational space of liminality and potential healing.

In each of the following stories I start with the often visceral lived experience of patients and follow with my own comment and reflection. In common with all my examples from clinical practice in which I am careful to maintain patient anonymity, I begin with a reflection that melds a number of similar patient voices which I name as being those of Kelly and Sian.

Kelly and Sian's stories

My reflection begins with the following heart-rending description which Kelly gave of her life history:

> *History*
> *of using crack cocaine and prescription drugs*
> *of prostituting herself to feed her habit*
> *of violence against her family, her self*
> *and others*
>
> *History*
> *of abuse from father and stepfather*
> *of the death of her mother*
> *and of her crime*
> *of being brought up by her aunt, her uncle and others*

History
of trashing her room and threatening staff
of cutting herself again and again with whatever she can find
of anger, pain, hurt and frustration
not knowing who she was, or is and might be

Kelly's story continued with a description of what I understood to be her liminal place, the threshold upon which she placed her hope for the future, albeit born from the depths of her pain and distress, and therefore the concomitant possibility of healing.

In this moment
I listen to Kelly talk about her parents and her love for them
I listen to her speak of her deep hurt for what they did and said
I listen to her confusion and shame
her desire for love and freedom

In this moment
I listen and offer Kelly my presence, my being, my care
I listen, I summarize the trauma, reflect back the pain and anger
I listen and wonder, about her future months in this ward
her desire for love and freedom

In this moment
I listen to Kelly speak of her need to believe in God and of moving on
I listen and seek not to judge, to hold the space for her and for me
I listen intently to her tell more of her story yet
not knowing who she was, or is and might be.

I perceived Kelly's experience as being both terrifying and hopeful. I saw my role as being alongside Kelly, and, to the extent that it is ever possible to do so, to seek to understand and become aware of her lived experience. I approached this liminal place of 'anger and pain' and 'desire for love and freedom' by 'listening'. I listened with the intention of holding the space that was created between us. This space is the essence of person-centred relational care.

As I write I am reminded of attending an international conference on religion, health and spirituality in Switzerland in 2010. At that conference a former chief nurse from Norway stated that after several years of seeking to use the best methods of applied nursing psychology to motivate nurses she had decided the only concept she could reliably depend upon was love. The response from the audience was largely negative, with a number of clinicians walking out of the conference hall. One of those who stayed responded by saying that as love cannot be operationalized as a concept it cannot be measured. As a concept within health care it is therefore at best naïve and at worst deeply problematic. I remember being deeply moved by the presentation and shocked by this response.

The 'supine' responses from staff as I entered the ward to see Sian had a similar effect on me.

I walk straight to the office and enter with my fob
I'm met by silence
'Hello, I'm Guy the chaplain,' I say. 'Sian has asked to see me, is this a good time?'
The member of staff appears attached to her computer
'Yes, sure, go knock on her door'

I exit, wander round the ward, looking for someone else
I feel sure it would not be a good move for me to knock on Sian's bedroom door

And later,

Sian appears unsettled, nervous and anxious
She says she's angry at the staff, angry at God, angry with herself
'I cannot see how things will change, not after several years, with my section due to be
extended for another six months on Friday'

She pauses,

'Will I ever get out of here?'
We speak of Sian's fear, her desperation and her desire to move to a place of more intensive care
To be noticed, for everyone to care
'You're desperate, you feel afraid and you feel angry and ignored'
I wonder if Sian's anger will erupt in the here and now.

My reflections on working with Kelly and Sian show that I was offering a loving response. This being the case, it can be said that my intention in the work that I do with patients and staff alike is to express love.

As indicated earlier (see Chapter 2, section 'The implications for developing psycho-spiritual care in health care practice'), love defined theologically as agape is often translated from the Greek as 'unconditional love'. According to Thorne (1991), Rogers' (1951) concepts of 'unconditional positive regard' and 'empathy' in Person-Centred theory have the same meaning as 'unconditional love' and are consequently vital components of healing. Simone Weil stated that 'our love for others expresses an abiding concern for their wellbeing. The love of our neighbour in all its fullness simply means being able to say to him [*sic*], "what are you going through?'" (1951, p.97). With Kelly and with Sian I was seeking to listen to, understand and empathically respond to what they were 'going through'.

Kelly and Sian also speak about their guilt and shame and in our conversations they, along with so many of the patients I meet, express a deep sense of guilt. From within the traditions of faith the divine is often represented as a violent, vengeful being that requires sacrifice or bloodlust as the most effective way in which people can find ultimate salvation and therefore healing. An example from the Christian tradition is the theological strand of interpretations of salvation as being through the 'blood of the cross of Jesus'. In contrast, Alison (2003) suggests that God is unconditional love who does not demand repentance as a pre-condition to receiving forgiveness and that ultimately salvation is a process of the discovery of being loved by God who is Love. My training and experience, and my spiritual and pastoral care responses to Kelly and Sian, were based on an understanding that all of us are on the same continuum; we all need to find ways to experience ourselves as being free from what binds us, to be loved, loving and creative. Kelly and Sian in their different ways expressed their belief in God. Kelly's own perception of herself was of someone who had committed the most awful atrocities for which she could never forgive herself and which might not be forgiven, even by a God of love. My training and experience and therapeutic responses to Kelly and Sian's self-image have the same root in that I interpret my reflection as an attempt on my part to convey the fact that, despite all the seeming evidence to the contrary, there is the possibility of a positive force at the centre of their lives, just as there is in mine. In terms of my practice this positive force is based on the Person-Centred theory of 'the actualizing tendency'. This can be described as the tendency in all of us for growth and development, even when under severe threat. It is not to be confused with Maslow (1968), who saw actualization as a state that could be attained. Rather, it is about developing the right conditions for self-healing and wholeness to happen, even when life is especially dark and frightening. According to Bohart, the implications of the actualizing tendency are that as patients or clients 'are able to think and experience in an open, supportive relationship, they are able to use their growth capacities to move forward in finding solutions to their problems' (2013, p.97). My reflections suggest that it is the living out of this hope, the enormous potential for change, that matters to me. By expressing this hope, I believe it to be possible that Kelly and Sian may find some level of self-acceptance that enables their guilt and shame to diminish. As a chaplain providing psycho-spiritual care, my responsibility was to be alongside them, to be with them as best as I could, to 'listen and offer my presence, my being, my care…'

Relationship, presence and intention and a lamentation of despair

Alan is someone who is very vulnerable. He is on a high-dependency ward, has had several outbreaks of anger/threatening behaviour and is 'desperate for care', with a desire to be put in a place where he can be attended to constantly. He has a faith and wants God to help him and (according to his psychologist) he feels the need for constant 'Godly care', and yet has an acute sense of God's absence. I have seen Alan several times and each time he appears to be despairing. I wonder how he perceives me and my role. Over several months, we have very similar conversations about him losing his faith, the perceived lack of support from staff and his paranoia. I find it difficult to know how things will progress for him but also know that I need to continue to be present and try to engage as best I can.

On this occasion, I'm told by a nurse to use the seclusion room to see Alan. A seclusion room is normally used for locking patients in on their own as a consequence of harmful behaviour. Alan comes from his room, where he tells me he has been for several hours.

> *'I feel so angry.'*

> *'Who with, Alan?'*

> *'Angry with myself, with this place, with God – but I can't be angry.'*

> *'You can't be angry?'*

> *'I'm trapped.'*

> *'It's easier to stay in bed – getting up late this morning was good for me. I can stay in bed until the afternoon some days [pause] I don't know what to say.'*

> *At this point I hesitate to leave the ensuing silence too long, as Alan appears very agitated (on a previous occasion, it had seemed as if he was about to hit his head and fists on the wall). I seek to distract him without avoiding the subject.*

> *'You've talked before about your meetings with the psychologist and how you tell her how angry you are – how's that going?'*

> *'It's OK.'*

> *'And the other staff?'*

> *'There's Anne, she's religious, and she told me a bit about her family and so on.'*

> *'She's a nurse?'*

'Yes – I asked if she would come to my CPA [Care Programme Approach] and support me, and she said yes, and then she didn't turn up.'

'That's very upsetting.'

'I don't know what to say. I'm so angry.'

Alan appears very angry and agitated again. I decide to risk keeping the silence and as I do so he puts his face in his hands and cries. For the first time, I have a real sense of a person completely trapped inside himself.

'I'm sorry. I'm sorry.'

'It's OK. You have nothing to apologize to me about.'

'I'm so angry but if I kick off all they say is, "Well, we'll leave you to hit the chairs [in the seclusion room in which we sit] if you want to".'

'It was my sisters' birthday last week.'

I remember that he had told me about a present he had bought for his sister.

'An important day. Have you managed to give her your present yet?'

'No, I expect she will come soon' (there is real sadness in Alan's voice at this point).

Pause

'I'm so angry.'

Pause

'I can never be myself here, the real Alan.'

'It's hard to be yourself. I'm wondering what the real Alan is like. I have a sense that you care about other people.' (While being caring is not part of the conversation, I somehow intuitively feel this is important, and also true!) 'When I come onto the ward and whenever you come out of your room I also notice that the other patients often greet you warmly.'

Pause

'The other patients are OK. They're friendly enough, though they can be very loud – so it's hard to escape. I try to help if I can.'

'You feel it would be good to escape from people.'

'Do you know anywhere I could go to apart from here?'

'I guess it's difficult with your section, but once you are well then there will be other options.'

'I don't know if I will ever get out of here and have an ordinary life back in Cardiff with my friends.'

'Do your friends keep in touch?'

'Yes, though they have mental health issues too, so it's difficult for them.'

Pause

'I was in therapy the other day. And I was asked to write or draw what I felt. And I drew something and the therapist had a look and said, they look like tears. I said "Are they? I don't know".'

Pause. I'm aware that lunch will shortly be served in the ward dining room.

'Would you like me to say a prayer before I go?' (Alan often asks for prayer at the end of a session.)

'Yes please.'

'What would you like us to pray for?'

'For healing and peace.'

We conclude with a prayer, and for only the second time in several sessions he takes the opportunity to pray as well and prays for me and my work. I thank him and leave, reporting in to staff before I go, though saying little about the narrative detail of our conversation.

There are several aspects to this encounter, albeit drawn from different sources: Alan's anger and depression; his desperate need to escape; his perception of me as someone who was interested in what he said and felt. As a whole the text feels like a form of lament and yet a lament that ends on a significant note of hope and the possibility of change. The paradox is that even in despair there is the possibility of a way out, even when that way out appears to be one of escape rather than recovery or, as Alan puts it, 'I can never be myself here, the real Alan,' and yet a few minutes later he requests a prayer for 'healing and peace' in the belief that God will hear his prayer.

Brodwin et al. state that 'it is the attention that care givers devote to the experience of menacing symptoms and grave loss as much as the technical interventions that improve outcome' (1994, p.13). It is this attention that is at the heart of my work. My attention to Alan's clear signs of distress and what may be described as his spiritual pain leads him to cry for the first time and to articulate his need. In Person-Centred counselling and psychotherapy this attention is understood as unconditional positive regard, the offering to the client of a fundamental acceptance of their worth and value. Mearns and Thorne offer a helpful definition:

Unconditional positive regard is the label given to the fundamental attitude of the person-centred counsellor towards her client. The counsellor who holds this attitude deeply values the humanity of her client and is not deflected in that valuing by any particular client behaviours. The attitude manifests itself in the counsellor's consistent acceptance of and enduring warmth towards her client. (2003, p.64)

The following three reflections further illustrate the potential for liminal spaces to become healing spaces.

The edge as a place of healing

The following describes my first encounter with the Trust's chief executive which illustrates an understanding of the importance of the liminal place of chaplaincy within the organization. This is followed by a contrasting meeting with a local parish priest in which I experienced disturbing feelings of disconnection and marginality in relation to parish ministry. Both occurred as part of my induction to the Trust.

> *I hear myself described as a healer*
> *or at least by implication*
> *by the chief executive no less*
> *and I'm flattered.*
>
> *And yet, have I not forgotten something?*
> *the ministry of healing is at the forefront of what I do*
> *I'm so used to dressing it up*
> *as recovery*
> *or spiritual care*
> *or accompaniment*
> *or the Person-Centred approach.*
>
> *I know healing is all of the above*
> *and yet this man is taking me somewhere I'm not used to describing*
> *especially to someone so senior in the NHS*
> *the ministry of prayer, the sacrament of healing*
> *I feel excited and surprised in equal measure.*
>
> *In this my first meeting he goes further*
> *describing my place in the trust as of crucial importance*
> *a role that is important for both patient and organization*
> *'spiritual care is clinical and yet not clinical,*
> *a crucial part of the organization and yet on the edge'.*

A liminal place?
a place of opportunity certainly
a healing place?
absolutely
and a privileged place.

Then we move to the personal
'tell me about yourself'
I tell my story in brief
my time in West London, at the Bucks hospitals,
at Bath hospice, at college in Salisbury, in Leeds…

He pushes me further
'what led you to do this work?'
and, 'how did you find yourself doing that?'
'what influences were there on your choice of career
your family, your childhood?'

I retreat in a hurry
I don't feel entirely comfortable telling him
this is not therapy after all…
and yet how the tables are turned, how strange
I take my leave, grateful
gently stirred up.

Two hours later
I have arranged to see a local parish priest as part of my induction into the local
area
Very friendly on the phone
and on meeting briefly at morning prayer.

I'm aware that our last meeting was cancelled
and there was that urgent e-mail yesterday
asking if we were still meeting.

A friendly hello and 'I can only stay a short time'
for very good reasons I feel sure
and yet the contrast with my earlier appointment
is extraordinary
A helpful conversation
and yet some uncertainty, ambivalence?
even suspicion, I'm not sure
'why have I asked her here?' seems the implied question.

I ask about being notified of the local clergy chapter meetings
'of course, though you may need to remind me…'
A different sort of liminal space for sure
a place that is hard to assess, to understand
that is more uncertain.

As I re-read the above, I am again moved by the fact that I felt more affirmed by and at home with the chief executive than I did with the local parish priest. While somewhat alarming at the time, I'm also struck by the chief executive's willingness to enquire about what motivates me personally and what influences there have been on my choice of career. Although, as I use the word 'career', I rather think he would be as comfortable about using the word 'vocation', as evidenced by his understanding and affirmation of my role within the organization. The contrast with the preoccupied busyness of the parish priest is stark and unsettling.

The question of whether liminal spaces are also healing spaces seems a congruent place for further reflection. The question is also relevant to my conversations with Lisbet. In this case, Lisbet had been referred to me by the occupational health department for support in the form of counselling. We had contracted to meet for eight sessions and this session was written after the penultimate session.

Being on the edge and being uncertain as to how to proceed

I feel we are on very sensitive ground with her experience of abuse very present but unable to be named. This combined with the fact that she came to this particular session expressing her nervousness about speaking, my awareness of her nervous fiddling makes me feel unsure as to how to proceed … I am aware that it will have taken a huge amount of courage for her to come to this point and say so. I feel torn about not being able to continue with further sessions, especially as Lisbet has herself said she feels that she is on the edge of something important that will potentially give healing, so enabling her to be 'the person she was created to be'. I also know that such healing will likely take time, something I am unable to give, owing to the constraints on my time.

It could be argued that the references to healing by Lisbet and the chief executive are what all therapy and spiritual and pastoral care is about. However, there can be particular moments of encounter within which profound growth and healing take place. Such moments are discussed by Rogers in terms of a way of being with clients that he calls 'presence', which he describes as 'an altered state in which his inner spirit has reached out and touched the inner spirit of the other … Profound growth and healing energy are present' (1980, p.24). Such extraordinary moments of potential healing are what Buber (1970) describes as 'I–Thou' moments. In this penultimate session with Lisbet I felt we were on the cusp of something that had the potential for profound healing. In my conversation with the chief executive he had referred to the healing aspects of my role. I found his words to me affirming of my vocation. We had arranged to meet as part of our respective inductions into the organization (he had started the week before me). I had come from an organization that had stretched to almost breaking point my belief in any kind of vocation to the work of health care chaplaincy to the extent that I was preparing to look for other, more 'secular', posts. Our conversation therefore became a healing moment for me. Both he and Lisbet affirmed and validated this aspect of my role in the organization. It is significant that while Lisbet came to me because I was a person of faith, most of our conversations had not focused on this aspect of her life. However, Lisbet had commented on the fact that it was precisely because I was a chaplain who was also a therapist that she could talk to me. This felt important and an affirmation of my role.

I have indicated above that healing can derive from liminal moments and that such moments may have elements of Buber's 'I–Thou' or Roger's 'presence' about them. The following encounter with Peter also suggests that this may be the case.

Amidst the pain a whisper is heard

A phone call to my office from a nurse
Peter – Christmas, acute depression, suicidal, self-harm, a fragile relationship
'He would like to speak to a chaplain.'

We meet
Peter curls up on a chair
I wait
and wonder what he will say.

We speak of his 'journey'
his past and present life with his family and friends
sometimes with God
sometimes not.

We speak of his hurt and pain and distress and loneliness
from God
from his relationship with his partner.

He says, 'no more!'
It cannot go on, things must change
And yet…

We speak of love
an absence of…
love of self
love from God
God.

I acknowledge his hurt
And a whisper, a thread
something calling
tentatively yet persistently.

Crises
and change
and possibility.

Yet Peter says that along with this hope comes his fear
his future is uncertain, unpredictable
'It's hard to accept the love of others and of God
without love of self'.

Peter presented himself to me as a very lonely figure. He had been diagnosed with severe depression, severe enough that he was self-harming. By his own admission his family relationships were deeply problematic. His relationship with his partner had just about broken down. He felt that he could not cope and had felt suicidal. In our encounter, it is clear that he knows things must change and is aware that he has a long journey to travel before he can find the healing and wholeness he clearly craves. I describe what seems to me to be the pivotal moment in our conversation as a 'whisper'. For me this was a moving moment of change, recognition and potential transformation. The vocation to which Peter tentatively refers, he described as the knowledge from an early age that he has a 'calling'. It is the 'threads' of this calling that are persistently 'whispering' to him, even in his wilderness experience. On reflection, I wonder if his healing began in that wilderness moment. Though I hasten to add at this point that I have no doubt that the nursing and medical team were also instrumental in supporting any such change. What was my role here? Was I exercising a spiritual and pastoral role or a therapy role or both? I suspect that it did not matter to Peter.

The following reflection derives from a professional knowledge seminar I attended at the Metanoia Institute (a counselling and psychotherapy training institute) in April 2013. In direct contrast with my reflections so far in this chapter, it takes the form of a third-person narrative about my practice but it also illustrates how liminality may be understood as a threshold or form of boundary dwelling.

Memory work seminar

In preparation for the seminar we were asked to write about something from our professional practice that we remembered well and which was especially evocative. Writing in the third person, I have taken the name Andrew.

> *Andrew went through the gate in the high-security perimeter fence. Monitored by a camera, which is operated by a person in an anonymous office, the gate led to a second fence and a second gate which Andrew opened with the largest key on his set of keys. He proceeded down some steps; then round a corner and, using another, second, smaller key, through a door; then through one more door and into the key lock where he deposited his set of keys; on then to a further automatic door; through the security area and the fingerprint identification gate that led to one more automatic door and a final revolving door which was controlled by a fob on his belt. He then walked through reception, yet another automatic door and into the outside world. This was a ritual he had done many times before.*
>
> *This morning though was different. It was Christmas Day and it was unusually quiet outside. The normal busyness of the entrance to this high-security hospital was replaced by the sound of birds and the wind in the trees.*
>
> *As Andrew walked towards the staff car park he noticed that the gates to the hospital cemetery were open, something he had not seen before. He walked over to the gate and paused. He was tempted to walk inside but something stopped him. Somehow and in a way he couldn't explain, he knew this was sacred ground. He also knew that this was not just because men and women lay buried here but because of what the place represented. In front of him lay some 1250 unmarked graves of former patients, all of whom would have been buried in the grounds of the hospital because this had become their home. Andrew felt himself being encompassed by something far greater than himself. A profound sense of awe and respect born out of knowledge of what each life represented for such an iconic and disturbing institution as Broadmoor Hospital. The relationship between the patients and staff he had been with just 30 minutes before was both profound and at the same time deeply disturbing. Andrew had been celebrating Christmas in the normally chaotic yet respectful setting of the hospital chapel. Before him*

was a scene representing hundreds of unknown lives, unspeakable horrors and untold stories.

Andrew went home to his own Christmas celebrations knowing that he had witnessed something extraordinary, something he could not put into words but which left him with a strange and profound sense of time and place and of grace and peace.

The contrast between the twin themes of celebrating the birth of Christ and that of remembering, albeit in anonymous graves, the lives of former patients seems almost too rich to do justice to in a necessarily short reflection. I shall endeavour to confine myself to reflecting on the fact that there is perhaps no more liminal place than that of celebrating Christ's Mass (Christmas) and remembering those who have died and been buried on the boundary of an iconic, not to say notorious, institution. That I had to go through such an elaborate set of security measures, a ritual in itself, to reach a point of serendipity seems to add a certain poignancy.

For Christians, the theological concept of Incarnation, that in Jesus Christ, God took a human form to become one with us, being born a vulnerable baby and a homeless refugee to parents (of whom Joseph may or may not be the father) who were dossing in some cattle shed demonstrates that God has a particular care for the marginalized and disempowered. If this is the case, then the patients at Broadmoor Hospital and elsewhere within mental health services are certainly included in this group. As a 'historical symbol', Macquarrie suggests that the Incarnation 'has an existential dimension in so far as it lights up for us our own being and our hitherto undisclosed possibilities of existence' (1977, p.272). Standing at an open gate before the graves of former hospital patients, I could not help but reflect on what this understanding meant for me and for all Broadmoor patients, both alive and dead. Referring to threshold as an aspect of liminality, Ward and Wild suggest that 'to be *between* here and there is to live in the faith that there is a future. To choose to be between here and there is to live in the faith that there will be a better future' (1995, p.30). While they have not chosen to be there, Broadmoor patients are where they are because health care professionals believe they have a better future. Nowadays, they are very unlikely to be buried in the hospital graveyard (in the five years I was working for that Trust there were only two such burials). It is hoped that they will have a future life before them, albeit one that, sadly, is likely to include stigma and discrimination.

On that Christmas morning, as so often, I found myself dwelling in a liminal place, on the boundaries between life and death, hope and despair, the institution and the outside world. The reflection makes me acutely aware of the extent to which I am a boundary dweller. I chose then as I choose now to be on the boundary of the institutional Church, employed by an NHS Trust that (leaving aside my conversation with my chief executive) sometimes disregards, misunderstands or is simply puzzled as to what I am doing there. I do so in the hope that there will be a better future. For me this work and ministry is a form of boundary dwelling, it is a liminal place, a threshold represented by the open gates of the graveyard on Christmas Day. My research into my practice was confirmation to me that my training and experience are rooted in this symbolic understanding. In this sense, and in the words of my reflection above, I believe I stand on 'sacred ground'.

Given the fact that I was also presiding at the Eucharist for Christmas morning it also seems certain that there is a place for religious ritual in my practice that will, when appropriate, take the form of sacramental care. Couture (1990) suggests that such ritual practices contribute to spiritual and pastoral care and counselling and psychotherapy in that they:

> hold together mind and body, word and action, logic and drama. They attend to the intrapsychic need for holding together ambivalent emotions…providing nurture and signification for the passage through the stages of the life cycle, and locate people in social institutions and in culture. (p.1090)

According to Turner, ritual also 'creates change within the community' through what he terms 'liminality and communitas', defined as 'intense experiences of social intimacy' (2008, p.6).

The links between the ultimate threshold of the cemetery gates and the drama of the story of the Incarnation are not only liminal and intrapsychic in nature but evoke ritual images of birth, life and death that are hopeful and ultimately celebratory.

While there is no direct link with counselling and psychotherapy, my experience of writing the narrative above also had an impact on my choice of research methodology. Livholts describes the characteristic of memory work as being 'work with concrete detailed memories following different steps of writing, discussing, rewriting, for the purpose of linking the everyday and mundane to larger ideas, norms and power relations in society' (2013, p.1). In this sense, it is a reflexive method for academic and professional development, including counselling and psychotherapy research, and one that I utilized in my autoethnographic approach.

The reflection below was written following a request to support two senior staff whose working relationship had broken down. It illustrates how, in order for two people to reach a place of resolution, liminality can also be a state or process whereby participants suspend their often negative responses to each other and seek to find solutions to the issues that have led to conflict. In this liminal phase the normal organizational and professional working norms do not apply and the participants enter a process of engagement with difficult thoughts and feelings focusing on the need for agreement and compromise.

My role in staff mediation

As I have indicated, my role includes a significant amount of staff support. On being appointed I was asked if, following the work of my predecessor, I would be prepared to be called upon to offer mediation. I gave a fairly ambiguous response as I was concerned that I did not have sufficient training or expertise. However, having later met with my predecessor and discussed this with him, he indicated that he used his psychotherapy and group work skills to support staff and that I should feel confident of being able to respond positively if asked.

I was asked by a senior HR advisor if I would support two senior staff in order to resolve some serious problems that had arisen and which had led one party to issue a grievance against the other. It was explained to me that as a result of the consequent investigation, mediation was one strand of a process that would also include individual reflective practice, coaching and adherence to team objectives. While not directly spiritual or overtly pastoral in nature, it is my experience that chaplains inhabit a unique place in the organization such that we can straddle different roles, and in my case I can use my psychotherapy training and pastoral skills to provide a context for people to genuinely meet each other.

Each of my mediation sessions began by setting the stage. Ground rules were established and an atmosphere conducive to respectful, productive discussion and conflict resolution was sought and, to a large extent, gained from each participant. In effect the setting of these ground rules signalled the beginning of the ritual stage that van Gennep (1960) and Turner (2008) call 'separation', meaning the entry into a liminal state where the usual social rules and conventions do not apply. The ground rules could be said to signify the creation of a space that transcends the normal professional interactions of each participant. Turner describes this liminal space as 'anti-structure', meaning a social environment in which the normal social rules are inverted. He focused a great deal on hierarchies and power. This focus may equally be applied to the participants in mediation.

Regardless of the disputants' relative status in the Trust, they were expected to abide by the ground rules. Both followed the same rules, such that they were required to listen and not interrupt each other.

The conclusion to mediation could also be said to exhibit ritualistic features. There is a set of mutually agreed solutions formalized in an agreement. The signing of the 'contract' served to mark the end of the liminal phase and a reintegration into the norms of the organization, an organization that it is hoped will be changed by the participants agreeing to change their behaviours and relationships with each other. To a large extent, I think this was achieved, though in this case the complexities associated with differences in cultural attitudes left me wondering how the relationship would progress.

My responses, based on the work of my predecessor, could be said to be pastoral in the broadest sense. I was seeking to support staff who were in some distress and whose personal and professional wellbeing was under threat. I was asked because of my comparatively independent role in the organization and because of my particular training in both spiritual and pastoral care and counselling and psychotherapy. In terms of my training and experience as a therapist, Forlenza (1991) suggests a possible parallel process. I am clear that psychotherapy and mediation are very different processes and therefore must have distinct boundaries. However, my reflections suggest that I used the skills of clarification, summarizing, normalization of feelings and validation, as I do with a client. The challenge for me was to integrate my psychotherapeutic skills into the mediation process without losing sight of the separate goal of mediation, which is to find solutions rather than attempt to turn mediation into therapy. This need for clarity about the role led to my subsequent training as a mediator. Although they may be chaotic or unsettling, it is liminal places that also hold the potential to foster change, growth and creativity. Out of the chaos, new things can be born.

The following is an example of how co-creating a video became an opportunity for developing a new creative perspective on the work of spiritual and pastoral care. It describes how the process of construction needed to be shaped through an organic form of creativity that had the 'betwixt and between' experience of entering a liminal space at its heart. I also point out the wider implications of this experience for developing Person-Centred arts-based practice as a vehicle for spiritual care.

The relationship of spiritual and pastoral care to the arts

I had asked that as part of the revamp of Trust inductions, the chaplains might be able to produce a film of their work. The communications manager agreed to this and Nina from the Trust communications team volunteered to work with us. At an initial meeting, we bounced around ideas as a team and Nina supported us with her ideas and thoughts. This led to a draft script, an exciting partnership with an artist and some local patients, and the collection of a group of photographs to be used as a backing for part of the script. A second meeting was convened, dates were arranged, scripts were revised and re-timed and it was agreed that we should find a service user and a staff member to illustrate our work.

One of the significant features of this project was the sheer hard work, collaboration, energy and commitment of all involved. It felt like a wonderfully creative day that could herald so much more in terms of conveying the importance of contemporary spirituality to health care. While in retrospect I feel as if I was getting slightly carried away with myself, the following comments illustrate my feelings at the time:

> *It was great to be back in touch with my own creativity. I need to do more! I'm reminded of just how important music, art and indeed film are at conveying spirituality and to my mind spirituality's relationship with psychotherapy in terms of healing and wholeness. We have yet to add another vital component which is that of story. This will be provided by a member of staff with whose team I facilitate weekly reflective practice and a patient with whom my colleague has been working. Again I am reminded of the power of people's experience, of connection, of the importance of wellbeing to human flourishing and the vital part we can play in enabling this to happen for people. It is also the place in which both spiritual and pastoral care and psychotherapy as healing arts lie. Isn't this at the heart of the compassionate care that the NHS is so keen to promote?*

In her book *The Creative Connection: Expressive Arts as Healing*, Natalie Rogers (1993) suggests that:

- everyone has the potential to be creative

- the process of creation brings transformation and healing

- when engaged in expressive arts feelings as sources of energy can be focused in order to 'be released and transformed'

- movement, art, writing, sounding, music, meditation and imagery lead us into the unconscious; this can enable the expression of new aspects of self and thus reveal new knowledge and awareness

- there is a connection between our 'life force' or soul and the 'essence of all beings'

- consequently, the inward journey allows us to discover our 'essence' or 'wholeness' in its relatedness to the outer world, and the inner and outer world unite.

If, as I do, one accepts the validity of Rogers' analysis, the importance of creativity to spiritual and pastoral care and health care cannot be overemphasized. The challenge for me and my fellow chaplains is to find ways to facilitate and support patients, staff and carers who are dealing with change and uncertainty in an increasingly stressful world. Art and narrative are widely recognized as ways of knowing about ourselves as human beings. If space and time are set aside for intentional creativity, then this too can become a liminal place. This can become a place where it is indeed possible to let go of the familiar in order to be open to the possibility of new and emerging reality, spiritual or otherwise.

In this chapter I have given examples of different kinds of liminal experience in my practice. I have suggested that liminal spaces, while being marginal and sometimes chaotic, are also spaces that contain the seeds of healing, wholeness and recovery. I have said that as both therapist and spiritual and pastoral carer, I perceive that my responsibility is to express love, a love interpreted in Person-Centred terms as unconditional positive regard and empathy. Such therapeutic responses enable the person providing psycho-spiritual care to stand alongside patients, carers and staff as best they can, to listen and to offer their presence, their care and their being. In this way cathartic 'I–Thou' moments of profound healing or growth may take place and people's spiritual needs can be addressed.

References

Alison, J. (2003) *On Being Liked.* London: DLT.

Anthony, W. (1993) Recovery from mental illness: The guiding vision of the mental health service provision in the 1990s. *Psychosocial Rehabilitation Journal,* 16(4), 11–23.

Bohart, A. (2013) The Actualizing Person. In M. Cooper, M. O'Hara, P. Schmid and A. Bohart (eds) *The Handbook of Person-Centred Psychotherapy and Counselling.* Basingstoke: Palgrave Macmillan.

Brodwin, P., Good, P., Good, M. and Kleinman, A. (1994) *Pain as Human Experience: An Anthropological Perspective.* London: University of California Press.

Buber, M. (1970) *I and Thou.* Translated by W. Kaufmann. New York: Charles Scribner's.

Couture, P. (1990) Ritual and Pastoral Care. In R. Hunter (ed.) *Dictionary of Pastoral Care and Counselling.* Nashville, TN: Abingdon Press.

Denham-Vaughan, S. (2010) The liminal space and twelve action practices for gracious living. *British Gestalt Journal,* 19(2), 34–45.

Di Nicola, V. (2010) States of exception, states of dissociation: Cyranoids, zombies and liminal people. An essay on the threshold between the human and the inhuman. *The Family Therapist: Journal of the Chilean Institute of Family Therapy*, 6, 10–32.

Ferguson, R. (2001) *George MacLeod: Founder of the Iona Community*. Glasgow: Wild Goose Publications.

Fonagy, P. (2004) Psychotherapy meets neuroscience: A more focused future for psychotherapy research. *Psychiatric Bulletin*, 28, 357–359.

Forlenza, S. (1991) Mediation and Psychotherapy: Parallel Processes. In K. Duffy, J. Grosch and P. Olczak (eds) *Community Mediation: A Handbook for Practitioners and Researchers*. New York: Guilford Press.

Francis Report (2013) *The Mid Staffordshire NHS Foundation Trust Public Inquiry. Chaired by Robert Francis QC*. London: The Stationery Office.

Livholts, M. (2013) *Reflexive writing for academic and professional development: The memory work method*. Unpublished introduction at Professional Knowledge Seminar, 22 March, Metanoia Institute, London.

Macquarrie, J. (1977) *Principles of Christian Theology*. London: SCM Press.

Maslow, A. (1968) *Toward a Psychology of Being* (2nd edition). New York: Van Nostrand.

Mearns, D. and Thorne, B. (2003) *Person-Centred Counselling in Action* (3rd edition). London: Sage.

Rogers, C. (1951) *Client-Centered Therapy*. London: Constable.

Rogers, C. (1980) *A Way of Being*. Boston, MA: Houghton Mifflin.

Rogers, N. (1993) *The Creative Connection: Expressive Arts as Healing*. Palo Alto, CA: Science and Behavior Books.

Thorne, B. (1991) *Person-Centred Counselling: Therapeutic and Spiritual Dimensions*. London: Whurr.

Turner, V. (2008) *The Ritual Process: Structure and Antistructure*. Piscataway, NJ: Transaction.

van Gennep, A. (1960) *The Rites of Passage*. Translated by M.B. Vizedom and G.L. Caffee. London: Routledge & Kegan Paul.

Ward, H. and Wild, J. (1995) *Guard the Chaos: Finding Meaning in Change*. London: DLT.

Weil, S. (1951) *Waiting on God: The Essence of Her Thought*. Glasgow: William Collins Sons & Co.

4

Developing Psycho-spiritual Care as an Aspect of Holistic Health

It is clear from my work that there is much to be done if a truly integrated approach to health care that is inclusive of spiritual and pastoral concerns is to be provided. This chapter explores this apparent gap in practice and provides further evidence of the close relationship between spiritual and pastoral care and psychotherapy.

In an article published in the *Journal of Health Care Chaplaincy*, Webb, Toussaint and Conway-Williams suggest that 'the fields of psychology and religiousness/spirituality, while different, are strikingly similar' (2012, p.57). Citing Kugelmann and Belzen (2009), Reisner and Lawson (1992) and Koenig (2009), they also suggest that 'both fields have attempted to address the human condition in an analogous fashion [and that] over the course of history, psychology, sometimes referred to as the secular priesthood, and spirituality have largely worked in concert with one another' (p.57). However, starting with Freud, many within the fields of psychology and psychotherapy have also dismissed spirituality, sometimes virulently. Examples include Horton (1974), Mandel (1980) and Ellis and Grieger (1986). Ellis in particular has garnered a particular reputation for dismissing religion. In his theory of rational-emotive therapy he states, 'the conclusion seems inescapable that religiosity, on almost every conceivable count, is opposed to the goals of mental health' (1986, p.42). Nevertheless, the evidence suggests that in recent years spirituality, and by association the spiritual needs of patients, staff and carers, has been rediscovered. Lyall states that 'it is a paradox of our time that in the midst of a society which is supposed to be increasingly secular and materialist, there has been a revival of interest in what is broadly called "spirituality"' (1994, p.28).

Orchard's research indicates that 'there is broad acceptance that spiritual care is now an integral component of a holistic approach to care giving'

(2001, p.3). Significant attention has also been given to the education and support of health and social care staff regarding the spiritual needs of their patients and clients. Examples would be the launch in 2009 of the British Association for the Study of Spirituality (BASS), the development of the Centre for Spirituality Studies at Hull University and the launch in 1999 of the Royal College of Psychiatrists (RCPsych) Special Interest Group on Spirituality which is now one of the RCPsych's largest member groups. Within the field of counselling and psychotherapy, the last 20 years or so has also seen a burgeoning number of books, articles and research on spirituality within therapy, for example Grof and Grof (1989), Wilber (2000), Moore and Purton (2006), West (2011) and Thorne (2012). Particular mention should also be made of transpersonal approaches such as psychosynthesis that seek to integrate spiritual understandings within a framework of psychotherapy. The principal architect of psychosynthesis is Assagioli, and the spiritual goals of 'self-realisation' and 'interindividual psychosynthesis' (1993, p.7), understood as a convergence of human biology, psychology and spirituality, are central to his theory.

Much of this interest has also been developed within the field of palliative care, where the term 'psycho-spiritual care' has been used to suggest that spiritual care has a direct link with emotional care and the 'total care' advocated by Cicely Saunders (1996), the founder of the modern hospice movement. In 1984, Barnard suggested that the term 'psycho-social care', which had come to refer to any non-medical intervention, should be replaced by the term 'psycho-spiritual care'. In a similar way, Cassidy describes 'spiritual accompaniment' as a delicate task which 'requires that we find out where each individual patient is both emotionally and spiritually and work with them in that place' (1988, p.1). Saunders, Barnard and Cassidy advocate an integrated and therefore holistic approach to care. The question remains, however: how do health care staff come closer to understanding and meeting individual spiritual needs? Sims (1994) suggests that psychiatrists should routinely ask each patient about spiritual topics such as aims, goals and values. However, my research evidence suggests that the integration of spiritual care into a holistic approach to care in this way is rare. I give a number of examples of this later in this chapter, including my experience of joining the Trust Clinical Advisory Group, co-facilitating a series of teaching sessions on spirituality and end-of-life care to a group of district nurses and what I describe as the 'missing ingredient' in caring for Clare.

In the field of psychotherapy, Pargament is one of the foremost American writers on spiritually integrated psychotherapy. He writes, 'psycho-spiritual questions are words that contain sacred qualities, such as peace, courage, solace, sustenance, devotion, faith, hope, love, letting go, forgiveness, regrets, despair and suffering' (2011, p.218). Hume, citing Cox and Grounds (1991), also illustrates this relationship in saying, 'the experience of mental disorder itself may involve a kind of suffering and inner abandonment that can barely be comprehended, and echoes the cry, "My God, my God, why hast thou forsaken me?"' (1999, p.109).

In my own research, this cry is also echoed in Steve's responses to the suicide of a close relative:

> *Where is she, what's happened to her?*
> *Is she in the spirit world?*
> *Is she a lost spirit?*
> *Is she condemned for killing herself?*
> *I worry about her*
> *The questions go round and round in my head like a tape recorder*
> *I've got to know; can you help me!?*

My conversation with Steve illustrates a number of similar enquiries from members of staff. As indicated previously, staff support is a key part of my role and much of the evidence within this chapter derives from sessions I have had with staff, both individually and in groups. The chaplaincy provision of staff support is replicated throughout the NHS in recognition that staff also have spiritual and pastoral needs. For example, the Cambridge University Hospital NHS Foundation Trust's website (2013) states, 'We offer pastoral care and support to all members of staff and their families. This is a unique service offered to staff of all disciplines.' Pastoral needs come into focus when staff have a crisis or experience a profound change in their lives or when they simply need the time and space to process some of the complex challenges and sometimes overwhelming demands of their daily work. The need to support staff also illustrates the symbiotic nature of the compassionate care of patients and clients with that of our own self-care. Wright argues that 'without a loving connection to another human being it is too easy to disconnect, to see the other as an "it", separate from us, allowing us to commit all manner of malice' (1997, p.31). This compassionate connection is called for in the Department of Health's national nursing strategy *Compassion in Practice* (2013), but it is often hard to uphold if as staff we are insufficiently self-aware or unable to sustain the often conflicting demands of an ever-changing, politically charged, under-resourced and consequently highly demanding role of care giving within the National Health Service.

A missing ingredient?

It is my contention that working in partnership with other professions should help mutual understanding and enable a shared approach to patient care. In practice, of course this is not always easy to achieve. The following scenario is based on a number of similar responses to different patients. In the scenario, Clare is a patient with an eating disorder, and Geraldine is her clinical psychologist. With Clare's permission Geraldine referred Clare to me for spiritual support. The following reflection highlights the need for a more integrated approach to patient care, namely psycho-spiritual care.

My sessions with Clare were very brief, lasting sometimes ten minutes or less. Clare talked about a number of deeply disturbing and, on the face of it, frightening images of heaven and hell, which for her raised issues about guilt and forgiveness. Many of these images and others she subsequently revealed were only told to me. My concern was whether or not these needed to be shared with others in the multi-disciplinary team who were caring for her, in particular her psychologist. I asked Clare if she might be willing to do this and approached Geraldine with this in mind. Both Clare and Geraldine indicated to me that they would be willing for the three of us to meet. The following is my reflection on that meeting and the 'missing ingredient'.

The chairs are arranged in a room full of chairs
I decide to begin.

'I thought it would be useful to meet
Clare has divulged some graphic images
I think these are important and Clare would like them to be acknowledged and understood.
I wonder if we need to understand what our respective roles are and decide with Clare what is the best way forward?
Clare states that she has not mentioned these disturbing images before
She wants to bring them to you.
I am here to bear witness
to see how we may work with them, you or me or both
together to hear Clare
for the first time'.

'Ah', says Geraldine
'Clare has a long history
But my role is to work with her eating disorder with the present.'

Geraldine goes on 'It's very difficult...
I asked for your involvement
because I hoped you would be able to work with some of the religious issues.'

'Yes, but of course the religious issues cannot be separated from all the other
aspects of her distress' I say
'We need to hear from Clare
but I wonder if these issues are at the heart of her pain.

I'm also wondering if there is a big gap in her care
and if so how that might be addressed.
Clearly I could go on seeing her
what will you do?'

'A few more weeks and then she will move on' is the response.

'But she will need help and while I have at her request found a
church for her to
attend, I think she needs long-term support/therapy' I reply.

'Very long term with all sorts of issues of dependence, transference and likely
regression
Let's ask Clare what she wants.'

Clare arrives,
All three of us acknowledge what has been said.

What is my role and how do I relate to the multi-disciplinary team/to Geral-
dine?
I could continue to see Clare
But this needs to be understood and acknowledged by the team
otherwise I'm on my own!

We end with us all agreeing on a number of tasks.

I know the wider team will not have the time or the resources...
Something vital is missing.

It is clear that Geraldine needed to focus on the present, whereas it seemed to me Clare was willing to explore some of the issues of her past that were impinging on her present. It is equally clear that I was expected to fulfil the role of the chaplain who is only there to speak about her religious needs. However, the evidence from Clare is that she could not separate these from her other emotional needs; what I was offering was a form of psycho-spiritual care. However, in this instance this care could not be integrated into a holistic approach to responding to all of Clare's needs.

Referral of a community patient

Similar issues are highlighted in the following reflection. John, a community patient, had also been referred for 'spiritual support'.

> *I remain puzzled. John doesn't seem to have any obvious signs of his long-standing mental illness and I am unsure as to what my role is in supporting him – though he clearly valued my visit, as his care co-ordinator made a point of saying so in the patient notes. I feel that the visit went well, especially as this was our first meeting. We spoke about the absence of family and his feelings of isolation and anxiety. I am also left feeling somewhat conflicted. While John clearly is in need, I am unsure as to whether he needs a professional response from a chaplain or whether he needs local volunteer support/friendship. It is also a long way for me to travel to see John, taking most of an afternoon. The issues seem to be as follows:*
>
> - *What am I and what is the multi-disciplinary team hoping to achieve by my going to see John?*
>
> - *Re above, I need to clarify the reasons for referral from the care co-ordinator.*
>
> - *How often should I visit?*
>
> - *What is the nature of John's anxiety? I need to understand more about this.*
>
> - *What are John's expectations? Chaplain (religious searching) or therapist (bereavement counselling – John indicated that he wanted some support as his mother had recently died) or in some sense both?*
>
> *John is certainly lonely and anxious but seems to be looking forward to days when he can get out, which seems positive. I am left with a dilemma as to how often I should visit or indeed whether I should visit again. When I asked him what he would like from me he indicated that he still had some bereavement issues he'd like to talk through.*

The above seems a long way from holistic care but highlights some of the issues facing us as chaplains. In particular, we might hope to be regarded as extended members of the multi-disciplinary team but are often left working in the dark as to the different expectations from both referrer, in this case the care co-ordinator, and patient. Again the issue was raised as to whether I was there as a chaplain (the referral for 'spiritual support') or therapist (for 'bereavement issues') or both.

Being lost and the process of being found

A more congruent approach that is the conjunction of pastoral care with counselling is illustrated in the following example of a one-off session with a member of staff. Steve was referred to me by Occupational Health for general support. The reflection starts at the point where Steve begins to explain why he has come.

Steve tells me that his sister committed suicide last year
he has been signed off sick with 'severe anxiety and depression'
he thought the inquest would be the end, a form of closure
instead it was the beginning.

'I feel like I'm in a bog.
I'm lost and frightened that I won't ever find myself again,' he says.

Lost is such a powerful all-embracing, terrifying word
I wonder at how frightened Steve is likely to feel in the room at that moment and
how it may be for him to say that he feels lost to me a stranger
as this is the first time we have met
I repeat the phrase 'frightened I won't ever find myself again'
I pause, and then wonder aloud at the sinking nature of a bog
Still quiet but more determined this time Steve desperately asks me

'Where is she, what's happened to her?'
'Is she in the spirit world, is she a lost spirit, is she condemned for killing himself?'
'I worry about her. The questions go round and round in my head like a tape recorder'
'I've got to know – can you help me?'
'I went to a christening once and tried to ask the minister but it was too hard.'

My first response is to invite him to tell me more,
'That sounds terrifying – as if you also are trapped'
And yet it is clear – there is no more to tell, Steve is here for a reason and wants to know.

'One hundred years ago the Church used to say that if you ended your own life you had sinned,
the God I believe in does not condemn, I believe your sister is at peace
and I'm conscious that for you the questions have gone round and round...'

Steve straightens up, lifts his head, gives a small smile and says
'Thank you, I really needed to know that, thank you so much
I didn't know who to ask, if only I'd come to see you sooner
I wouldn't have tortured myself, I didn't know you see'
Somehow and in some way it feels as if Steve is reaching out across the room
the contact between us feels almost electric
as if he is reaching out with his very self
'Thank you for coming' I say – 'Thank you for trusting me with your story'
Steve pauses by the door, looks at me and holds out his hand.

It's not a complete handshake, more a holding of fingers
I have a strong sense that Steve has begun to release himself from the bog.

In all three examples of Clare, John and Steve I am seeking ways in which psycho-spiritual care may be integrated into a holistic approach to a compassionate care that takes account of the whole person that is body, mind and spirit. In the first two examples, it seems I was somewhat thwarted. In the third, in what was for me a meaningful encounter with Steve, there were the signs of being able to respond to the whole person. However, a complicating factor is that all three had been diagnosed with conditions that seem to suggest a particular approach, namely cognitive behavioural therapy (CBT): for Clare who has an 'eating disorder' and who needs to address her weight, John who has 'paranoid schizophrenia' and Steve with 'severe anxiety and depression'. I hope that along with Carl Rogers, my practice is about realizing a person's potential for healing and wholeness, rather than limiting their treatment to a focus on the physical/psychological (Clare), mental disturbance (John) or emotional wellbeing (Steve). I wholeheartedly concur with Roger's hypothesis that 'if I accept the other person as something fixed, already diagnosed and classified, already shaped by his [*sic*] past, then I am doing my part to confirm this limited hypothesis. If I accept him as a process of becoming, then I am doing what I can to confirm or make real his potentialities' (1967, p.55). However, the evidence from my practice suggests that I am working in a health care environment that sometimes unnecessarily pathologizes care. It is often a service that is at best ambivalent about integrating spiritual care into the overall care that is offered to patients.

The alarm is for you
The alarm calls out
And again it demands your
Attention your care

Your patient 'kicks off'
You wearily react as
The pattern repeats

Now listen take heart
Your vocation is true that
Alarm is for you.

I received an invitation to run a staff support/reflective practice group in the Trust's psychiatric intensive care unit (PICU). The above haiku was written in response to the first session. The session revealed the often violent and distressing scenarios that ward staff have to deal with on a daily basis. My feelings were summarized as follows:

- awe at the extraordinary commitment to the one extremely challenging patient who is being almost constantly restrained, 'in hold'

- a strong sense of wanting to support this group as far as possible

- wonder at the terrific sense of humour shared by all the staff, tinged with a concern that one or two staff might feel left out by this (though that was not immediately apparent)

- concern that this was a very short period of time; we started late and eventually had only 35 minutes, and yet a lot seemed to be crammed into that time

- concern that expectations might be raised: the ward manager said afterwards that was the best staff support session he had experienced.

At the time the staff were supporting 'one of the most challenging patients the trust had ever had to work with'. This was a patient who was in constant danger of severely self-harming. Alongside him were 14 other very unwell patients. Underlying everything was an anxiety that patients had been and could again become violent. Amidst the apparent chaos and challenge represented by the alarm constantly going off (and the immediate response of several staff) I had a sense that, while exhibiting real care and dedication, staff were in danger of losing a sense of themselves and their own needs, especially the need to replenish themselves. Owing to the unrelenting pressure of their day-to-day work they were finding it difficult to stand back and reflect on what was happening to them and to their patients. I also wondered whether the invitation to me to facilitate the group was symbolic of this need and therefore of what the ward manager referred to as the 'spiritual dimension' of their lives and the lives of their patients. I am clear that for this group I was there as a chaplain who is also a therapist. I suspect that I also represented something 'other', the spiritual side of Person-Centred compassionate care. As Lartey says, compassionate care must be:

> directed towards a greater awareness of the complexity of the physical-spiritual holism that lies at the heart of human nature…for care to be compassionate it needs to be attentive to all the dimensions of our human existence…personal, physical, social, cultural and spiritual. (2012, p.297)

Working on the premise that there is a direct relationship between the care of patients and the care of staff, then my engagement with staff support is directly linked to the development of psycho-spiritual care as an aspect of holistic health. This link between care of staff and care of patients is made explicit in the Department of Health's nursing and midwifery strategy *Compassion in Practice* which states that:

> The health and well-being of staff is essential. Treating each other well is fundamental. The link between the values and behaviours that staff are shown by their employers, managers and peers and the way they in turn treat others, including their patients and users of the service, is very clear. Ensuring staff feel valued, cared for and communicated with is essential. (2013, p.10)

My reflections on my practice suggest to me that one of my roles is to help ensure that staff feel valued and cared for in order that the respect and dignity of patients is upheld and empathy is maintained.

Kitwood (1997) has been recognized as being instrumental in developing person-centred care within health care. Kitwood, inspired by Buber and cited in Baldwin and Capstick, writes that to care for another person is:

> to respect their unique qualities and needs; to help protect them from danger and harm; and – above all – to take thoughtful and committed action that will help to nourish their personal being… No one can flourish in isolation; the well-being of each one is linked to the well-being of all. (Baldwin and Capstick 2007, p.241)

Buber's insights have been taken up by psychotherapists of all modalities, for example Assagioli (1998), Mearns and Cooper (2005) and Spinelli (2005), as a way of reflecting on the 'I–Thou' quality of relational depth when working with clients.

Supporting staff groups

In day-to-day experience, however, Buber's comments on wellbeing are tested when confronted by violence such as that which occurred on one older adult ward where a member of staff was seriously assaulted by a patient. I was asked to facilitate a staff 'psychological de-brief'. I had a sense that I was required to mind the gap. By this I mean that I was being asked to be attentive to the potential gap between being able to provide compassionate care that is truly holistic and inclusive of all aspects of wellbeing and an absence of such person-centred care and the possibility of relapsing into a silo mentality. In my reflection, I write that I was disturbed to hear about the challenging nature of the unit and the effect this was having on staff morale and the ability of the ward to care for some very unwell patients.

In the foreword to *Compassion in Practice*, the Chief Nursing Officer for England and the Director of Nursing at the Department of Health state that:

> The six fundamental values – care, compassion, competence, communication, courage and commitment (the 6 C's) – resonate strongly with both staff and people who use our services, across the whole range of health and care settings…staying connected to these values is what gives us the strength to keep doing this challenging work every day. (2013, p.11)

The strategy defines compassion as 'how care is given through relationships based on empathy, respect and dignity – it can also be described as intelligent kindness, and is central to how people perceive their care' (p.11). 'Intelligent kindness' strikes me as being central to the work of all care staff and pertinent to my experience on the elderly care ward. My reflection at the time contained the following sentence: 'Being able to support staff in this way is a significant step forward in bearing witness to the importance of the existential questions and concerns of patients within each groups' care and as part of their own self-care' (Harrison 2016, p.129).

Dealing with existential questions and concerns is demanding and takes a certain amount of wise thought especially when, as in this instance, consideration needs to be given to some complex ethical and cultural issues. My observation above is also pertinent to an equally distressing and challenging period for another group of nursing staff, a children's nursing team who had been supporting a young child and his family over a number of months in the latter phases of his illness prior to death. There had been a number of cultural and religious complexities that were exacerbated by a specific parental request that cardiopulmonary resuscitation (CPR) should be used in order to ensure that there was every possibility of extending the child's life. It was clear to me that the staff had been highly respectful of this decision. However, the emotional cost to them and to members of the family was immense. My role as pastoral carer and therapist was to help them process their difficult thoughts and feelings in order that they could maintain their levels of empathy and respect and focus on the many other demands on their time, energy and resources. I suspect that this would not have been possible without my training and experience in *both* psychotherapy and pastoral care. The final reflection in my reflective practice notes is as follows:

Everyone shared (no one was silent though all were given the option to listen if they wanted) and everyone in the group came to a point of tears, distress, sadness and mourning. There was a recognition that each one could not but bring themselves into a relationship of practical and emotional care for each patient, though it was understood that this was costly and questions were raised about being professional.

I felt privileged to be witnessing the group nurturing and caring for one another with an honesty that was somehow raw and yet beautiful at the same time. There was a particularly poignant moment when the nurse most involved with the patient spoke to her manager (who was also in the group) and reflected back just how supported she had felt.

By way of contrast, the reflection that follows illustrates one of the common dilemmas inherent in constructing a possible model of psycho-spiritual care, namely, the inability of some staff to understand, for a variety of reasons, the nature of my role on a ward. In this reflection, it is manifested in my lack of confidence in the ability of some staff to understand my responses to patients (here exemplified as Jane) and therefore my role in patient care.

Waiting for Jane

Jane had struggled for many years with her understandings of God's judgement and retribution.

Jane wants to die
She has tried many times to end her life
On each occasion she has told me that she is too afraid
Fear disables her, paralyses her, crushes her at every turn.

I enter the ward
The staff nurse tells me wearily,
'Jane has had her stomach pumped again'
I ask if Jane would like to see me,
She says 'yes'.

I entered the room in which we have been placed
Jane seems withdrawn, head down, arms folded into herself,
unwilling or unable to look me in the eye
I close the door
She moves her head very slightly
indicating to me that she is aware of my presence.

I wait
Experience tells me that Jane will speak in her own time
I wait what seems an eternity
much longer than usual
Leaving me
wondering whether to break the silence.

Aware of her frail, vulnerable, wraith-like appearance
I feel drawn to say something out of my own need
'I'm sorry' or 'let me help you if I can'
I wait
The silence seems to envelop the room.

Then
softly, as if gently awaking from a coma, Jane speaks
she tells me that she has sinned and deserves to die
God has judged her and found her wanting
She deserves to die, she will die next time
And yet, if she dies she says she will go to hell
'suicide is also a sin'.

I want to cry out
'God is a God of grace who embraces us with His love'
Instead I say, 'It sounds terrifying, as if you are trapped
— frozen with fear.'

Again we wait
and we wait
until the noises of the ward outside the room
disappear into the silence.

Jane asks me in a still small voice
'Will you take my funeral?'
I am shocked by the question
yet deeply moved by her request
I take a deep breath and say with all my being
'Yes Jane, I will take your funeral.'

Later
I wonder what the nursing and medical staff
might make of my 'collusion'.

We sit in silence for several minutes
until she briefly looks me in the eye and says in a whisper
'Thank you'.

After a few moments I leave the room
saying that I will be back in a few days
I ask whether she would like me to see her again
'Yes please' she whispers as she raises her head
She looks me in the eye once more.

This narrative depicts the kind of deeply moving, intimate meeting that I experience in my work. It bears testament to the need to attend to the psycho-spiritual care of sometimes the most vulnerable patients.

In terms of constructing a realistic approach to developing psycho-spiritual care, one possible way forward is to utilize the Recovery Approach. The Recovery Approach, as discussed in Chapter 2, is described by Anthony as 'a way of living a satisfying, hopeful and contributing life, even with the limitations caused by illness' (1993, p.11). It is notable that much of the literature on recovery-orientated practice, not least first-person accounts from service users, refers to spirituality. One such example is Clay, who states that:

> We who have experienced mental illness have all learned the same thing… We know that we have learned the bare bones of spirit and of what it means to be human… There is something to be learned here about the mystery of living itself, something important both to those who have suffered and those who seek to help us. We must teach each other… Knowing that it is often the wounded healer…who is most able to help others… From my experience of madness, I received a wound that changed my life. It enabled me to help others and to know myself. I am proud that I have struggled with God and with the mental health system. (1999, p.35)

By adopting a Recovery Approach to care it is possible to listen to patients' stories of 'the bare bones of spirit and of what it means to be human', in such a way that we discover their spiritual side. It will also help other members of the multi-disciplinary team to understand and thereby develop confidence in my role and expertise in psycho-spiritual care. One example of this approach is in relation to Jason.

Pastoral care and the psychotic patient

Jason's story provides an insight into his spiritual needs, which seem to me to be clear, even when he has been given the label 'psychotic'. One of the first principles of the Recovery Approach is that as a patient he had a story to tell and that as an accompanying member of staff I wanted to hear it.

Jason says that as I'm the chaplain he would like to talk
He straight away tells me that he used to be very clever, especially at physics
So clever that from an early age he had special tuition.

I tentatively say, with the emphasis on the first word, 'Used to be clever?'

'Oh yes but not any more
especially not since my sister died last year
she used to support me with everything.'

We pause. Then in a dramatic gesture with his head
John indicates that he spent all her money 'on coke' – 'tens of thousands of pounds'
Quickly his statement is followed up with
'I would do anything for my sister, I'd even hit someone!'

Every part of me is alert to the drama of the moment
I want to say 'That's a hell of a lot of money'
I don't intend to touch the 'I'd even hit someone'
I'm uncertain what to say so remain silent.

Jason quietly says, 'I just want to see my sister'

I say, 'You really miss your sister' and then from I'm not sure where
'She supported you in so many ways
you would have done anything for her.'

Jason takes a deep breath
He takes out a notebook and pen and writes as he says,
'I was born in… my date of birth is…
my sister was born in… her date of birth is…'
And continues with his son and his daughter and ends by saying,
'I'm doing this so I don't forget.'

'Like it's hard to remember' I say
At which Jason jumps up saying, 'I have to have a cigarette – will you come with me?'

I say that I am happy to go into the courtyard whilst he has a smoke
Instead, to my surprise
Jason sits down.

I wonder about his sister
I wonder what he makes of my presence in the room with him

I wonder at his need to remember and what anxiety fuels this compulsion to write it all down.

'I really, really, really want my sister' says Jason
We sit together whilst he sobs
Then and only then does Jason leave the room.

Listening to Jason's story and others like it has supported the development within the Trust of 'exploring your spiritual side' groups. Following the work of Louis (2006), I had piloted this work with occupational therapy colleagues in my previous post. The following is a description of the purpose and chosen approach.

> The group deliberately did not have specific treatment aims and objectives, but there was a strong desire on the part of the facilitators… to allow patients a 'safe place' to talk about deeply personal issues with facilitators who would validate contributions in a non-judgemental, empathic way, and would encourage the other members of the group to do the same. The group facilitators suggested a thematic approach: illustrating spiritual development as an allegorical journey that we all take; drawing on resources, overcoming struggles, finding and showing compassion and forgiveness, maintaining hope and reflecting on our progress. (Harrison 2010, p.6)

The process of establishing these groups, which have since evolved and been developed by my chaplaincy colleagues, has been the catalyst for establishing two important principles as they apply to psycho-spiritual care. These are, first, the importance of developing multi-disciplinary approaches and second, that when integrated into the principles of the Recovery Approach, Person-Centred spiritual care can contribute significantly to the wellbeing of patients.

The effects of suicide: A pastoral response or psychotherapy?

I have already discussed how my work includes staff support, and the following extract illustrates the potential development of psycho-spiritual care with staff. The following piece of reflective practice relates to my work with Mary and describes her capacity to process the effect of her daughter's suicide whilst trying to cope with a very challenging work environment and the complexities of home/work balance.

I first of all describe my feelings as follows:

I felt almost overwhelmed by the sheer volume of what Mary has to face on a daily basis and wonder how she is still standing. At the same time more generally I marvel at the human spirit and how in Mary's case she has kept going, but wonder at what cost!

I also feel a deep compassion with a sense of wanting to make things all right for Mary, though know that I cannot and that it would not be helpful to try. I am though determined to offer her Roger's Person-Centred core conditions to the best of my ability. When we met, I wanted with all my being to support Mary if I possibly could.

I am aware that Mary is on the brink (if she is not already falling over the edge) and feel a sense of responsibility and associated anxiety that she may not be able to find the wherewithal to carry on, not that I detect any suicidal signs, more a case of if and when she stops Mary may completely collapse!

I describe some of the issues as being:

- *There is a clear need to spend significant time to work through the myriad forms of grief and loss and associated feelings of needing to care for all around her like a good nurse, to the possible neglect of her own feelings and sense of identity.*

- *The above is combined with the day-to-day need Mary has to care for her family's basic needs.*

- *My position in the organization is not completely neutral. I also know the stresses and strains faced by her manager and other managers.*

- *I wonder about Mary's spiritual needs. Does she, for example, believe in a God of love?*

- *I need to take my understandings and feelings to supervision. It would be easy to get caught up in a parallel process of feeling I need to care for Mary rather than support her in determining how best to care for herself.*

Once again, this reflection raises the issue of the boundary between my role as a trained therapist, chaplain/pastoral and spiritual carer or both. I am clear in all my interactions with patients and staff that I am a chaplain and that it is as a chaplain that I am meeting them. However, it is not possible to factor out or bracket my training and experience as a therapist and the concomitant insights they give to each and every encounter. What is also clear to me is that in the context of the psycho-spiritual care I offer, I am developing Pargament's claim expressed in the introduction to this chapter, that 'psycho-spiritual questions are words that contain sacred qualities' (2011, p.218). According to Pargament, examples of sacred qualities as they apply to my interaction with Mary could include courage, devotion, love, despair and suffering. In other words, it is possible to move between the different worlds of therapeutic care, spiritual wellbeing and the sacred; worlds where both suffering and healing manifest themselves.

While the previous reflection explores issues in the development of psycho-spiritual care in relation to staff support, similar challenges are reflected at the level of the organization. The following is a reflection on my first meeting of my Trust's clinical advisory board (CAB). This is a bi-monthly meeting of all the senior clinicians within the Trust. I include this reflection because it exemplifies some of the dilemmas associated with my organizational role as a senior leader who seeks to place issues of psycho-spiritual care onto the Trust agenda. It is presented as a piece of reflective practice that includes my feelings, a summary of the issues and a brief reflection on what action I took.

The Trust clinical advisory board

FEELINGS

I was delighted to be asked to attend and feel affirmed by my line manager in being invited and being seen to be included. The welcome from clinicians was, I felt, cordial. However, I also detected some surprise and uncertainty as to what I could contribute to the meeting. The question of what I could contribute was also one I felt acutely. I was given an item on the agenda. While being affirming and a great opportunity for me, no such item was given to some of the other senior staff, for example the senior occupational therapist or physiotherapist! I therefore felt rather exposed and a little embarrassed.

I also felt somewhat at sea. Many of the clinical management issues were very technical and highly evolved in their telling and consequent discussion. Much of the time I felt unsure how to contribute.

In summary, the issues were:

- *How to integrate spiritual and pastoral care into the mainstream of clinical care, for example care pathways that are still overly medical and neglect the emotional and spiritual dimensions of care.*

- *How to challenge senior clinicians, some of whom are suspicious and/or lacking in any understanding of my role or purpose.*

- *How to enter an overly technical and possibly bureaucratic agenda, much of which I simply don't understand.*

- *Are there unconscious attempts to keep the agenda management and clinically focused?*

- *If so, how do I seek allies (for example head of occupational therapy) in seeking to re-balance the focus of the agenda so that it is patient led and therefore both inclusive and holistic?*

REFLECTION

The areas with which I am most familiar, that is, spiritual and pastoral care and associated issues such as compassionate care, values-based care and support for staff when considering issues such as change management, were only ever brought to the table by me. I felt a lone voice. This was compounded by my own personal challenge to make my presence felt, whilst being true to my naturally quieter more reflective self.

I will need help and support in making appropriate interventions that will be heard. I will also need to seek allies and suspect that along with the head of occupational therapy one or two of the heads of nursing will be open to talking about issues that are more spiritual in nature.

While the concept of psycho-spiritual care may be alien to many who sit on the CAB, I realize that, despite my struggle to find my voice and make myself heard, I have been given a significant opportunity to present both myself and the department I lead. I was appointed to my present post precisely because of my training and skills in counselling and psychotherapy *and* spiritual and pastoral care. The idea of developing any concept of psycho-spiritual care is predicated on my ability to be able to find allies and develop partnership working within the CAB, within the variety of clinical teams around the Trust and within the medical model of care that is still dominant within health care. The question of precisely how this might happen is still an open one. Whereas psycho-social care is universally accepted as an all-encompassing term that seeks to hold together the social, interpersonal and cultural aspects of care within a psychological framework, psycho-spiritual care within mental and community health care is a virtually unknown concept. Barnard states:

> The term 'psychosocial' has come to refer to a host of issues in health care. Its wide, indiscriminate usage in referring to almost any non-biophysical aspect of illness obscures or distorts the experience of illness as a 'crisis of meaning'. The term 'psycho-spiritual agenda' is introduced to emphasize the problems of meaning associated with illness, and to avoid the potential reductionism, pathological skew,

and interventionist bias of conventional 'psychosocial' analyses of the illness experience. (1984, p.74)

If we accept that this is true it enables the possibility of exploring and examining the questions of meaning and value that often occur when someone is diagnosed with a life-limiting or life-challenging illness. For some patients, illness might be described as a crisis of meaning and therefore of spiritual distress as an aspect of pain. The question remains as to how I present this as a possible model for consideration by senior clinicians and multi-disciplinary teams across the Trust, whether at the CAB or elsewhere.

In this chapter I have discussed the gap between the theory and practice of what I describe as the psycho-spiritual care of patients and clients. I have indicated that much recent counselling and psychotherapy and health care literature suggests that spiritual care is a vital component of holistic care. However, in my discussion I have shown how the evidence from my practice is that there is often an absence of an integrated approach to care that is inclusive of spiritual concerns. Finally, I have highlighted a number of questions. These include:

- How can spiritual care be integrated into a health care service that is often ambivalent about the role of the chaplain?

- How can a model of psycho-spiritual care be developed that embraces spiritual care and counselling and psychotherapy and thereby responds to the needs of patients and staff such as Clare and Steve?

- How can health care staff be supported in embracing 'compassionate care' and thereby be enabled to step closer to understanding and meeting individual spiritual needs?

These questions along with many others will be explored in Part 2.

References

Anthony, W. (1993) Recovery from mental illness: The guiding vision of the mental health service provision in the 1990s. *Psychosocial Rehabilitation Journal*, 16(4), 11–23.

Assagioli, R. (1993) *Psychosynthesis*. London: Penguin.

Assagioli, R. (1998) *The Act of Will*. London: Psychosynthesis and Education Trust.

Baldwin, C. and Capstick, C. (2007) *Tom Kitwood on Dementia: A Reader and Critical Commentary*. McGraw-Hill: Open University Press.

Barnard, D. (1984) Illness as a crisis of meaning: Psycho-spiritual agendas in health care. *Pastoral Psychology*, 33(2), 74–82.

Cambridge University Hospital NHS Foundation Trust (2013) Chaplaincy: Top of FormBottom of FormPromoting Best Practice in Health Care Chaplaincy. Available at www.cuh.org.uk/chaplaincy, accessed on 9 December 2016.

Cassidy, S. (1988) *Sharing the Darkness*. London: DLT.

Clay, S. (1999) 'Madness and Reality. In P. Barker, P. Campbell and B. Davidson (eds) *The Ashes of Experience: Reflections on Madness, Survival and Growth*. London: Whurr Publications.

Cox, M. and Grounds, A.T. (1991) The nearness of the offence: Some theological reflections on forensic psychotherapy. *Theology*, 94(758) (March), 106–115.

Department of Health NHS Commissioning Board (2013) *Compassion in Practice: Nursing, Midwifery and Care Staff Our Vision and Strategy*. London: Department of Health.

Ellis, A. and Grieger, R. (eds) (1986) *Handbook of Rational-Emotive Therapy, Vol. 2*. New York: Springer Publishing Co.

Grof, C. and Grof, S. (1989) *Spiritual Emergency: When Personal Transformation Becomes a Crisis*. Los Angeles, CA: Tarcher.

Harrison, G. (2010) Exploring your spiritual side. *Thresholds*, Spring, 4–7.

Harrison, G. (2016) *The relationship between counselling and psychotherapy and spiritual and pastoral care in the role of a health care chaplain: An autoethnographic narrative case study evaluation*. Unpublished DPsych final project. Metanoia Institute and Middlesex University.

Horton, P. (1974) The mystical experience: Substance of an illusion. *American Psychoanalytic Association Journal*, 22(1–2), 364–380.

Hume, C. (1999) Spirituality: A part of total care? *British Journal of Occupational Therapy*, 62(8), 367–370.

Kitwood, T.M. (1997) *Dementia Reconsidered: The Person Comes First*. Buckingham: Open University Press.

Koenig, H. (2009) Research on religion, spirituality, and mental health: A review. *Canadian Journal of Psychiatry*, 54(5), 283–291.

Kugelmann, R. and Belzen, J.A. (2009) Historical intersections of psychology, religion and politics in national contexts. *History of Psychology*, 12, 125–131.

Lartey, E. (2012) Pastoral Theology in Health Care Settings: Blessed Irritant for Holistic Human Care. In M. Cobb, C. Puchalski and B. Rumbold (eds) *Oxford Textbook of Spirituality in Health Care*. Oxford: Oxford University Press.

Louis, E. (2006) Exploring your spiritual side. *Journal of Health Care Chaplaincy*, 7(2), 21–29.

Lyall, D. (1994) *Counselling in the Pastoral and Spiritual Context*. Buckingham: Open University Press.

Mandel, A. (1980) Toward a Psychobiology of Transcendence: God in the Brain. In J. Davidson and R. Davidson (eds) *The Psychobiology of Consciousness*. New York: Plenum Press.

Mearns, D. and Cooper, M. (2005) *Working at Relational Depth in Counselling and Psychotherapy*. London: Sage.

Moore, J. and Purton, C. (eds) (2006) *Spirituality and Counselling: Experiential and Theoretical Perspectives*. Ross-on-Wye: PCCS Books.

Orchard, H. (ed.) (2001) *Spirituality in Health Care Contexts*. London: Jessica Kingsley Publishers.

Pargament, K. (2011) *Spiritually Integrated Psychotherapy: Understanding and Addressing the Sacred*. New York: Guilford Press.

Reisner, A.D. and Lawson, P. (1992) Psychotherapy, sin, and mental health. *Pastoral Psychology*, 40, 303–311.

Rogers, C. (1967) *On Becoming a Person: A Therapist's View of Psychotherapy*. London: Constable.

Saunders, C. (1996) A personal therapeutic journey. *British Medical Journal*, 313(7072), 1599–1601.

Sims, A. (1994) 'Psyche': Spirit as well as mind? *British Journal of Psychiatry*, 165(4), 441–446.

Spinelli, E. (2005) *The Interpreted World: An Introduction to Phenomenological Psychology*. London: Sage.

Thorne, B. (2012) *Counselling and Spiritual Accompaniment: Bridging Faith and Person-Centred Therapy*. Chichester: Wiley-Blackwell.

Webb, J., Toussaint, L. and Conway-Williams, E. (2012) Forgiveness and health: Psycho-spiritual integration and the promotion of better health care. *Journal of Health Care Chaplaincy*, 18, 57–73.

West, W. (ed.) (2011) *Exploring Therapy, Spirituality and Healing*. Basingstoke: Palgrave Macmillan.

Wilber, K. (2000) *Integral Psychology: Consciousness, Spirit, Psychology, Therapy*. Boston, MA: Shambhala Publications.

Wright, S. (1997) Holistic health. *Nursing Times*, 93(17), 30–32.

PART 2

Aspects of Psycho-spiritual Care in Health Care Practice

Introduction

The Symposium and Beyond

William West

The five chapters in Part 2 of the book are written by five health care professionals, of various backgrounds, who share a holistic view of the person. Consequently, they work in ways that include the spiritual aspect of patients in their care. In March 2016 I chaired a symposium held at Woodbrooke Quaker Study Centre in Birmingham at which, in private, earlier versions of these chapters were presented by these five authors. Each draft chapter had a written response, and these responses are also included here. These responses were also presented at the symposium, followed by a time of discussion and reflection.

At the end of the symposium I was left frankly full of admiration for the quality and quantity of the health care undertaken by the participants, and their surprising good humour despite the workload and other challenges they faced. As Rachel Freeth, one of the participants, states in her chapter, 'Hearing about the experiences of other attendees at the symposium heightened my awareness of how challenging and costly it can be for those of us who are trying to incorporate a spiritual dimension into our work.'

I felt a bit of a fraud since my own experience of working in the NHS dated back to 1972, when I worked 'behind the scenes' writing computer programs. However, as a recent in-patient following a bicycle accident, I could, and did, offer a patient perspective (further explored in West 2015), as did several of the participants.

My tentative conclusions at the end of the symposium were:

- We shared personally and professionally at a pretty deep level in ways that were capable of accepting differences.

- It seemed useful to work with what spirituality means to our patients rather than impose a definition on them.

- Spirituality for many people involves meaning making.

- Using diagnosis to distance us from our patients, while understandable, is not helpful.

- Can we find opportunities, within the NHS as it currently stands, to take forward this acceptance of the part spirituality can play in the care of patients? The reply was affirmative!

What was common to all participants was their ability to reflect honestly on their practice, including their experiences and understandings of the role spirituality can play for the patients (and sometimes staff) involved. One of the common features of each of these chapters is the participant's use of anonymized examples of their work with particular patients to both illustrate the point(s) they are seeking to make and also, equally important, to ground their writing in actual clinical practice. The other striking features they share with us are the impact on themselves of the work with patients, the role of their colleagues in their work and the part played by the wider context of the health care setting.

Rachel Freeth reflects on the spiritual dimension in mental health care and the struggle for meaning. In her chapter, she states: 'I am interested in how spiritual considerations may shape understandings of illness and give meaning to a variety of mental and emotional experiences.' It seems to me that counselling, and mental health care as a whole, and spirituality and the major religions of the world share the common aim of being a response to human suffering. Both have an explanation for human suffering and pastoral ways of responding to suffering, and have developed techniques to minimize current suffering and to reduce future suffering.

Of course, the word 'spirituality' means differing things to differing people. Most people see religion as the structures within which some people locate their spirituality, and spirituality as personal experience and understanding. The crucial thing is what the client or patient means by the word 'spirituality'. Equally crucial is that some people describe the phenomena that many would call spiritual in non-spiritual terms.

Isabel Clarke's chapter together with Sean O'Mahony's response invite us to re-think and re-consider our views of psychosis, including the role spirituality might well play in the crisis the patient experiences and in their recovery. This presupposes health care professionals have an understanding of spirituality and the key part it plays in many people's lives.

Isabel Clarke's questioning of psychosis reflects research from the USA into therapists' attitudes to clients reporting mystical experience (Allman et al. 1992). This research study invited therapists to view a description of a would-be client who reports a mystical experience with some disturbing features. The results showed that those with a negative view of mystical experiences would take a negative view of the patient's experience. Those with a positive view of mysticism would tend to ignore the disturbing features presented. Lukoff (1985) suggested that we could use a DSM-5 (American Psychiatric Association 2013) classification of mystical experiences on a spectrum from mystical experiences with psychotic features through to psychosis with some mystical experience. This has unfortunately not been taken up.

It is not just psychosis and psychotic diagnoses that need careful consideration. There are concerns about the over-use of diagnoses of depression, which seems influenced by class and ethnicity (Edge and West 2011). Such diagnoses are rarely viewed through a spiritual or religious lens, despite notions from the Middle Ages onwards of the 'Dark Night of the Soul' denoting a spiritual crisis in which the person feels abandoned (West 2004).

In the run-up to the launch of the DSM-5 in 2012, there was a fierce debate about mental health diagnosis and treatment. The British Psychological Society issued a statement in which it stated that it:

> recognizes that a range of views exist amongst psychologists, and other mental health professionals, regarding the validity and usefulness of diagnostic frameworks in mental health in general, and the Diagnostic and Statistical Manual (DSM) of the American Psychiatric Association in particular. The Society for Humanistic Psychology (Division 32) of the American Psychological Association (APA) has recently published an open letter to the DSM-5 taskforce raising a number of concerns about the draft revisions proposed for DSM-5 which has, to date, been endorsed by 12 other APA Divisions. A major concern raised in the letter is that the proposed revisions include lowering diagnostic thresholds across a range of disorders. It is feared that this could lead to medical explanations being applied to normal experiences, and also to the unnecessary use of potentially harmful interventions. (British Psychological Society 2011)

However, while we can welcome health care practitioners with a clearer understanding of spirituality and of the role religion might usefully play in their patients' lives – and there is US research showing that working with religious patients' belief systems can be helpful (Payne, Bergin and Loftus 1992) – it is possible that the patient's beliefs can be part of their problem. The potential limitation of religious pastoral care being offered to someone doubting their faith was discussed by one of the participants in a recent research study (West and Goss 2016).

Bob Health and Kate Butcher led us into the world of words, music and the compassionate spirit, particularly in the context of end-of life-care. Recently, the creative use of music with people living with dementia has been widely covered in the media, building on the work of health care professionals (Wall and Duffy 2010).

Gavin Garman and Emma Louis, whose presentations focused on mindfulness, left me with the following conclusions:

- of the need to be mindful

- of how to make best care of patients possible

- of the need for patients to put experience at the heart of their treatment and of being aware of our own potential (as health care practitioners) to provide leadership and direction to self and others.

Mindfulness is clearly an approach whose time has arrived, with it being used across a range of health issues, as well as an approach that can promote good health (Melbourne Academic Mindfulness Interest Group 2006). This harvesting of techniques from religious traditions to promote health has a long pedigree, for example in the ongoing use of yoga and Tai Chi. The increasing popularity of retreats in a variety of religious settings is another example of resources from religious traditions that can be put to use without the participants having to belong to the religion involved.

Steve Nolan, writing as a chaplain, advocates non-religious spiritual care, which as it happens probably represents the views of the majority of people in Britain, where organized religion, among many groups, especially young white people, is in decline but belief in God and a sense of personal spirituality remains. Judy Davies, another chaplain, writing in response, makes a striking statement, among others: 'Recently, I was stopped in the corridor by a senior nurse who had walked the ward for a whole morning, not making eye contact, wearing a tabard that said, "Do not disturb: nurse on drug round". She said, "I'm glad you're here. You're a visible reminder of the things that can't be measured."'

In conclusion, in many ways this was a tough symposium, as reflected in the following chapters, with no easy answers to taking forward an agenda to develop, indeed to embrace, spirituality within health care in Britain. However, the determination, commitment, courage and sheer hard work being undertaken by the participants was inspiring and left me with some hope for the future of spirituality in health care. If I have a future need for in-patient health care, I would only wish for one of these authors to be involved in my treatment!

References

Allman, L.S., De La Roche, O., Elkins, D.N. and Weathers, R.S. (1992) Psychotherapists' attitudes towards clients reporting mystical experiences. *Psychotherapy*, 29(4), 654–669.

American Psychiatric Association (2013) *Diagnostic and Statistical Manual of Mental Disorders* (DSM-5). Washington, DC: American Psychiatric Association.

British Psychological Society (2011) *British Psychological Society Statement on the Open Letter to the DSM-5 Taskforce.* Available at www.bps.org.uk/sites/default/files/documents/pr1923_attachment_-_final_bps_statement_on_dsm-5_12-12-2011.pdf, accessed on 1 September 2016.

Edge, D. and West, W. (2011) Mental health and 'The Big Society': Where do counselling psychologists and therapists fit in? *Counselling Psychology Review*, 26(2), 17–23.

Lukoff, D. (1985) The diagnosis of mystical experiences with psychotic features. *Journal of Transpersonal Psychology*, 17(2), 155–181.

Melbourne Academic Mindfulness Interest Group (2006) Mindfulness-based psychotherapies: A review of conceptual foundations, empirical evidence and practical considerations. *Australian and New Zealand Journal of Psychiatry*, 40, 285–294.

Payne, I.R., Bergin, A.E. and Loftus, P.E. (1992) A review of attempts to integrate spiritual and standard psychotherapy techniques. *Journal of Psychotherapy Integration*, 2, 171–192.

Wall, M. and Duffy, A. (2010) The effects of music therapy for older people with dementia. *British Journal of Nursing*, 19(2), 108–113.

West, W. (2004) *Spiritual Issues in Therapy: Relating Experience to Practice.* Basingstoke: Palgrave.

West, W. (2015) On becoming (a) patient. *Journal of Critical Psychology, Counselling and Psychotherapy*, 15(2), 96–103.

West, W. and Goss, P. (2016) Jungian influenced therapists and Buddhists in dialogue. *British Journal of Guidance and Counselling*, 44(3), 297–305.

5

The Struggle for Meaning

Incorporating a Spiritual Dimension in Mental Health Care

Rachel Freeth

Introduction

Long before I first picked up a medical, let alone psychiatric, textbook, I was interested in healing. The potential for living organisms to heal after being damaged or injured has fascinated me, as does considering the conditions that may enable or enhance the healing process. I was particularly interested in the human psyche and where religion may fit into the healing process. My main frame of reference at the time was that of Christian pastoral care, having grown up in a household engaged in pastoral activities underpinned by Christian faith. However, my understanding was fairly simple, and I certainly didn't appreciate the great variety of concepts, meanings, cultures and contexts relevant to healing. While my knowledge and understanding is still limited, and my interest still biased towards Christian spirituality, 20 years of clinical practice as a psychiatrist and a co-existing allegiance to Person-Centred therapy has considerably developed and shaped the way I now think about healing.

I share the commonly accepted view that healing involves the concept of wholeness, incorporating body, mind and spirit (or soul), however we think of or describe these. Also essential to my understanding is the social and cultural setting in which a person's process towards wholeness occurs.[1] Even accepting these basic assumptions, the topic of healing can be approached from many academic, clinical and helping disciplines, within or without a religious context. Ultimately then, I see myself on a never-ending exploration of how healing can be conceptualized and what it may involve.

---

1. I view wholeness as a process and not a fixed state or destination.

The main aim of this chapter, however, is to explore what I have come to view as an important aspect of healing – *the desire and quest for meaning.* The arena in which I shall explore this is that of mental health care, where I aim to show how within any clinical encounter is a web of meanings. For example, diagnosis may be a major focus from which questions of meaning arise. The specific roles of mental health professional and patient also carry meaning, as well as the relationship between helper and patient. Specifically, I will explore where the quest for meaning incorporates a spiritual dimension. I am interested in how spiritual considerations may shape understandings of illness and give meaning to a variety of mental and emotional experiences. I shall offer something of how I have come to view mental disturbance and some reflections on how I see my role and task as a psychiatrist. In this it will be evident that I am heavily influenced by humanistic psychology and in particular the values and philosophy of the American psychologist Carl Rogers and the Person-Centred approach he developed.[2] I will also note briefly how my own 'way of being' as a helper (to borrow a phrase often used by Rogers) has developed through my own struggle for meaning, making reference to the concept of the 'wounded healer'. Finally, I shall offer some reflections from the symposium for which I prepared the paper on which this chapter is based.

Much of what follows stems from my clinical experience as a psychiatrist. However, some of these reflections also reflect a striving towards ideals that a lot of the time seem unachievable. There are many reasons for why there is frequently a gulf between (my) ideals and the realities of clinical practice. Throughout this chapter, I shall draw attention to some of the main challenges, tensions and obstacles I have encountered that contribute to this gulf. Some of this relates to the profession of psychiatry and some to the nature and organization of UK mental health services as I have experienced them in the NHS.

Meeting Jack

I shall begin by describing my work some years ago with a young man called Jack (not his real name, and some details have been altered), as this will help me to illustrate the many faces of meaning within mental health care, particularly its spiritual aspects.

---

2. The term 'Person-Centred' in this context relates very specifically to a theory of personality and therapy with a particular philosophical underpinning. It is regrettable that today the term is more commonly used within organizations as a buzz-word or sign of political correctness, which in my view renders it fairly meaningless.

Jack was in his mid-twenties when I first met him. This was in the setting of an out-patient clinic as part of my duties working within a community mental health team. Jack's previous psychiatrist had moved on and the only information I had about Jack before meeting him was to be gained from a thick pile of notes and about ten minutes in which to skim through them. The main points I quickly gathered from the notes were that he had been given a diagnosis of bipolar affective disorder and had previously been admitted to a psychiatric hospital several times, usually involuntarily (i.e. detained using Mental Health Act legislation). Since his last admission two years ago, he had been followed up only by a psychiatrist seeing him approximately every three months. The medical notes mainly recorded issues related to medication, particularly that Jack was reluctant to take medication on a regular basis, despite the psychiatrist's efforts to persuade him that he needed it to prevent a major relapse and further hospital admissions. On more than one occasion it was also recorded that Jack 'lacks insight' into his disorder, implying he denied having a mental disorder, with the further implication that he was therefore still mentally ill.[3]

From the outset, Jack seemed reasonably at ease talking to me, and I experienced him as very willing to describe his ongoing visual and auditory experiences, which he actually referred to as hallucinations. Sometimes what he saw and heard was of a sinister and disturbing nature, but more often these sensory perceptions were pleasant and a source of strength and comfort. Examples of the latter included hearing beautiful singing that had an ethereal quality, or seeing beautiful and intricate mosaics on street pavements. On some occasions these experiences were accompanied by a tremendous sense of wellbeing when he felt overwhelmed and enthralled by the beauty of the universe. It seemed to him that he was part of a divine play and that his own part was full of significance and meaning. He felt a sense of being deeply loved by the universe and of having a profound sense of connectedness. So how did I understand Jack's experiences?

Beyond the medical model

Within health care settings, particularly in Western cultures, the medical world view (often referred to as the 'medical model', or 'bio-medical model') is currently dominant. Very simply, in this model physical or mental 'problems' for which health care is sought are construed as pathology,

---

3. Doctors often link the patient's ability to accept a psychiatric diagnosis with how well or unwell they are, as illustrated by this statement in another patient's notes: 'Her mental state improved, and she was able to acknowledge her underlying diagnosis of bipolar disorder'.

described in terms of symptoms which, following assessment, lead to a diagnosis according to a medical classification system. A psychiatrist, like other doctors, is trained to use this model – that is, to follow a particular method of assessment and examination towards the goal of diagnosis and then treatment.

In Jack's case, many of his mental experiences were indeed described in his medical notes as symptoms of illness. His perceptual phenomena were recorded as hallucinations and as 'evidence of ongoing psychosis'. His feelings of elation and wellbeing were interpreted as an 'abnormally elevated mood'. His sense of being part of a divine play was described as either 'over-valued grandiose ideas' or 'grandiose delusions'. The psychiatric textbooks would clearly tell you that Jack had many of the symptoms of bipolar affective disorder in its more severe form, for which mood-stabilizing medication is the standard treatment. But is this the only way of thinking about and interpreting his experience?

In fact, despite what his medical notes said, Jack didn't reject the diagnosis of bipolar affective disorder and he did recognize that he was vulnerable to severe mental disturbance and distress. Rather, what he rejected was framing his experiences *primarily* as medical symptoms, or pathology,[4] using medical language. He rejected seeing himself as mentally ill or as having some form of mental disease, which meant that he didn't view himself as having a condition that necessitated medical treatment in the form of 'corrective' drugs. As Jack talked about his mental experiences with me, particularly his perceptual phenomena, it was apparent that they were deeply meaningful to him. And if his hallucinatory experiences were meaningful, albeit often puzzling, even those that were sinister, why should he see them as in need of modification or eradication by medication?

What I think Jack and I both shared was a recognition that the medical model, with its underlying assumptions (e.g. notions of deficits that need correcting, and its current emphasis on biological theories of mental illness) is *just one model*, albeit a very powerful one. While it is also the model on which a clinical encounter with a psychiatrist is expected to operate, over the years I have come to adopt a view of illness and disorder that rejects the reductionism of many biological and psychological theories. I believe scientific discoveries have shed valuable light on how we understand mental and brain functioning, but when thinking about illness and disorder it is crucial also to take account of a person's social context,

---

4. In the original Greek the word 'pathology' is not the study of abnormality, as it is commonly taken to mean, but the study of suffering, which considerably broadens its meaning.

relationships and their cultural background, past and present. In fact, I would foreground the socio-cultural aspects.

In terms of my own theorizing and understanding of mental disturbance, I am drawn to the personality theory developed by Carl Rogers and his co-workers, which is not a deficit model of disturbance but instead a growth and developmental model. Theories of mental disturbance are developed within this overarching growth model. Rogers uses the term 'actualizing tendency' to describe his belief in an inherent tendency within all living organisms to 'develop all its capacities in ways which serve to maintain or enhance the organism' (Rogers 1959, p.196).[5] This theory is commonly viewed as the 'foundation block' on which Rogers' theory of therapy and Person-Centred forms of helping is based, where the aim is to provide the optimum environment to enable people to grow (or, to express it in more technical language, to facilitate the actualizing tendency in the direction of constructive potentials). In practice, this means providing a facilitative relationship in which the helper consciously strives to embody particular attitudinal qualities. I shall say more about these qualities shortly.

Rogers (1980) also regarded the actualizing tendency as part of an overall 'formative tendency' of the universe towards increased order and interrelated complexity. Such a belief could imply that the world is intelligently created and has purpose, pointing to the existence of a divine being or creator. It also resonates with spiritual ideas of interconnectedness.

Needless to say, the terms 'actualizing tendency', or even 'growth', tend not to be spoken in clinical encounters in psychiatric settings, where the medical jargon of 'disease' and 'disorder' are more common parlance. However, I believe it is important when using terms such as 'illness', 'disease' and 'disorder' to be attentive to the variety of meanings these and related words generate. Meanings of mental illness are frequently negative, for example suggesting moral weakness or failure. Particular diagnoses can be loaded with negative meaning – personality disorder and schizophrenia being obvious examples. The issue of diagnosis was a significant topic of discussion between Jack and me. His diagnosis had impacted him greatly, holding for him mostly negative meaning. For example, he had experienced the hurtful judgements of his family and various other forms of social exclusion and stigma, not least within the workplace. This seemed

---

5. This theory does not see growth and development as inevitable, but just recognizes the tendency towards it. In adverse conditions the tendency leads to stunted or distorted development.

a high price to pay for a diagnostic label that didn't really explain very much or help him to understand himself.[6]

My questioning of the prevailing medical and psychiatric discourse and unwillingness to privilege the traditional language of symptoms and diagnosis does of course create difficulties and tensions for me in my work as a psychiatrist (although how much I voice my critique in my workplace depends on the situation). I am aware of authoritarian voices telling me that my job is to 'psycho-educate' the patient, meaning in effect to endorse the importance and 'truth' of psycho-diagnosis, to help the patient to see things from a medical viewpoint (to 'foster insight') and to accept treatment. I am well aware that by holding the medical model lightly and acknowledging its limitations and potential for harm, I may at times risk accusations of medical neglect by colleagues more rigidly wedded to the medical world view, as well as professional alienation. To challenge or critique the medical model, as a doctor, is risky. The risk of misunderstanding or alienation is also, of course, faced by health care professionals wishing to attend to and incorporate the spiritual dimension in their work.

Symptoms or spiritual phenomena? The relationship between spiritual experience and psychopathology

Jack wanted to understand his experiences and to make sense of what he had been through. He was, like many patients, looking for explanations. 'Why?' is a question that presents in many clinical encounters, even if not clearly articulated, for example 'Why has this happened?' or 'Why me?' But as the previous section highlighted, for Jack, as for many people experiencing mental disturbance and distress, a medical framework alone is insufficient because it does not begin to address these kinds of questions. The medical model offers plenty of theories, for example biological and psychological, that are attempts to explain pathology, often in a linear 'cause and effect' manner, but it doesn't address questions of a more existential or spiritual nature – questions of meaning.[7] This can be a challenge for psychiatrists in all sorts of ways. For one thing, we have little, if any, training in how to respond to issues of an existential nature. And even biological explanations

---

6. While for Jack a psychiatric diagnosis did not hold any positive meaning, this is not the case for other patients. For some, a diagnosis seems to provide a sense of being understood and known, at least initially, thus having a therapeutic or healing effect. Diagnosis also increasingly acts as a gateway to services.

7. This could be described as the distinction between the biological and the existential 'why'.

of mental disorder lack conclusive scientific evidence to back them up. It is especially challenging when some patients want answers with a ring of certainty. Actually, Jack did not impose on me such a demand. Despite wanting explanations, he was willing to embark on a more open-ended exploration that tolerated uncertainty, ambiguity and confusion. In my own clinical experience this is unusual (increasingly so as our culture looks to science and technology for clear answers). It is also not often that I meet patients who themselves initiate questions that are explicitly spiritual in nature. I have found that many patients are very reticent about bringing spiritual or religious themes into discussion with me, for fear of being judged or pathologized. Even when I gently invite people to talk about any spiritual and religious issues or concerns, I still often sense a hesitation in them to do so.

One of the questions that Jack raised with me was whether some of his experiences that psychiatric textbooks would label as psychopathology could instead be described as spiritual in nature. In particular, he wondered whether some of his perceptual phenomena – those auditory and visual experiences that gave him a sense of deep wellbeing, peace and connectedness – could even be described as mystical experiences. Certainly, history reveals that many forms of hallucination, and other mental experiences such as various emotional states, thoughts and beliefs, have been understood in many cultures as having spiritual significance and meaning, for example as spiritual or divine messages. For example, the Christian mystics Julian of Norwich and Teresa of Avila, in the fourteenth century and sixteenth century respectively, recorded in great detail their visions, which for Julian was a 'revelation of divine love'.

As well as individual mental phenomena, the totality of a person's illness experience may also be understood within a spiritual framework. For example, Jack wondered whether his mental vulnerability was some sort of spiritual gateway to a different realm of reality, leading to a different understanding of himself and his place in the world. Could he describe his illness, therefore, as a form of 'spiritual awakening' (e.g. as described in the work of Grof and Grof 1991 or Razzaque 2014)? This possibility gave him a sense of meaning and significance that he had never experienced before. Many people have reported that illness (mental or physical) has led to the development or deepening of a religious faith or spiritual practice, in which illness is viewed as a positive transformational process, although not necessarily when going through it. It is also the case, however, that for others illness can seem utterly meaningless and lead to a profound questioning or loss of faith, which compounds their suffering.

My work with Jack is just one example of the interface between psychopathology and the spiritual dimension. I think it demonstrates how the quest for meaning through illness can lead to an engagement with explorations of a spiritual nature. However, spiritual and religious issues may present in mental health care settings in myriad ways, not always in such an obvious way as with Jack. Clearly this interface is highly complex, and there is not space to explore it further here, other than to note that many thinkers have sought to understand the relationship between psychopathology and spiritual experience, for example William James in his classic work *The Varieties of Religious Experience* (1902). Today there is also increasing interest in and attempts to explore and understand this area.[8] There are many fascinating questions about how we understand human experience and whether there is a difference between psychopathology and spiritual experience, and, if so, how we may make the distinction.

While there is a place for continuing to develop theory and concepts to help us understand this complex interface, it is arguably more important just to be aware of whether patients have spiritual and/or religious beliefs and their potential meanings and implications. This chapter, taken as a whole, affirms the importance of taking seriously a spiritual dimension in mental health care, but I also want to note another two reasons why it is important to be alert to when spiritual and religious perspectives have meaning for patients. The first is that it will influence what kind of help people want or will agree to. Some people may welcome the involvement of someone in a more formal religious capacity such as a chaplain, to complement other forms of care such as medical interventions. Such a person could become a very important member of the multi-disciplinary team for some patients. In contrast, where a medical viewpoint is rejected by a patient in favour of a religious explanation of mental disturbance, it is unlikely that they will voluntarily or without coercion accept medical help. This can create some of the most challenging clinical situations.

Another major reason I want to take seriously people's spiritual or religious beliefs is that for many they are a source of comfort, anchoring and hope. Therefore, if my aim is to facilitate healing, it seems obvious to me that I should recognize that source of hope, whatever it is. (It would also be important to be aware of the danger of blind or naïve optimism or when delusional beliefs are having an impact.) Damage has been done by mental health professionals who have been indifferent to or dismissive

---

8. Examples include the work of the Spirituality Special Interest Group of the Royal College of Psychiatrists and the work of Isabel Clarke (2010) on psychosis and spirituality.

of patients' religious or spiritual beliefs. Such responses might be the result of negative attitudes, although they may also simply be the result of professionals feeling that they lack the skills to talk about religious or spiritual beliefs or concerns.

Finally, I want briefly to highlight a couple of additional challenges I think are relevant when seeking to integrate a spiritual dimension into an understanding of mental disturbance. They also serve to emphasize further the complexity of the territory we are in.

Challenging dualistic thinking

I am aware of a noticeable tendency when speaking about a spiritual dimension to compartmentalize it. What does it really mean to view human beings holistically and not to split off the spiritual or religious from the mental and physical realm? The conceptual challenges of countering the tendency in Western cultures of dualistic thinking are, I think, formidable. Health care professionals wanting to develop concepts and a framework that are truly holistic are likely to be hampered simply because of the way health care services are now organized and delivered. The application of standardized care pathways through which services are delivered (in the interests of achieving, for example, pre-determined outcomes and targets) are by their nature compartmentalized, mechanistic and linear and therefore deter a deeper, integrated and truly holistic approach to care. The health care culture and systems within which we work profoundly influence our habits of thinking.

The issue of language

Related to the above is the issue of language. Medical language is different from spiritual and religious language, even though medicine and religion have in the past been more closely aligned. I often feel linguistically challenged, in considering the language I use not only with patients, but with colleagues too. As a psychiatrist practising at a time when biological and materialistic perspectives are dominant, when scientific terminology is afforded superiority, to talk about meanings and incorporate spiritual language that is by its nature subjective, vague, more tentative and often ambiguous, can feel very uncomfortable. To use spiritual language can at times feel as though I am speaking a foreign and alien language. Furthermore, mental and spiritual phenomena will always in the end defy verbal expression. Often there just are no words to convey experiences that are, at a fundamental level, mysterious.

Person-Centred psychiatry in action

What I have written so far should have given some flavour of what I bring both theoretically and philosophically to my work as a psychiatrist, particularly with regard to the spiritual dimension. In this section, I want to draw out further a few more of the implications for how I practise as a psychiatrist. The key question here is how my psychiatric practice reflects my own spiritual values and beliefs, although providing an answer is far from straightforward and I can only touch on this briefly. As in the previous sections, I will also draw attention to how organizational factors impact upon me.

In considering my practice as a mental health care professional, I need to make a distinction between the tasks and activities that specifically relate to my role as a psychiatrist, and those that are relevant to all mental health professionals. However, while it is possible to delineate a number of tasks normally assigned to psychiatrists, such as making a diagnosis or prescribing medication, there is much that I do that is less clearly defined and not exclusive to the role of a psychiatrist. One of the challenging issues that faced me when working with Jack was precisely that of being clear what my role was, and when I may have been in danger of straying into territory that might best be met by other professionals with the relevant knowledge and expertise.

It is also worth acknowledging that over the years my role has become increasingly narrowed to what at times feels like that of a technician with the function of achieving SMART goals (SMART being an acronym for Specific, Measurable, Achievable, Relevant or Results-focused, and Time-bound). The broader, unmeasurable, therapeutic and relational aspects often now seem little recognized and have become devalued. This is because the psychiatric profession currently embraces not only a scientific and technician-like identity, but is also a reflection of wider organizational and political demands. It is simply more expedient that I work within the narrow confines of diagnosis and treatment, because that way I can see more patients. Economic efficiency and maximizing productivity seems to be the top priority for health care organizations today, as it is for most organizations and businesses operating on market economics.

So how did I work with Jack? As well as attending to the more obvious medical tasks such as discussing medication, particularly its effects and potential uses, I also considered whether Jack should be referred for some form of psychological therapy, and whether he might find it helpful to talk to a priest or other spiritual/religious professional. As is so often the case, however, actions are taken according to the resources available.

In the end, we decided not to pursue a referral for psychological therapy. This was partly because what he was looking for was a space to explore his questions of a more existential and spiritual nature, while much of NHS psychological therapy these days is a version of the medical model, with a problem-solving and treatment-orientated emphasis. Furthermore, Jack and I had developed a relationship of mutual trust which seemed right to capitalize on. Indeed, I believe it was our relationship that played an important part in his process.

The therapeutic or helping relationship has always interested me, and the model of relationship I am most drawn to is that articulated by Carl Rogers and his co-workers, with an emphasis on the attitudinal qualities of the helper. The Person-Centred approach to helping relationships also most encapsulates my own spiritual values.[9] I could say, therefore, that my work as a psychiatrist, or my 'spirituality in action', is expressed in the way I relate to others and the nature of the therapeutic relationship I try to facilitate. This manifests in a particular approach to understanding people, which is to enter as fully as possible into their frame of reference. With Jack, then, what seemed important was not to evaluate or categorize his symptoms by seeing him through a medical lens, but to get to know how he saw things and what informed his perceptions. This is a key feature of the Person-Centred approach and is core to a person-centred understanding of empathy.

What can be so powerful about this kind of empathy is that it endows the other person with worth, or what Rogers termed 'positive regard'. It is like saying, 'I want to understand how you see things because I value you.' Empathy, then, becomes a vehicle for conveying an attitude of respect and fundamental valuing of the other.

This way of working is characterized by a form of listening that is highly concentrated, attentive and involves both the intellect and emotions. I believe this kind of listening is qualitatively different from much that is taught to doctors and other health care professionals, where the emphasis is on developing techniques that can be used in an instrumental way, for example, to gather information. In contrast, my aim is to embody certain attitudinal qualities, those known as congruence, unconditional positive regard and empathy, which are a *principled* expression of certain values and beliefs about human beings, such as their intrinsic worth (intrinsic worth is to me an ontological notion), capacity to grow, and the right to

---

9. It is a remarkable feature of the Person-Centred approach that it appeals to practitioners of many spiritual and religious persuasions.

self-determination.[10] In other words, how I behave towards others is a reflection of what I believe about them, for example whether I believe they have an innate trustworthiness and wisdom, where my task would then be one of facilitating this. It is also a reflection of my belief in human beings' need for connectedness and a sense of belonging, which so many patients entering the mental health system profoundly lack. On this, Rogers wrote, 'To my mind, empathy is in itself a healing agent…it releases, it confirms, it brings even the most frightened client into the human race. If a person can be understood, he or she belongs' (Rogers 1986, p.126).

Putting all this in a more explicitly spiritual framework, these relational qualities and attitudes are nothing less than an expression of love, of the kind described in many religious traditions and philosophical systems. For a Christian, unconditional positive regard (sometimes described simply as acceptance), for example, may be seen as the embodiment of the unconditional love of God. Jesus Christ has been described as the greatest listener and empathizer with the human condition who has ever lived.[11]

It must be said, however, that for human beings to love and accept others unconditionally can only ever be an aspiration. While the attitudes and kind of listening I have briefly outlined characterize much of my practice, there are many things that make this enormously challenging and sometimes impossible. The role of a psychiatrist in itself presents limitations. Some tasks I undertake will not be experienced by patients as therapeutic, particularly in situations that involve coercion and forms of control. And, of course, it can be argued that the kind of listening I have described is not the task of a psychiatrist but more that of a psychotherapist or counsellor. It is also the case that some forms of mental disturbance, such as severe psychotic illnesses, present a formidable challenge to the establishment of relationship and connection, let alone a therapeutic one. Furthermore, it is immensely challenging, if not impossible, to embody the attitudinal conditions of unconditional positive regard and empathy towards individuals whose behaviours are disturbing, frightening, confusing or repugnant (see Freeth 2007 for a more in-depth exploration of these challenges). To be congruently in touch with my own inner world of thoughts and emotional reactions towards the other in these situations is also a challenge.

10. There are major implications here regarding the use of control and coercion within mental health care settings.

11. For example, the prophesied Messiah is described in the book of Isaiah in the Old Testament as a 'man of suffering and acquainted with infirmity', that is, one who entered into the human condition and knew profound human suffering – physical and emotional (Isaiah 53.3, New Revised Standard Version).

Many other barriers to listening, however, are created by organizational factors. My own experiences of mental health service environments are that they are not conducive to the development of compassion or to being able to offer attentive, empathic listening. In my own role this is often due to the sheer weight and nature of demands placed upon me – in simple terms, to overload. Combine this with a blame culture, and insufficient support and supervision, and working in a relational way becomes risky – particularly the risk of burnout. But it is more than feeling overloaded and unsupported that creates distress. It can also be due to the profound conflict of my values and ideals with the 'operational goals' of the organization. The painful question I increasingly ask myself is whether I can continue to be a spiritually sensitive and relationship-orientated psychiatrist in an organization that pursues a business model and not a service one, and that in general does not recognize or value the concept of healing.

My own struggle for meaning

In this section I want to offer a few thoughts on how my particular professional journey has played a part in my own quest for meaning, as well as how my sense of meaning comes through the *way* or *how* I do what I do.

The notion of vocation seems to me entirely appropriate to use here, despite the increasingly rare use of this term within the medical profession today. I didn't always want to train to become a doctor, but once at medical school I had a very strong vocational sense that I would work in the area of mental health. There are a number of reasons why I was drawn to psychiatry, but one of them was as a response to my own wounds. The 'wounded healer' is a psychological and spiritual concept I readily embrace, in which wounds may become sources of growth and healing. They can therefore be of value. How I have drawn on my own wounds in my professional life has endowed them with meaning.[12]

I see my own vocational path, then, as that of a wounded healer. This path has been strewn with obstacles and many difficult questions and inner conflicts about the nature of my work as a psychiatrist and what I can continue to do. In particular, I have had to confront the risks and personal vulnerabilities (the costliness) involved in working the way that I do. The fact that I went on to train as a counsellor also suggests that I found something profoundly missing working in NHS mental health settings, which includes its limited ability to recognize and relate to human beings

---

12. It is also important to be aware of how wounds may play out in unhealthy ways when we are in helping or caring roles.

as whole persons and to listen in depth. I think the issue I am grappling with here is one of personal and professional authenticity and integrity. To bring my full personhood, or my full self, into my work environment feels risky, but not doing so feels more risky.

If my vocation is 'a response of the heart and soul', as I have heard it described, in which I use my self, in relationship, as a healing agent, inevitably this involves much more than having knowledge, skills and competencies. It is much more than what tasks I perform. It involves being prepared to be alongside others in distress and being vulnerable. I find it much easier to do this as a counsellor than as a psychiatrist. But in both I see myself on a journey of both woundedness and meaning. At times this feels like a journey of profound paradox.

Reflections from the symposium

It was a rewarding experience to prepare a paper for this symposium. I also found it an exceptionally challenging one, as it seemed like an existential process that prompted examination of my core beliefs and values. The symposium also created an opportunity for papers to be read and responded to in an immediate and direct way. I am particularly grateful to fellow psychiatrist and psychotherapist Dr Melanie Bowden, who was invited to offer her reflections on my paper, which I will draw on in this final section and quote her directly.

Melanie shared her own personal struggles responding to the way care is conceptualized and delivered, commenting that as 'an individual it has been a challenge to hold onto faith and meaning in a work context'. She also drew on her psychotherapy experience and offered some theory about how organizations, particularly health care organizations, operate and create the kind of challenges we found ourselves reflecting on.

One of Melanie's reflections is how as health care professionals we encounter many languages. She put this as follows:

> There is possibly what could be called 'normal language' which we might share with patients and staff as we go about our day. There is health care language, psychological language, psychotherapeutic language, medical language, human resources language and managerial language. I feel there is a particular language of the NHS. This evolves with time and certain words become fashionable as time passes. New buzzwords appear such as 'safeguarding' and have great power.

What seems particularly significant, again in Melanie's words, is how 'meaning feels lost from the discourse. The language is of pathways not people, targets not truths, goals not God'. She also noted how meaning *between* these many languages can also easily be lost and create barriers.

Referring to the work of Isabel Menzies Lyth (1959, 1979), and Obholzer and Roberts (1994), she also drew attention to the very important issue of how organizations such as the NHS struggle to respond to the suffering, fear and anxiety it is presented with, and how easy it is to become overwhelmed. A consequence of this is the way organizations unconsciously set up various defences and strategies to cope with or ward off the threat of intolerable feelings such as the fear of death. Examples of such defences include depersonalization, categorization, denial of significance of the individual, and detachment and denial of feelings.

Another of Melanie's observations was how 'management models seem to have become more influential over clinical care'. An example is the manualization of care, which is an increasingly prevalent feature of health care delivery. Business and economic considerations – market forces – also inform management models. One of the consequences, in Melanie's words again, is that 'worth becomes equated with making money and the appearance of care becomes more important than true achievement of care'.

The question this leads to is simply how do we respond to suffering in a way that is healthy and mature? How can we ensure that we are sufficiently safe and secure to practise competently and creatively? Drawing on the ideas of psychoanalyst Donald Winnicott (1965), Melanie commented that 'a person cannot play or create if they are instantly asked to justify the cost or value of what they are doing or if their actions are consistently labelled, managed or at worse judged'.

This raises the issue of self-care and ensuring that our own needs, including our own wounds, are attended to. One implication of this, which Melanie observed, is that helpers need to find a way of dealing with the organization. Many of us attending the symposium spoke about our struggles with the organization in which we work, experiencing at times a sense of working in an alien and hostile culture. Hearing about the experiences of other attendees at the symposium heightened my awareness of how challenging and costly it can be for those of us who are trying to incorporate a spiritual dimension into our work. Others shared how their way of working may be in conflict with the predominant values of the organization (which are not necessarily reflected in mission statements). Yet it is clear that despite the challenges we want to find a way of working that expresses our values and enables us to care, incorporating spiritual dimensions. Melanie was hopeful: 'I do feel that at every level of care whether it be the individual, service or organizational, I see attempts to bring meaning and goodness popping up despite the pressures we are under.'

To conclude, there seemed to be a yearning among many of us at the symposium to be able to bring more spiritual language into our work, despite the risk of being ignored or belittled. There was a valuing of the concept of healing rather than that of cure, which involves being able to face the reality of suffering and be with it. For me this means being what the word 'psychiatrist' means in Greek – a 'healer of the soul'– and to work in 'sacred space'.

References

Clarke, I. (ed.) (2010) *Psychosis and Spirituality: Consolidating the New Paradigm.* Chichester: Wiley.

Freeth, R. (2007) *Humanising Psychiatry and Mental Health Care. The Challenge of the Person-Centred Approach.* Abingdon: Radcliffe Publishing.

Grof, C. and Grof, S. (1991) *The Stormy Search for the Self: Understanding and Living with Spiritual Emergency.* London: Mandala.

James, W. (1902) *The Varieties of Religious Experience: A Study in Human Nature.* New York: Longmans, Green and Co.

Menzies Lyth, I. (1959) The function of social systems as a defence against anxiety. *Human Relations,* 13, 95–121.

Menzies Lyth, I. (1979) Staff Support Systems: Task and Anti-Task in Adolescent Institutions. In R.D. Hinshelwood and N. Manning (eds) *Therapeutic Communities. Reflections and Progress.* London: Routledge.

Obholzer, A. and Roberts, V.Z. (eds) (1994) *The Unconscious at Work: Individual and Organisational Stress in the Human Services.* London: Routledge.

Razzaque, R. (2014) *Breaking Down is Waking Up: Can Psychological Suffering be a Spiritual Gateway?* London: Watkins Publishing.

Rogers, C. (1959) A Theory of Therapy, Personality and Interpersonal Relationships as Developed in the Client-centred Framework. In S. Koch (ed.) *Psychology: A Study of a Science: Vol. 3. Formulations of the Person and the Social Context.* New York: McGraw-Hill.

Rogers, C. (1980) *A Way of Being.* Boston, MA: Houghton Mifflin.

Rogers, C. (1986) Rogers, Kohut and Erickson: A personal perspective on some similarities and differences. *Person-Centred Review,* 1(2), 125–140.

Winnicott, D. (1965) *The Maturational Process and the Facilitating Environment.* London: Karnac.

Acknowledgments

With particular thanks to the Reverend Dr Guy Harrison for inviting me to contribute to the symposium, Dr Melanie Bowden for her reflections on my paper, and my fellow symposium attendees for a rich sharing of experience.

6

Spirituality, Psychosis and the Journey of Life

Isabel Clarke

When asked to give a talk about spirituality, I generally start by stating that I am not going to offer the usual menu of definitions from respected authorities. Instead, I ask the audience to reflect on how they know that an experience of theirs is spiritual or not. This points to the reality that some of the most crucial knowledge, for instance judgements about relationships, is not well captured by words and formulae; it is grounded in feeling and requires creative and poetic use of language to begin to express it. Spirituality is at the heart of this category as, I would argue, it is a sense of relationship with that which is beyond; both deepest and furthest, but out of the limited and limiting reach of human language.

Because of this inaccessibility to the precision of scientific language, spirituality has been marginalized in our reductionist times. This has always intrigued me as I have from a young age experienced the spiritual dimension as important, at the same time as having a healthy respect for science, so throughout my life I have pursued this conundrum. In my youth, I studied medieval history – a period when spirituality and religion were seen as vital to the health of the whole community, though mainly delegated to the clerical and monastic caste. Taking up psychology later, one of the questions I wanted to get to the bottom of was: where did spirituality fit in? The other question, the one that propelled me into this study because of the experience of a friend, was about how human beings are so prone to breakdown. I asked: what is going on there? I felt there must be a better way of meeting it than my friend's dire experience with hospital. Interestingly, I discovered that the answer to both questions fit together when viewed through the lens of the cognitive science-based model of cognitive architecture on which I now base my understanding of the human being, namely Interacting Cognitive Subsystems (ICS; Teasdale and Barnard 1993).

A challenging model of the mind

When I read Teasdale and Barnard's book, *Affect, Cognition and Change*, I found the answer to the question about human frailty. As I came to understand more fully the implications of this model of brain architecture, painstakingly constructed from the morass of data on memory, coding and information-processing bottlenecks coming out of cognitive science, I realized I had the answer to the spirituality question as well. To oversimplify massively (and it is the utter complexity of this model that has prevented the wide dissemination of this understanding), the modular human brain, with different circuits managing different functions, is integrated by two overarching meaning-making systems. One collects information about perception, the body, the emotions – in summary, 'the heart'; the other, evolutionarily newer, system only deals in the verbal side, 'the head'. The emotional, 'implicational' system looks for information on threat and value to the self; it makes connections. The verbal, 'propositional' system can manage precise distinction and context (it is the only one that tracks time). I hypothesize that it is the addition of the propositional system that gives us our human sense of self-conscious individuality. Importantly, the two systems share control, passing it from one to the other. As Teasdale and Barnard write, 'there is no central executive' (pp.63, 78). In other words, there is no boss. And the character of our experience changes according to which one is dominant.

This is the basis of how I now understand the human being, and of how I work clinically. When the implications of this model are fully faced, they are quite challenging, but when the challenge is accepted, a lot of puzzling factors start to fall into place. Subjectively we feel as if we are unitary and in control. Recognizing that this is not the whole story makes it possible to see how dependent we are on roles and relationships to give us our sense of who we are. Our very selves are 'work in progress' – the implicational looking out for threat and position, information that is registered at the gut level. Normally we are only marginally aware of this: a flutter of discomfort when someone implies criticism, an affirmed feeling in response to the opposite. However, when those vital supports in terms of important roles and relationships are threatened or crumble, the feeling is more powerful. No wonder that mental health breakdown is associated with times of transition and relationship breakdown. Further, because the 'implicational' looks out for threat and disregards time, when things are difficult, past threatening situations are added to the current challenge. Thus, the impact of past trauma and adverse circumstances on vulnerability to breakdown is explained in a way that makes sense in terms of evolutionary survival

– being hypersensitive to threat ensured that in simpler times, but such overreaction spells disaster in terms of mental stability. The wonder is not that people are prone to breakdown; more that most of us manage to hold what is a wobbly balance pretty well a lot (but not all) of the time. I have explored these ideas in more detail in my book, *Madness, Mystery and the Survival of God* (Clarke 2008).

Interacting Cognitive Subsystems and spirituality

This model also offers a way into understanding spirituality. Each of the subsystems is associated with a different character of subjective experience. When both are working smoothly together (our usual waking state) we are capable of precise, logical thought and planning, with emotional considerations in the background. The 'propositional' is dominant. When under threat or pressure, in love, and so on, the 'implicational' and emotions can take over. The propositional has a filtering effect on our perceptions, making everything more manageable and handleable. The implicational is the default system and so can take over more fully. When this happens, we lose the filter. Everything becomes larger than life, more connected, more meaningful; it acquires a supernatural glow – in short, it feels more spiritual.

My sense is that when grounded in our implicational, we have the facility to step outside our safely bounded individuality into an area of experience that is at the same time more connected and holistic, and less safe and contained. In our implicational mode we cease to be isolated individuals and the sense in which we 'are' relationship is brought out; we become part of the whole.

The paradox is (and this is the place of paradox where 'either–or' logic breaks down) that we need our filtered, propositional, capacity to manage real-world relationships – and indeed normal life. The spiritual experience of awe and wonder at the immensity of the universe, for example, is like stepping over a threshold – I have adopted Thalbourne's term, used by Claridge (1997), of 'transliminal' for this area of experience – which just means 'across the threshold' in Latin. If you can manage that threshold and pass easily backwards and forwards across it, all is well. You can have a life-enhancing spiritual experience and come back to the boring, ordinary world. However, it is all too easy to get stuck on the other side. In these circumstances, with the usual boundaries and certainties dissolved, the experience becomes frightening, disorienting and disintegrative. This is the type of experience that can attract the label of psychosis.

Bringing psychosis and spirituality together

It was the conundrum of two very different outcomes representing the same area of experiencing that I tackled in my first book, *Psychosis and Spirituality* (Clarke 2010). When I started to look into it in the 1990s, the subject seemed to attract one question: how do we distinguish between a nice spiritual experience and the nasty illness, psychosis, as the two can, inexplicably, often seem very similar? For me, this was fundamentally the wrong question, and it was my mission to turn perceptions around towards the recognition that both represent the same area of experiencing with differences in what the individual brought with them to the experience, and their ability to move in and out of it or not. The edited book brought together research and perspectives from a number of disciplines to support this position. I was helped to this perspective by the conjunction of my familiarity with the Christian spiritual literature, studied as part of my medieval background, and the stories of early breakdown I heard from the people with long-standing mental health problems, usually labelled as 'chronic schizophrenia', whom I worked with as part of my job as a clinical psychologist in a psychiatric rehabilitation service.

These people often related ecstatic experiences when everything appeared to come together, now long ago – after which everything went just as catastrophically wrong, and they ended up stuck in the system. I was aware that the medieval saints and mystics had a more powerful containing narrative for their transliminal experiencing, and usually good support for daily living through monastic communities when taken up with higher things. On the other hand, like my informants in the hospital, the initial breakthrough (breakdown?) often came at times of illness and transition – times when the bonds of regularity and relationship that hold the self together were looser. With the growing awareness of the role of past trauma in psychosis (Read and Bentall 2012; Varese, Smeets and Ducker 2012), it is possible to see how the ease of intrusion of past adversity at such times will have intensified that loosening.

Viewed in this way, it ceases to make sense to see psychosis as an illness. It is more a stage in the journey of life, a possibility that opens up when the straight way ahead has become blocked. This might occur because someone is dissatisfied with the meaninglessness of their current life (as, for example, Saint Francis and the Buddha were) and seek growth and inspiration; they might be driven to seek escape when life is intolerable – in both cases that escape may be sought through spiritual practice, but equally it could be through mind-altering substances, a not to be recommended fast track to the transliminal, popular in our society! Or the intolerability, probably helped by past trauma and current adversity ganging up, might be such that an individual is catapulted without warning into that other dimension beyond the threshold. For an example of a personal account that illustrates this perspective most engagingly, see Hartley (2010).

The importance of this perspective

Do these distinctions matter? I would answer, 'yes'. My therapy clients in the rehab service knew that their experiences were significant. Until then they had been told that they were just symptoms of an illness, so it made a great difference to have them validated as part of a tradition of mystical visions, even if what had followed was a disaster.

More generally, there is a telling research literature that demonstrates unarguably that the way in which someone makes sense of their experiences, the societal context around them, makes a great difference to whether these remain as an episode that they can move on from, even learn from, or a disaster from which they do not emerge (e.g. Brett 2010; Heriot-Maitland, Knight and Peters 2012; Brett et al. 2013). This ties in with the message coming from epidemiological research as early as 1985 and persisting to the present day (Warner 1985, 2007) that recovery from so-called 'schizophrenia' in traditional society was more rapid and less prone to relapse than in advanced societies. There must be lessons here for the way to treat people – lessons that we in the West are remarkably slow to learn.

Spirituality and the journey of life

I will return later to how I have tried to incorporate this learning about the importance of how the individual makes sense of their experience into clinical work with people who have been given a diagnosis of psychosis within an acute mental health service. I now want to consider the implications of looking at human beings and spirituality in this way from the wider journey-of-life perspective. I have referred above to the way in which the traveller can become bogged down, lose their way, or find the path ahead blocked. Remember that according to this model, the self is work in progress, and is partially constituted from existing roles and relationships. These can become too restrictive to allow development. The individual can find themselves with nowhere to move. Alternatively, these external props might shift dramatically. This could be in an adverse direction – major losses, whether of people, role, place, and so on – or it could be positive: for instance, the destabilizing effect that sudden massive fame can have on someone.

Wherever, for whatever reason, the props holding the sense of self and containing the person so that everything feels calm and 'normal' dissolve or are broken out of so that there is an urgent need to reconstitute that vital containment. A state of psychic nakedness and vulnerability obtains. It is precisely at this point that the potential containment of that wider, spiritual, relatedness becomes vitally relevant.

Looked at from this perspective, spiritual care shifts from being a trendy box that any trust with an up-to-the-minute values statement needs to tick, to its rightful place at the heart of holistic care. It is a place that is relevant to all, but many would not recognize it under the label 'spiritual', a word that repels as many people as it enthuses. It is about recognizing that the human being only makes sense in a context of relationship, and this context gets its cohesiveness from love. The loving relatedness that the individual has experienced throughout their life is the foundation of the self, but too often this is a broken and damaged container. A sense of being of value and accepted, a vital part of something, much vaster and more magnificent, is actually a basic human need. For some it is fulfilled within the context of a religion, for others through a more diffuse spirituality, and in our society maybe for yet more, by a sense of valued role or pursuing valued aims in life – even through sports-based affiliation. In whatever form, that reaching beyond is essential to the healing that needs to take place when the framework of relatedness that enables us to maintain our wobbly balance in our bossless state has been ruptured and torn. Those of us who work in health services will recognize that torn state.

Reaching out to that broader context is not only important to help the individual to get through and regain their former functioning. It is an opportunity to draw upon wider sources of creativity, to bring newness into the equation. This is the fuel for growth and transformation. Many of the people I have worked with in therapy have said their mental health issues have assisted their growth as people. It has deepened their empathy and perspective and opened their eyes to a spiritual dimension to which they were previously blind.

Of course, for others, to look out to that wider view is simply too frightening, and they remain locked in a diminished state. The messages they receive from those around them about hope and potential or its opposite can be crucial for which way it goes. In my present and previous role, I work with people to help them to recognize that the understandable ways in which they are coping with their current intolerable internal state, which is usually made worse by the re-awakening of past trauma (e.g. withdrawing, or self-harm), are keeping them stuck, and to develop new and healthier ways of coping (Clarke 2009, 2015). Mindfulness is the key skill to learn here, to enable someone to connect with themselves and the world around them in a state of non-judgemental awareness. It is a skill that lies at the heart of finding that place of spiritual relatedness.

Transformative potential of psychosis

All that I have said about potential for growth, transformation and reaching out for creative resource beyond the limited self is especially true for the states labelled as psychotic. This perspective stands in sad contrast to the depressing messages that people often receive when they report such transliminal experiences. This is not to deny the adverse consequences for everyday functioning and potential for risk that such states can entail. People need support and containment when going through this sort of process. The destructive and disruptive potential of getting lost in the transliminal is clear. The transformative element is the other side of the coin, and this is honoured in traditions such as Grof's concept of 'Spiritual Emergency' (Grof 1988; Grof and Grof 1991).

Grof saw transliminal encounters, spontaneous or induced (by LSD in his earlier work, and later using holotropic breathwork) as a process of growth towards higher states of human consciousness. Such a viewpoint fits in with a well-established tradition in Buddhist literature. In the Christian contemplative tradition, such experiences are seen as encounters that can strengthen the connection with the divine and so confirm the devotee in resolve to pursue a Christian life. Both traditions, in common with Grof, recognize that such encounters can be negative as well as positive (cf. Chapters 6 and 7 in *Madness, Mystery and the Survival of God*, Clarke 2008, for more on this). Religious and spiritual traditions characteristically counsel adherents against becoming attached to transliminal experience for its own sake, rather seeing it as a path to spiritual growth and effective action in the world.

Mike Jackson, one of the first people to research the area of overlap between spiritual and psychotic experience (Jackson 1997, 2010, pp.139–155), has a more prosaic way of making sense of this, which I find eminently convincing. He argues that, at the point of impasse, when life appears to have led the individual up a blind alley, accessing the transliminal can reveal a new vista. He characterizes this as 'problem solving'. In terms of ICS, the problem-solving potential of the usual loop between the propositional and implicational subsystems is exhausted, and the wider resources of the implicational, which as we have seen, can extend beyond the individual, need to be accessed. The danger is that there are no guarantees or boundaries in this area, hence the potential for not returning smoothly to ordinary reality.

The suggestion is that the return will, in any case, not be to exactly the same place. The encounter with the transliminal has the potential to be truly transformative. It certainly dents faith in straightforward, propositional, either/or logic and opens the way to the mind-expanding, both/and logic of the transliminal (cf. Bomford 1999 for a discussion of these different logics). It can lead to the integration of aspects of the person that had become split off, usually by the dissociative process triggered by emotional pain. This is the link between trauma and openness to transliminal experience. Exposure to a sense of greater unity can be liberating and expanding both of consciousness and of compassion. On the other hand, as we have seen, it can go either way. The re-awakened wounds from the past can intrude into the present and take over, destroying that fine balance that we depend on to navigate human life.

The What Is Real and What Is Not approach

Between 2004 and 2012, I worked in an acute hospital and developed a therapeutic programme that builds on this perspective (Clarke 2013). We called it the 'What Is Real and What Is Not' group. It was delivered as a four-session group, for in-patients or those recently discharged and supported in the community, or individually. The programme was offered to anyone who was prepared to identify themselves as having experiences that others do not share, irrespective of diagnosis. These might be voices or visions (hallucinations, flashbacks), strongly held beliefs (delusions), or fears (paranoia). In inviting people to join the group, a new way of looking at symptoms was offered as well as coping strategies.

Schizotypy and 'unshared reality'

The approach is characterized by treating participants as the interested and intelligent adults that they are, and so presenting (briefly) research findings behind the key ideas. The programme first introduced Romme and Escher's (1989) idea of normalizing voice hearing and drawing on the coping resources of experiencers for mutual support, but extended to other unusual experiences, unshared beliefs and fears.

We then introduced the idea of openness to voices and strange experiences – the schizotypy spectrum – highlighting Gordon Claridge's research effort normalizing openness to this other way of experiencing given the right conditions (drugs, trauma, sleep deprivation, etc.), while recognizing that some people are more open to it than others (Claridge 1997, 2010). This offers a hopeful perspective as the research identifies positives, such as creativity and spirituality, associated with high schizotypy

– along with the greater vulnerability to psychotic breakdown, leading to discussion of the pros and cons of being a high schizotype.

The rest of the group programme aimed to provide strategies to manage openness to unshared reality and participate in the shared world, without necessarily totally rejecting the unshared. This contrasts with other mental health programmes which tend to aim at elimination of 'symptoms' (i.e. unshared experiences). The programme respects individual values, whether these reject unshared experiencing or see it as an integral part of identity, and stages in between. Where the individual sees what others label as psychosis as their access to a valued spiritual reality, this approach opens a way to dialogue. Where linked to a faith, discussion with the chaplain or other faith representative can establish whether or not someone's interpretation is normative. However, spiritual and mystical experience has always led people into unique experience, producing new insights that can be seen as challenging or heretical by orthodoxy. We are here operating beyond the realms of certainty.

In this way, the aims of the group were presented as something that would give the participants more control, but without having to reject their unique experiences or to accept a stigmatizing label. Medication was recognized as one of these means of control, and an important one, along with psychological coping strategies. Arousal management, which controls access to unshared reality, and mindfulness, are straightforward strategies that we could deliver in the hospital to help people to cope. Mindfulness for psychosis has a sound research base (e.g. Chadwick, Newman-Taylor and Abba 2005).

The Spiritual Crisis Network

Working for change within the NHS is slow. There is a parallel need for people to have access to a different message and a different sort of support from the outside – and that is why I joined with others, under the leadership of Catherine Lucas, in 2004, to found the Spiritual Crisis Network (www.spiritualcrisisnetwork.uk). We have remained a small movement, but visible chiefly through the Internet to the many who recognize that their experiences or those of people they are supporting cannot be written off as an illness, but do have important potential, given the right support.

At the moment, we can only provide that support via email because of limitation of resources. However, we hope to be able to expand that, and are connected with people all over the world in an International Spiritual Emergency Network, the embryonic ISEN, as well as like-minded bodies in the UK (e.g. Soteria). We have organized successful conferences in

Liverpool, Sunderland, Norfolk and London which spread the message to a wider public, including many health professionals, and provide training for the vital volunteers who answer the queries that come through our website. We are also closely associated with initiatives to transform mental health treatment and attitudes, under the embryo umbrella organization Revisioning Mental Health (formerly the New Paradigm Alliance). Watch this space!

Sean's following piece adds the valuable perspective of the clinician working at the coalface of NHS mental health service care delivery. He reflects on the potential and rewards of taking experience seriously as a spiritual journey as opposed to an illness to be eliminated. He also adds the necessary note of realism, given the constraints and existing orientation of the service, along with encouragement for the development of alternative narratives outside it.

A Response

Sean O'Mahony

I was asked by Guy Harrison to give a brief clinical response to Isabel Clarke's paper, 'Spirituality, Psychosis and the Journey of Life'. To give some brief context: I had attended a four-day course in spirituality and mental health care organized by Guy, and this generated a lot of interesting discussion and reflection, among other things, about how 'spiritual care' might be experienced and framed within organizations and clinical work. I work for an early intervention psychosis service in Oxford (EIS). The client group is mainly young (14–35), and often this is their first interface with health services. As can be imagined, those whom we support often present with a wide range of difficulties, and not just those classified as, for example, 'psychotic experiences'.

Isabel Clarke's paper was thoughtful, illuminating and complex, and it would be a wider task to respond to all the aspects that were covered by it. My experience suggests that the provision of spiritual care within community mental health and psychiatric practice is very peripheral. It barely gets a look-in. It can be left to somewhat 'idiosyncratic' individuals to pursue or raise the challenge of these experiences. This might be all right. However, in my experience, and in discussion with other colleagues, a number, and quite a large number, of the individuals we support are bringing these difficult, complex experiences relating to spirituality and psychosis to our door. It seems to me that as clinicians, in seeking to provide good care we have an obligation to discuss and explore with individuals the experiences they bring to us. Unfortunately, in clinical practice, including sometimes my own, this 'dialogue' can be closed down quite quickly. Part of the ongoing clinical work I do is to simply hold this 'space' open and to give individuals opportunity for reflection and exploration of what can be both quite confusing, distressing and fascinating experiences for them. In this regard the notion of 'going on a journey', which Isabel talks about in her paper, fits well with what I try to do in practice: that is, supporting someone through difficulties, being there when in deep need, and holding out hope for people, as well as 'sense making' and meaningful exploration of troubling, enlightening or transformative experiences, which can be particularly apposite in early psychosis work. It is a being-alongside, and I think is a shift away from what I could consider just 'case managing' or case 'co-ordinating' people, with its risks of framing all an individual's issues and experiences in a particular 'illness' category: that of 'psychosis'.

Evidence from my own work in discussions with individuals I support pinpoints that, for them, adherence to spiritual or religious ideas, for example, 'having faith' or a belief in a 'wider transcendence' as part of their experience, can sometimes mark a core part of their recovery. This is perhaps unsurprising, but the problem lies in the extent to which this in then taken on by clinicians as forming part of the person's 'care plan' or their recovery focus, and how this can be embedded in ongoing health and social care support.

Isabel Clarke says in her paper that there are many for whom we 'recognize that their experiences or those of people they are supporting cannot be written off as an illness, but do have important potential, given the right support'. Perhaps we are still learning what that right support is, and how this can be integrated within standard mental health provision. Within my own clinical practice and wider experience in the EIS I do think there are chinks of practice that try to incorporate where possible and help those we support with these aspects of their lives and experiences, but I would say it is not 'normative practice'. The 'elimination of symptoms' Isabel refers to in her paper remains the dominant and overarching principle of practice. But it seems to me and as part of my own practice that there is scope for the 'parallel' support, for the adoption in practice of creative exploration of psychotic experiences, their significance and meaning. I think there is the conjunct notion of supporting young people with existentialist and general 'humanistic' issues that confront those we support, and for those young people with psychosis this can be particularly acute. In practice, I do worry that if we 'close down' this dialogue, then we are not properly supporting or serving those we are meant to serve, and may be giving them a reduced and impoverished service, and missing something out.

I also, though, have to sound a note of realism. In front-line service provision there are many and multiple pressures and constraints. Notable examples would be constant pressures of time, higher caseloads, bureaucratic and administrative constraints, ongoing service reorganizations, staff changes and wider service changes, to name the most common. Sometimes trying to do the most important and key clinical work, including what we are discussing, can be frustratingly sidelined. These pressures will militate against doing the kind of 'spiritual care' that, as Isabel states, is 'relevant to all'. I often think such work is also hard, exhausting, and often does not come with some immediate benefits. It is a very different thing from, for example, supporting a person back into work. In EIS, though, a core component is active engagement, and part of this would be exploratory dialogue with individuals at their level and about their experiences, both 'spiritual and psychotic' – a dialogue that is grounded in attentive listening and open support.

Finally, as Isabel writes, 'Working for change within the NHS is slow. There is a parallel need for people to have access to a different message and a different sort of support from the outside'. I would agree with this and thoroughly endorse the parallel access to a 'different message', at least for some. Where this 'parallel message' is embedded, though, and who holds it, can be the leading question. In chaplaincy? In clinicians themselves? In third-party services or in the whole community? Perhaps all of these. It remains to be seen.

References

Bomford, R. (1999) *The Symmetry of God*. London: Free Association Books.

Brett, C. (2010) Transformative Crises. In I. Clarke (ed.) *Psychosis and Spirituality: Consolidating the New Paradigm* (2nd edition). Chichester: Wiley.

Brett, C., Heriot-Maitland, C., McGuire, P. and Peters, E. (2013) Predictors of distress associated with psychotic-like anomalous experiences in clinical and non-clinical populations. *British Journal of Clinical Psychology*, 53(2), 213–227.

Chadwick, P.D.J., Newman-Taylor, K. and Abba, N. (2005) Mindfulness groups for people with distressing psychosis. *Behavioral and Cognitive Psychotherapy*, 33(3), 351–360.

Claridge, G.A. (1997) *Schizotypy: Implications for Illness and Health*. Oxford: Oxford University Press.

Claridge, G.A. (2010) Spiritual Experience: Healthy Psychoticism? In I. Clarke (ed.) *Psychosis and Spirituality: Consolidating the New Paradigm* (2nd edition). Chichester: Wiley.

Clarke, I. (2008) *Madness, Mystery and the Survival of God*. Winchester: O'Books.

Clarke, I. (2009) Coping with Crisis and Overwhelming Affect: Employing Coping Mechanisms in the Acute Inpatient Context. In A.M. Columbus (ed.) *Coping Mechanisms: Strategies and Outcomes. Advances in Psychology Research* 63. Huntington, NY: Nova Science Publishers Inc.

Clarke, I. (ed.) (2010) *Psychosis and Spirituality: Consolidating the New Paradigm* (2nd edition). Chichester: Wiley.

Clarke, I. (2013) Spirituality: A New Way into Understanding Psychosis. In E.M.J. Morris, L.C. Johns and J.E. Oliver (eds) *Acceptance and Commitment Therapy and Mindfulness for Psychosis*. Chichester: Wiley-Blackwell.

Clarke, I. (2015) The emotion focused formulation approach: Bridging individual and team formulation. *Clinical Psychology Forum* 275, 28–33.

Grof, C. and Grof, S. (1991) *The Stormy Search for the Self*. London: Mandala.

Grof, S. (1988) *The Adventure of Self-Discovery*. Albany, NY: State University of New York Press.

Hartley, J. (2010) Mapping our Madness: The Hero's Journey as a Therapeutic Approach. In I. Clarke (ed.) *Psychosis and Spirituality: Consolidating the New Paradigm* (2nd edition). Chichester: Wiley.

Heriot-Maitland, C., Knight, M. and Peters, E. (2012) A qualitative comparison of psychotic-like phenomena in clinical and non-clinical populations. *British Journal of Clinical Psychology,* 51, 37–53.

Jackson, M.C. (1997) Benign schizotypy? The Case of Spiritual Experience. In G.S. Claridge (ed.) *Schizotypy: Relations to Illness and Health.* Oxford: Oxford University Press.

Jackson, M.C. (2010) The Paradigm-Shifting Hypothesis: A Common Process in Benign Psychosis and Psychotic Disorder. In I. Clarke (ed.) *Psychosis and Spirituality: Consolidating the New Paradigm* (2nd edition). Chichester: Wiley.

Read, J. and Bentall, R. (2012) Negative childhood experiences and mental health: Theoretical, clinical and primary prevention implications. *British Journal of Psychiatry,* 200, 89–91.

Romme, M. and Escher, S. (1989) *Accepting Voices.* London: Mind Publications.

Teasdale, J.D. and Barnard, P.J. (1993) *Affect, Cognition and Change: Re-modelling Depressive Thought.* Hove: Lawrence Erlbaum Associates.

Varese, F., Smeets, F. and Ducker, M. (2012) Childhood trauma increases the risk of psychosis: A meta-analysis of patient-control, prospective and cross-sectional cohort studies. *Schizophrenia Bulletin,* 38, 661–671.

Warner, R. (1985) *Recovery from Schizophrenia.* London: Routledge.

Warner, R. (2007) Review of recovery from schizophrenia: An international perspective. A report from the WHO Collaborative Project, the International Study of Schizophrenia. *American Journal of Psychiatry,* 164, 1444–1445.

7

Souls and Shadows

Words, Music and the Compassionate Spirit

Bob Heath

Regardless of what we believe, or don't believe, we will all at some stage face the prospect of confronting the great questions of life and death. This existential search for truth and meaning isn't contained by traditional time frames and there are few, if any, predictable boundaries. Indeed, rather than actively seeking out the questions, many of us will spend a great deal of our lives staying busy and distracted enough to avoid them altogether. But they are always there, nudging our moral compasses, tugging at the sleeves of our uniforms, adding the light and the shade, whispering to our souls and our shadows.

As health care professionals we will meet people for whom these time frames and boundaries may well have become more visible and clearly defined. Those of us who work predominantly with the dying can become very familiar with these shifting landscapes and the challenges that they can present. Avoidance becomes a less attainable option; time slips away, often at great speed. In supporting the dying we become familiar with these changes and the challenges that they raise; not just for the patients but also for ourselves. We will need to respond with professional integrity and compassion and we will need to do this at a time when our patients are seeking relationships that are both humane and authentic. And herein lies one of our challenges; as we attempt to respond with authenticity to death and dying, how might these experiences influence our own search for spiritual meaning and, in the context of caring for the patient, is it important or indeed helpful? Music therapist David Aldridge suggests that:

> in working with the dying and the chronically ill, we need to consider that which helps us to transcend our daily lives. Note that I am not separating practitioners and patients here, for we all surely face the great questions of life. (Aldridge 2003)

One of my favourite quotes from Carl Jung, and I have many, is 'One does not become enlightened by imagining figures of light, but by making the darkness conscious' (Jung 1945). This has always felt helpful when considering how to support people who are facing the end of their lives. Is this ultimately what our dying clients are trying to engage in, making the darkness conscious? It has certainly felt like that in many of my encounters with clients over the past 15 years or so. But, of course, there are many forms of darkness, and within each form the potential for many levels. And clients have important and sometimes very difficult choices to make about how much of the darkness to engage with. A few classic movie scenes spring to my mind where the hero on the very brink of death sees his life flash before him, a ten-second review of an entire life in colour and chrome, and then he's gone. Off to…wherever? But if, for instance, you are dying of cancer and all active, curative treatment has stopped these ten seconds can become ten weeks, or ten months. And then what do you do? Do you simply wait for the end of the movie, do you try to stop it now and freeze the picture or do you hit rewind and look at it again, frame by frame? Or do you try to make a new movie altogether?

I consider myself extremely fortunate because my particular therapeutic discipline can help me to encourage clients to be creative when trying to say the unsayable or think the unthinkable. I've lost count of the number of times where I've heard myself saying, 'I don't know the answer to that but let's put it in the music and see where it takes us.' And of course, music being what it is, it takes us to all sorts of places, often surprising and often at great speed. We all reveal ourselves in music. Whether we consider ourselves to be musical or not, human beings have a relationship with music that is as ancient as mankind itself and yet at the same time is as contemporary and relevant as this very moment. We are born into music; we always have been. There has yet to be a civilization uncovered that doesn't appear to have used music in some way as part of its social communicative structure. We know that our hearing is fully formed in the womb around 11 weeks after conception so that by the time we're born we are familiar with an aural landscape, including our mother's voice and the music that has been part of our early enculturation. Music is in essence the emotional landscape upon which we all play. It can sit at the very heart of our being and our knowing without ever really asking us to understand it. It can become the arms that cradle the very emotions that, often mysteriously, link us all together. We do not need to understand these musical processes to be a part of them; they are intuitive and inherent. Over the past two decades, technology has developed to the point where we can now see inside the human brain as people listen to and even create their own music.

The results are startling and may well lead us onto new discoveries about perception and cognitive disorders. However, as Oliver Sacks reminded us in *Musicophilia*, as exciting as the neuroscience is, we need to be alive to the danger that perfunctory clinical descriptions may well overlook the simple art of observation and as a result the richness of the human context can become ignored or even lost (Sacks 2008). By richness of human context it sounds like he's talking about spirituality to me – at least in the way that I've come to think about spirituality, as the humanness and the otherness in all things, definable or not.

Music and spirituality go back a long, long way. For the Ancient Greeks music was the great art of the Muses, promoting the development of both mind and soul (Hamel 1978). For the Native American and First Nations people of North America, songs were often seen as an individual's direct line to the healing spirits, the very breath that consecrates the act of life (McLuhan 1973). Influential figures such as Schopenhauer have ruminated on the unique power of music to speak not only to mankind's shadows but also to our very essence, our souls, and our spirit (Storr 1992). Music and song have always played a highly significant role in religious and cultural rituals. For some, songs and hymns can represent the very conduit to the God or gods they seek help from (Baker 2015). I can vividly recall the moment when as a chorister, aged 11, I burst into tears during a performance of the Magnificat much to the amusement of my fellow trebles and the annoyance of the choirmaster. It had sounded profoundly beautiful and I'd simply become both physically and emotionally overwhelmed. We live in a world where music is all around us, all of the time. And while some of this may not be to our taste, a deeper look into the material will often reveal the same search for love and meaning, hope and peace. I may at times turn to William Byrd for inspiration, and on another occasion I might reach for Tom Waits. The music couldn't be more different but the spiritual impact is always there.

Perhaps then it is little wonder that placing music therapy within the context of a hospice where people are dying will inevitably promote opportunities for patients to explore their own spirituality. And, of course, the hospice community famously encourages and embraces this. Spiritual care will be one of the main pillars of practice on offer alongside physical, psychological, psycho-social and emotional support. My own discipline usually sits within the psychological support team, but of course there are frequent crossovers, and I have spent many a long, helpful hour with hospice chaplains wrestling with difficult patient issues and indeed some of my own.

Today we operate in a society that craves and invests prolifically in 'science' while at the same time expressing its frustration with a perceived lack of patient-centred compassionate care. But surely compassionate care is not about the skills of provision but more about the skills of response: responding as human beings to need, whatever that need might be, and, if we can't respond, knowing who has the skills to respond. And, if this is our aspiration, in order to contain and cope with it we will need a profound generosity of listening and hearing, whatever form that might take. Dr Albert Schweitzer (2001) advised us to develop the art of letting our own individuality interact with the individuality of the patient. At the heart of these encounters will be our spirituality, our stories and beliefs, our responses to the very human longing for a purpose and for meaning. This corresponds deeply with my own philosophy and I spend a great deal of my time co-creating work with my clients. Whether improvising music or composing songs, relationships forged in music therapy can often feel highly collaborative. And it is during these creative collaborations that clients begin to explore their own spirituality: 'What has this all been for? Why is this happening to me? Where am I going? Am I really going anywhere?' They are looking for answers, they almost certainly know that I don't have them but they are still asking the questions and so my response has to be a willingness to accompany them. The music, poetry and songs that emerge from these encounters will often provide helpful insights into their search for meaning, spiritual connection and peace. And at the same time, I will need to be aware that the very tools of my trade can also accentuate difficult feelings such as sadness and loss and I will need to approach this work sensitively (Shea 2000).

Hannah

Hannah was in her late forties; she'd fought for ten years to regain the custody of her children and had finally succeeded. Within two months of setting up the new family home she had been diagnosed with cancer and had undergone surgery, chemotherapy and radiotherapy. When I first met her, she had just been told that there was no further treatment available. She'd pushed her consultant for a likely prognosis and he had reluctantly advised her that it would be likely that she would die within the next six to nine months. She was frightened and outraged by her colossal stroke of misfortune at a time when she felt that she was finally beginning to make some sense of her life.

At our first meeting, she sat in the far corner of the music room as far away from the musical instruments, and me, as possible. I was struggling to engage with her and when she did speak her voice was so quiet that I could barely hear her words at all. I invited her to come and sit at the piano and she simply shook her head. I asked if she would like to listen to some music and again she declined. Instead she reached into her bag, pulled out a sheet of paper and held it out to me. In small and precise handwriting she had written:

> I fall to my knees and I lay myself open
> Willing what I feel to be revealed
> Baring my soul I look for an answer
> Facing the sun.

Hannah was peering out of the darkness into a blinding sun, traumatized by the thought of having to face her own death at a time when more than ever, she wanted to live. She was clearly finding it too frightening to talk about, but she could write about it. As I tried to engage her in conversation she stood up, took the paper off me, picked up a pen and immediately wrote her second verse:

> How do you put the words to this tragedy?
> In a heartbeat a life can change
> Like sliding doors, whenever they're open
> We're facing the sun.

This pattern continued throughout our entire first session. Piece by piece Hannah was arranging her thoughts and by using lyrical poetry she was finding her own way to begin looking for some answers. The first real breakthrough came in our next session when I asked for her permission to sing the words. She looked astonished but didn't say no, so I went ahead and improvised a melody with my voice and a guitar. At this point, Hannah began to weep and repeated the words 'Oh my God' several times before drawing her chair next to mine and saying, 'Can we finish this?' She completed her song with:

> And we say what if, and we say if only
> But what can we really do
> We don't have the power to change the tragedy
> So we just go through.

> Well my question is, yeah, the big question is
> How am I supposed to deal with this?
> What happens if I will not be consumed?
> Facing the sun.

Over the following months Hannah wrote eight songs. Our pattern was always the same, although by now we were talking a lot and I'd come to learn a great deal about her history and the challenges she was now facing. Hannah always wrote the lyrics but always refused to engage in any form of musical creation, insisting that it was only when I wrote the melody and sang the words that she could feel able to truly own them for herself. While Hannah felt like this was a very natural way of working, I privately fretted about therapeutic principles and boundaries and took some of these to my own supervision. I don't recall ever voicing my concerns in our sessions but just a few weeks before she died Hannah arrived saying that she had written a song for me. I immediately felt uncomfortable and very tentatively unfolded the page of lyrics. She had written the title in bold letters across the top of the page: 'You Worry Too Much!'

Listening to the songs now as I write this some seven years later I notice that while it's my voice that's singing, it is Hannah's voice that I can hear clearly in all the words. And yes, my individuality is there in the music and the playing but now it somehow sounds and feels absolutely right. Hannah knew exactly what she needed from me and, despite getting in my own way at times, I had managed to respond.

Listening again has also prompted my own memories of her struggle and her death. Hannah had become a popular figure in the day centre and had developed some very close friendships with fellow patients. Several members of the multi-disciplinary team were also supporting her and the impact of her death had been widely felt throughout the hospice. I can vividly recall sitting in the day room with patients and staff as we took the time to mark Hannah's death and to share some of our memories of her. This was not an uncommon experience and it would often fall to me to provide some music or poetry as part of the reflective process. On this occasion, however, I was driven into silence, much as Hannah had been when I first met her. I struggled to cope with the impact of Hannah's death for some time and began to reconsider some of my own spiritual beliefs. Supervision helped me to work through some of my own feelings around injustice and unsolvable suffering but also helped me to acknowledge some of the other feelings that were present, including grief, compassion and love.

A few years ago, Robert Twycross, one of the pioneers of modern palliative medicine, once introduced me at a conference by saying I had the best and the worst job in the hospice. The best job because music can help me to get 'inside' the world of my clients very quickly, the worst because it can often be very difficult to get back out again. Perhaps there is something here about what happens to us as human beings when we share creative endeavours together. Certainly, relationships can be forged very quickly, and clients are frequently surprised by how soon they move from a position of 'I can't do any of this' to 'I can't believe that I am creating this.' In offering people the opportunity to bypass some of their cognitive rumination, their tricky minds if you like, we can help people to access another level of thinking and feeling and to express this in surprising ways. A technique that I have borrowed from creative writing and developed to support song creation is the acrostic (Heath 2014). This ancient and simple exercise helps clients identify a significant word or words and to explore them further by using the letters to begin each line of writing. Recently I was with a client who was trying to put into words how she felt about her treatment regime. She was struggling to balance her feelings about living and dying. On the one hand, she felt incredibly responsible for the people who loved her and who were living on hope and almost hope alone. On the other hand, she was exhausted by the treatment and wanted to tell the truth about how she really felt. I'd invited her to play the piano with me but even the simplest contact with the piano keys seemed to heighten her anxiety. I suggested an acrostic and having written the word 'chemotherapy' down the left-hand column of a sheet of paper I invited her to write freely using the letters to begin each line.

Chemotherapy

Come in next Monday to start your treatment
Hold on a minute; I need time to think
Everyone says just do as they say but
Monday's too soon
Oh!
There must be another way
Help me someone please
Except, there is no one
Ready or not it must go
Ahead
Poisoning begins on Monday
You've no other choice.

Nikki 2012

By creating this poem she was able to articulate her own feelings and subsequently share them with her family. With their support she was also able to make the difficult decision to discontinue the palliative chemotherapy.

Music therapy has, at times, been considered to be a rather esoteric form of psychotherapy, an art beyond words perhaps (Bunt and Stige 2014). And yet over the years I've come to see a great deal of my work as rather practical. We talk and listen, we do things together, we write things, we play them, we record them, and sometimes we share them with others. I do spend a great deal of time listening but at the same time I am aware that helping people to move into a creative space can often be very beneficial. Recently I've been involved in a great deal of debate around the differences between empathy and compassion. I'm not sure how helpful all of this is but perhaps for me it's helpful enough to believe that fundamentally it is compassion, not empathy alone, that compels us to act. Empathy can be exhausting; it can confront us with endless examples of unsolvable suffering and leave us wrestling with a sense of moral and spiritual injustice. However, if empathy drives us to compassion then we can act. By acting we can make a difference, not only for our patients and clients but for ourselves too. Perhaps we can also emerge richer and safer for it.

I can remember the first time I used a 'lolly' sponge to moisten the lips of a dying woman with whom, two days previously, I'd been singing and playing. The connection felt profound; I was still feeling sad, but no longer helpless. This may seem like a very small gesture in the great scheme of things and it is certainly something that I have repeated on many occasions, but the impact of that first experience has stayed with me for 15 years.

The work that clients create at the end of their lives can be profoundly beneficial, not only for themselves but for those they leave behind. Their songs often talk to us of people experiencing themselves in new ways, trying to express their own compassion, making new and surprising discoveries, seeking and at times finding peace and reconciliation (Heath and Lings 2012).

Ruth

Ruth was a woman in her early forties and was married with two children. She had been diagnosed with a brain tumour, and when I first met her at home, she had been struggling to communicate. Both she and her husband were fine musicians, and Ruth also had a career as a music teacher. I was very aware that the brain tumour was robbing Ruth of her facility to play the piano and this first meeting had felt difficult and sad. We were all musicians together and the sense of loss, although not verbalized, was palpable. Following some treatment, she recovered a little and was able to begin attending sessions with me at the hospice. Over a period of several months, despite the difficulties she was encountering, Ruth was able to compose music and write songs that not only expressed what she was experiencing but also her deep faith, her spirituality and her very realistic hopes for the future.

I don't think I've ever met anyone quite as courageous as Ruth. She approached the end of her life with honesty and a gentleness that was truly inspiring. As her condition worsened over the last months of her life I was able to visit her at home. and with the help of her husband we were able to revisit some of the music that she had been creating. I was always very nervous about these visits and looking back I think it was partly because I was simply furious about what was happening to Ruth and her family. However, on each occasion Ruth, with her gentle presence and humour, held and encouraged by her husband, made these visits feel joyful, almost transcendental.

Ruth's condition began to deteriorate quite rapidly but, with her husband as translator, she was still determined to be creative and was writing what would be her final song. As she lost more and more of her ability to communicate with words she also became aware that some of the people around her, including some of the medical staff, had stopped listening to her. Despite the confusion she was experiencing, she was able to use her lyrics to express exactly how this felt and she called this song 'Hello, It's Me':

HELLO, IT'S ME
Hello it's me, it's so frustrating Hello, hello, what are we doing?
Hello it's me, it's so frustrating Hello, hello, why aren't you there?
Hello it's me, trying to find another way
If there's only just words it's so illogical
Hello it's me, trying to find another way
Feels like everybody else is moving on
Well I don't know, I don't know.

Crazy misleading, what we believe in
Bring us up to date with medics tell us all we need to know
Crazy I'm crying, honest I'm trying
Keeping things afloat when things just don't make sense.

Hello it's me, trying to find another way,
Been here a long time it's been good and bad for me
Hello it's me, trying to find another way
Feels like everybody else is moving on
Well I don't know, I don't know.

Hello it's me, trying to find another way
I'll take a guess at what you're meaning working round the intricacies
Hello it's me, trying to find another way
I don't know where to go but I'll just keep going on
And I don't know, I don't know
Hello it's me.

Ruth and her husband posted the song on YouTube[1] where many people, including the families of others who were suffering with degenerative brain illnesses, including Alzheimer's disease, were able to listen to it. True to her nature, one of Ruth's final acts was to reach out to others and help. I consider myself blessed to have had the opportunity to work with Ruth and continue to stay in touch with her family and, from time to time, still get the opportunity to play music with her husband.

Ruth and the many other people I've worked with over the past 15 years have given me the opportunity to share a part of their own creative spiritual journeys. And in sharing these I have been gifted a legacy of three hundred or so songs, all of which in their own way express something of the human experience of living and dying. I'm often asked if this just isn't a bit too much. Haven't I filled my life with too much loss and sadness? It certainly doesn't feel like that. The people I've encountered over the past 15 years have given me the opportunity to become safe with my compassionate self and to explore human spirituality from many different viewpoints. I haven't always shared their convictions, their beliefs or their faith but they've consistently taught me that I didn't really need to.

I recently visited a very poorly client on the oncology ward and I asked him what he was reading as I peered down at the book laying open on his knees.

'From Darwin to Behaviourism,' he replied, 'I'm trying to figure out what to think about God, and Heaven and an afterlife, that kind of stuff.'

'Is it helping?' I asked.

'Well, yeah, it is in a way,' he replied. 'There's lots of stuff on classical conditioning, how we respond to things, you know, what we set ourselves up for in life.'

'So…what have you decided?' I asked.

'Well, it's pretty straightforward actually,' he replied, 'I figure I can afford not to believe in any kind of afterlife because when I die if there is no Heaven or land of souls,' – he said these words with some sarcasm

---

1. www.youtube.com/watch?v=OoKjoWXviaY

– 'only nothingness, then I won't know anything about it and it simply won't matter.'

He paused for a moment, smiled and then said, 'And if there is an afterlife, then I get to go, "Holy ****! What a result!" It's a kind of win-win situation as far as I can tell.'

We laughed together, and I said, 'Great! Well that's sorted then.'

Kate Butcher's response to the above when presented at the March 2016 symposium prompted much interesting discussion around compassion and spirituality, their place in modern nursing and, perhaps most interestingly, how we obtain the opportunity and the permission to act with professional authenticity.

A Response

Kate Butcher

There is so much debate, and at times confusion, in nursing literature about what spiritual care *is* that to unpick it is a huge task. However, reading Bob's paper helped to articulate on a personal level how it is that I can offer care to patients approaching the end of their life in a spiritual manner.

Bob states early in his writing that we need to respond to patients in a compassionate manner, and with integrity, and that at this point in life patients are often looking for a humane and authentic response from health care professionals. Compassion is an essential of nursing care, I believe; without it we become robotic in our approach and lack the human contact. 'Compassionate care,' Bob writes, 'is not about the skills of provision but more about the skills of response: responding as human beings to need'. Although spiritual care encompasses compassionate care, I believe it is more than this.

It is easier to examine the concept in terms of patients to whom we have offered care, and Hannah's case study brought to mind a patient I cared for – Eva – and how I experienced a brief moment of my nursing practice when caring for her when I knew that I had offered spiritual care:

> *A woman in her mid-30s, Eva was younger than I. She was imminently dying but her behaviour and conversation with the staff belied this fact. She talked of when she was 'better', when she got married, when she started work again; she was loud in her expression of needs, seemingly unaware of the surrounding ward environment... The nurses I was working with were all younger than she was, and they were struggling with what was perceived as denial and unrealism on Eva's part; they didn't know how to respond to her conversations and began to attribute them to 'the drugs talking'.*
>
> *I was new to the clinical environment, so in the way it often happens in nursing teams I gravitated towards offering care to Eva (and giving the other nurses some respite). Eva's physical needs were huge – pain, frequent haemorrhages, agitation, hunger followed by vomiting, to name but a few – and so it would have been easy to only 'do' care for Eva. But one afternoon, after her physical needs had been met, I pulled up a chair and sat in front of her as she perched precariously on the*

edge of her bed. I predicted, and I think that she did too, that the next period of agitation was looming close, so we just sat in a moment of quiet.

Slowly she leaned forward until her forehead was touching mine, and we remained like that for probably less than a minute, though it felt like much longer. She broke the silence by saying, 'You know, don't you?' All I needed to reply was, 'Mmm...' She nodded.

From a professional perspective, I felt that new ground had been broached through this interaction, that a façade had been breached, even if temporarily, and that an acknowledgement by Eva of her situation had occurred. I felt that this was what offering spiritual care could be, giving space and time, helping a patient to understand the situation.

I did not shy away from sharing in her distress during that episode of care, and that act was understood by Eva.

But moments such as this cannot be acknowledged from a purely professional point of view. We all carry our unique personal perspectives with us too, and it was on a personal level that we also made a connection. We were human beings connected for a moment in time.

Eva married her fiancé in the hospice the next evening, then requested sedation to manage her agitation, achieved a degree of peace and died two days later. I will never know if that shared moment was a catalyst for those events or not, but I know that a meeting of spirits happened and it mattered to us both. The connectedness we felt in the moment wasn't of a physical nature, nor a meeting of minds, but a meeting of the essence of our humanity.

Whereas Hannah was quiet and withdrawn when meeting Bob, Eva was loud and insistent, yet in both of these situations there was a tangible need for human contact. Both women responded to the act of sitting next to them, an act that can demonstrate so much in such a simple way – no power hierarchy, available time, a willingness not to hide behind the mask of the profession but to be as one human to another. Bob suggests from his reading of the topic that 'at the heart of these encounters will be our spirituality' and to this thought I respond positively. I experienced a very strong sense of my spirit[1] having met Eva's spirit in this moment and it was profound for me as a nurse (I needed a brief moment of time to compose myself before responding to other patients on the ward). My individuality was there, as Bob suggests.

Nursing literature can define spiritual care in existential terms and theories, can relate it to or separate it from religion, can describe it in ways that seem to make it even more indescribable, yet it is also documented

---

1. For those with a religious faith, the spirit may be conceived as being of a divine nature, or it could be understood as that which makes us unique.

in accessible and tangible ways. Some of these are around being able to help patients to find meaning in the present situation, about having the openness and willingness to 'get to the core' of a person. In that one act, I felt I understood Eva on a different level than most of the other nurses, and that she understood that in me she would find a part of the help that she was seeking. The challenge of defining spiritual care is owing to the subjective and personal nature of the concept that is interpreted in a unique way by each individual.

I reflected as I read Bob's paper, using a simple cup of tea as my focus… I poured the milk into a cup of hot strong tea. I watched it disperse through the tea, starting with a definite streak of white, which quickly became a swirl with the appearance of vapour trails. The tea turned from a uniform dark brown into a myriad of lighter browns. The vapour trails became more defined, more like rivers under the surface, forming mysterious patterns, ever changing in response to the temperature of the receiving liquid, and outside forces such as movements of the table. It was beautiful to watch.

The milk formed a bubble on the top of the tea, at the centre. It moved around in tiny, seemingly random, patterns around the centre point. It seemed to take an eternity, though in reality it was probably only seconds, to change pattern shape; it seemed to be skating or dancing on top of the liquid, tracing all manner of patterns, seemingly unfocused in its intention. Slowly, so slowly it seemed, it traced a complete circle about two-thirds of the diameter of the cup, then miraculously it settled back to the centre point and just stopped.

I looked at the wider picture of my cup of tea again, and saw that the milk had now dispersed throughout the tea, non-distinct but having permanently altered the cup of tea, not only visually but also in taste, temperature and smell.

I wondered as I drank, though, was this small insignificant event in a snatched five minutes of my day really a metaphor for our spiritual life? It is so difficult to define in words a meaning that has universal agreement, but it struck me that the cup of tea captured the essence of my thoughts totally.

Our spirit spreads throughout our whole being, crafting each of us into a unique individual. It grows and flows throughout our lives, sometimes more discernible, sometimes just a presence, uncapturable yet ever present. Sometimes we see in moments of pure emotion, good or bad, our spirit dancing across the surface, clear for all to see, like the bubble. Much of the time it is at work changing us from beneath the surface, a dynamic presence in our life that is often overlooked. Some of us may be too busy, too caught up in the present demands of life to ever be aware of it, and it may need a catalyst to bring it to our attention.

Ideas for demonstrating spiritual care in nursing practice include listening, honesty, authenticity with others, respect – any and all of these can be present in the day-to-day actions of a nurse, easily overlooked and beneath the day's surface, but every once in a while, they are apparent at the surface, as in the case studies of Hannah and Eva.

A Response

Bob Heath

In the early part of this chapter I referred to Jung's assertion that we become enlightened by confronting our own darkness rather than avoiding it. The case studies and reflections that followed were my attempt to illustrate just a few of the myriad ways that we as human beings begin to peer into the darkness in search of comfort and meaning. Perhaps the greatest commonality in my chapter and Kate's response is the suggestion that our personal authenticity as health care professionals can, and often does, have a huge impact upon the quality of care we provide. Our definitions and interpretations may differ, but we both acknowledge the tugging of the soul and the shadow and continue to listen and wonder.

Note: All case study material contained in this chapter has been anonymized and full permission for its use has been obtained.

References

Aldridge, D. (2003) Music therapy and spirituality: A transcendental understanding of suffering. *Music Therapy Today*, February. Available at www.wfmt.info/Musictherapy world/modules/mmmagazine/issues/20030218101523/20030218102425/SpiritMTTFeb2003.pdf, accessed on 10 December 2016.

Baker, F.A. (2015) *Therapeutic Songwriting: Developments in Theory, Methods and Practice.* London: Palgrave.

Bunt, L. and Stige, B. (2014) *Music Therapy: An Art Beyond Words.* Hove: Routledge.

Hamel, P.M. (1978) *Through Music to the Self.* Shaftesbury: Element Books.

Heath, B. (2014) Acrostic in Therapeutic Songwriting. In B.E. Thompson and R.A. Neimeyer (eds) *Grief and the Expressive Arts: Practices for Creating Meaning.* London: Routledge.

Heath, B. and Lings, J. (2012) Creative songwriting in therapy at the end of life and in bereavement. *Mortality: Promoting the Interdisciplinary Study of Death and Dying*, 17(2), 106–118.

Jung, C. (1945) The Philosophical Tree. In C. Jung, *The Collected Works of C.G. Jung, Vol. 13: Alchemical Studies.* New Haven, CT: Yale University Press.

McLuhan, T.C. (1973) *Touch the Earth: A Self-Portrait of Indian Existence.* London: Abacus.

Sacks, O. (2008) *Musicophilia: Tales of Music and the Brain.* New York: Vintage.

Schweitzer, A. (2001) *The Quest of the Historical Jesus.* Minneapolis, MN: Fortress Press.

Shea, J. (2000) *Spirituality and Health Care: Reaching Toward a Holistic Future.* Chicago: The Park Ridge Center.

Storr, A. (1992) *Music and the Mind.* London: HarperCollins.

8

The Mindfulness of Caring

Gavin Garman and Emma Louis

Introduction

Jon Kabat-Zinn (1994) defines mindfulness as 'paying attention in a particular way, on purpose, in the present moment and non-judgementally' (p.4). This chapter suggests that paying attention to patients, families, colleagues and oneself in this way can be a great help in the provision of compassionate health care.

A quick gaze around the spirituality or religion section in a high street bookshop (or a search on Amazon for most of us) will leave you in little doubt that there is a market for something called 'mindfulness'. There are guides on mindful meditation, mindful parenting, mindfulness at work or creativity and mindfulness. Mindfulness for beginners, for men, women, children, the anxious, the frazzled and, of course, 'for dummies'. There's even mindful colouring and dot-to-dot mindfulness. Mindfulness is a term that has captured the public imagination and one that is at risk of becoming a brand and a 'cure-all'.

Many of the tenets of mindfulness have changed little from the teachings of the Buddha through to the writings of teachers in the Buddhist tradition such as Thich Nhat Hanh (for example, *The Miracle of Mindfulness*, 1991a, first published in 1975) and recent textbooks on approaches to treating depression. Mindfulness has been applied to become a form of cognitive therapy and is used to treat stress, chronic pain, depression and psychosis (Segal, Williams and Teasdale 2002; Chadwick 2014). Many of these treatment interventions use an eight-week structured group programme. However, completion of a formal eight-week course of therapy is not required for us to start to bring mindful practices into our everyday practice as health professionals.

There are small practices that can become part of our working lives that enable us to centre ourselves and bring us back to the present moment. These small practices are perhaps easy in comparison to the 'formal' practices of regular meditation or participation in a *sangha* (a Buddhist community), which many would struggle to commit to, or to maintain. Mindfulness gives us simple tools that can be easily shared and used.

This chapter is written by a mental health nurse, Gavin, and a hospital chaplain, Emma, and will include accounts of our personal experiences to portray how the practice of mindfulness can shape our interactions with others. Mindfulness teaches that all people and events are interrelated. Nobody exists separately from everybody else. Equally, our work selves and experiences are interrelated and only exist in relation to our non-work selves and experiences.

Psycho-spiritual care seeks to link the spiritual, emotional and physical dimensions of life. This holistic approach, which is about exploring, understanding and caring for the whole person and their experience of life, has much synergy with mindfulness. Mindfulness practices are about awareness of body, thoughts, feelings and how we respond to our environment. It is also definitely to do with human flourishing, living life to the full and nurturing wellbeing. This is partly why mindfulness has 'worked' for us or made so much sense in both our personal and professional lives. It seems to bring everything together in a non-threatening, holistic and compassionate way and fits gently and easily with what we are about as clinical and spiritual care teams.

Mindfulness can be a way of health care professionals contributing to or embodying psycho-spiritual care. It can be a way of facilitating the more spiritual side of care that is open to all, as you don't need to swear 'fealty' to any particular religion to practise it. Mindfulness can be the place at which different traditions and professions can all meet.

Through story and reflection, we seek to show how mindfulness, used as a tool or as an approach in nursing, is essentially about how we are with those we encounter. It is about being present and being interested, practising compassion and kindness and not leaping to judge or label the behaviour, thoughts or actions of others or ourselves. These would seem to be key elements of psycho-spiritual care, whether it is coming from nurses, chaplains, psychologists or any other person involved in someone's care.

A retreat with Thich Nhat Hanh

Gavin Garman

A question and answer session took place on the fourth day of the retreat. The four hundred participants gathered in rows in the main hall. A space at the front by the podium was reserved for children and young people.

Thay (Thich Nhat Hanh) entered the hall with his ceremonial retinue, and they made their way slowly up the side aisle and onto the stage.

Attendants helped to settle Thay into a central, seated position, adjusting the robes on his shoulders and around his folded knees. The bell master invited the bell to sound, we had a moment of silence and then questions were invited from the audience. The children were allowed to go first; once their section was finished they could go and play with the monks and nuns and skip the less interesting questions from their parents.

One of the children who asked a question was a young boy who looked to be around 12 years of age. He took his turn to approach the stage and sit next to Thay. Thay greeted him and asked him for his question. The young boy's voice was broadcast by speakers through the hall.

'Have you reached enlightenment?' he asked. 'And if so, how?'

A wave of laughter swept the room. Thay breathed with the question for a while. He then gave an answer which has returned to my thoughts many times. It was a simple answer, even a predictable one, but on that day and in that room it had a profound effect on me. He said (words to the effect that), 'We can all experience enlightenment every day. It is not a very mysterious state. If we drink our tea mindfully, that can be a moment of enlightenment. When we eat, or sit and meditate, or wash our dishes mindfully, all of these can be moments of enlightenment.'

I had heard Thay and his monks and nuns say similar things in the past, but on that occasion it hit home and I felt that I had understood the answer in a deeper and more meaningful way. Enlightenment was within my grasp. Not as an impossibly difficult goal that might be attained after years of study and months of leg-aching meditation. But right then and there. Any time and anywhere, in fact. Not to say that it was easy, but it was self-evidently true, in the same way that exercising to feel well is a simple idea that may be hard to maintain in practice.

We can all experience enlightened moments of mindfulness. They are sitting inside us every time we return to our breath. If you were to ask me now if I am enlightened, I would ask you if you would like a cup of tea.

A nurse's experience of mindfulness
Gavin Garman

When presenting the basics of mindfulness, I find there is one analogy that captures everybody's imagination. I ask, 'When you are driving to work, a journey you have done a hundred times and know very well, do you sometimes find that you have driven a few miles and have no memory of the journey? You must have made turns and negotiated roundabouts but don't remember doing so?' At such times we are travelling on automatic pilot with our minds elsewhere. Considered by mindful eyes, this is an example of living a ghost life, a life in which we are not fully present. By attending more carefully to the everyday activities we all do, we can bring ourselves back to the real world. When we do so, we find that the real world is a beautiful, rewarding and fascinating place.

The tool that we use to return ourselves to the present moment is something that is in us all the time, essential to life but largely ignored unless we experience problems with it: namely, our breathing. We can return at any time to our calm centre by returning to our breath. The best way to develop this skill is by meditation.

Any activity can become a meditation. We are used to the image of someone doing sitting meditation, but I tell the audience there is walking meditation, doing the washing up meditation, brushing your teeth meditation, eating dinner meditation and, of course, tea drinking meditation. All of these can save us from despair and fear at work and can be used with our clients.

Jon Kabat-Zinn (1990) in his book *Full Catastrophe Living: How to Cope with Stress, Pain and Illness Using Mindfulness Meditation*, describes an eight-week course that was adapted by Segal, Williams and Teasdale (2002) in their book *Mindfulness-Based Cognitive Therapy for Depression*. The eight-week course includes exercises such as the mindful eating of a raisin, body scan meditation guided by CDs, pleasant events calendars, mindful movements, looking at automatic thoughts and identifying signs of relapse. Participants receive CDs to aid their practice at home, including one that guides them through the 40-minute body scan. During a body scan, individuals lie down and move their non-judgemental attention through their body, noticing how each part of the body feels.

The course has been successfully run in prisons and hospitals. I have seen trails of slow-moving walkers outside one of our day hospitals. But a formal taught eight-week course is unlikely to form part of most practitioners' experience. It becomes another group that patients disappear into. On the eight-week course I attended, one of the themes that emerged in our discussion was that it was easier to integrate everyday mindful practice into our lives than to do the 'bigger stuff', meaning the 40-minute meditations and yoga exercises.

And perhaps the small things can be more helpful in our working hours than lying down for a body scan in the evening. As a nurse, I have always felt (hoped?) that it was the everyday interactions that I make with my patients (and I am thinking of in-patients in forensic settings) that build and help them find their own way to recovery. Patients spend most time with other patients, then with nurses and nursing assistants. It is the nursing staff who ensure that somebody gets out of bed in the morning, that they are washed and dressed and their room is reasonably clean, that they have meaningful activities to do during the day, that their physical health is monitored, that they have some money in their pocket, that they are encouraged to get out and be as independent as possible and keep in touch with their friends and family. The less obvious therapeutic interventions can occur whilst watching television together in the evening, walking in the grounds or playing pool.

Just as these interventions can foster a therapeutic experience for our patients, so they can scupper it if not done genuinely or from the heart. Patients have said to me that they know who wants to be at work and who they feel is 'there for the pay cheque'. And we can lose our way over the years if we do not attend to our interactions over the kettle or medicine pot.

Cultivating mindfulness enables us to be fully present when talking to our patients. Individuals can tell if our thoughts are elsewhere. We may start to think of the many things we need to do before the end of the shift, the notes we have to write and the report we have not yet begun that is due in tomorrow. Yet dwelling on the fantasy of those plans does not help get them done and it takes our focus from the person we are talking to.

The Buddhist concept of deep listening occurs only when our minds are quiet. It is not about formulating judgement or labelling what the other is telling us, or thinking how to describe the conversation when we write up our notes at the end of the shift. It is about being open and receptive to what lies beneath the words we are being told. How often have patients said that what helped them was having someone to talk to, someone who listened? Do not become distracted by the compulsion to think ahead to your response to the patient, planning what CBT tool might be useful on this occasion. Sit quietly and just listen. When people experience deep listening, it may lead to a sense of oneness, in the listener and the speaker. Of course, we may need to challenge or seek to re-frame the way our patient is looking at their situation, but we need not jump to that resolution. It is too tempting to think that we have heard something like this before and leap to the conclusion of what is the right thing to say at these times.

My interest in Buddhism first led to action whilst I was a university psychology student, before I had begun my nurse training. With a friend who was studying theology, I first attended evening classes on meditation and went to see a lecture in London by the Dalai Lama. Then, ten years ago or so, I encountered the teachings of Thich Nhat Hanh. His words spoke to me in a way like nothing else I had encountered. Crystal clear as a mountain lake, Thay laid out the beauty of the world in a way that resonated for me and showed me that it was possible to find lasting peace within myself. Even better, it could help me go to work on a Monday morning with a smile on my face, and when somebody attempted to ruin my mood and sour my day by firing a broadside across the meeting room table, I could stand and watch the cannon ball drop harmlessly into that clear mountain lake. The ripple it made might be big, but would not last long and would only be a light lapping at my feet by the time it reached me standing on the shore.

I can recall two times in my life when I felt an overwhelming sense of relief. One was at the age of 13, when I saw the heavy metal band Motörhead play at the Crawley Leisure Centre. As the deafening music bludgeoned me about the head, I looked around at the denim- and leather-clad crowd losing their minds and felt utterly understood and amongst friends. I was unhappy at school and suddenly I had found that there was an entire subculture out there that would welcome me with open arms, understanding how I felt and how difficult the rest of the world was. It sheltered and saved me then and continues to save me now. The second relief came with the measured, kind and inviting words of Thay.

Thich Nhat Hanh is now 89, and his health is failing, but his writings have found their time. His teachings have been converted into many books, such as *The Miracle of Mindfulness* (1991a, first published in1975) and *Peace Is Every Step* (1991b), in which he describes practices that can return us to the present moment. Thay introduced the term 'engaged Buddhism' to capture the need for Buddhists to actively seek to help others. His followers were persecuted and murdered in the Vietnam War as they sought to protest against the war and to aid those villages worst hit by the conflict.

His concept of engaged Buddhism is akin to one part of the Buddhist Eightfold Path to Enlightenment, that of Right Livelihood. The Buddha encouraged his disciples to make their living in an ethically positive way that does not cause harm. Most of us spend a large amount of time at work, and it can be a task to try to ensure our work is a help and not a hindrance to spiritual practice. Mental health patients often drift to the margins of a society that in many quarters does not understand or accept them. To care for forensic patients who have committed serious crimes, who do not want your help and who may abuse or attack you is to seek to love the unlovable.

I have a teaching session on mindfulness that I have delivered in a number of settings to audiences from ward nurses to the health and safety team to members of the executive board and teams of hospital nurses in the former Soviet republic of Georgia. I explain that the concept of mindfulness is found in the original teachings of the Buddha. The Buddha was, of course, a man and a wealthy one at that. Born into royalty, he was married off and had a son before his ruminations over the triumvirate of mental health problems: the existence of death, disease and old age. After finding his path, he became a spiritual leader. His popularity brought enemies and there were some soap-opera-worthy attempts to discredit him by a woman claiming to bear his child, and the planting of a dead body in one of his camps. However, his teachings have persisted and prevailed.

A chaplain's experience of mindfulness

Emma Louis

I am an ordained priest in the Church of England. I have also been profoundly affected by the Zen Buddhist monk Thich Nhat Hanh and his teachings on mindfulness. Thay leads an international community of people trying to live mindfully and peacefully, and offer that as a way of life to others wherever they come from, whatever their background. It is in this context I first came across the language of mindfulness, through what we might call a spiritual or faith route (although neither of those words, 'spiritual' or 'faith', are commonly used in Buddhism). As my mindfulness journey continued I discovered Jon Kabat-Zinn, and others, who have incorporated mindfulness into a more secular Western approach to responding to the suffering that accompanies mental distress or physical pain in the health care setting.

I've always been fascinated about the relationship between the roots of mindfulness and what it has become now in the health care context, and in how people who experience mindfulness respond to those roots. I am very happy sharing the benefits of mindfulness with or without reference to its roots, depending on the context. I have also enjoyed discovering more about what looks like mindfulness in other spiritual or faith traditions apart from Buddhism, for example 'watchfulness' in the fifth-century Christian tradition and in Sufism. I have co-facilitated days for chaplains and other health care professionals on spiritual care and mindfulness to explore that very area.

However, I am aware that for some people, who choose not to follow any particular faith or spiritual tradition, or have beliefs and views that are very different from a more Eastern outlook, these roots can cause concern. With my team's broad approach to spiritual care, where we say we are there for people of all faiths and beliefs, or for those who don't align themselves with a particular tradition, mindfulness seems to provide a way of encompassing the spiritual dimension without necessarily referring to it, or requiring anyone to be a follower of a certain religion. Occasionally there is a bit of unease that, in our Trust, mindfulness has ended up being closely aligned with the spiritual care team, but on the whole, it seems people sense that it kind of fits – even if they can't articulate that.

Whenever I am involved in facilitating mindfulness or speaking about it (even with people of faith) I don't tend to use the language of spirit or spirituality, or even spiritual care. That kind of language is also seldom used in the books I have read about mindfulness. I feel very clear that mindfulness itself is not a religion or a 'spirituality'. It is not asking you to believe a creed, believe in God or not believe in God! It isn't that mindfulness itself is Buddhist or Christian or Hindu. It is just mindfulness. It is an approach to life and offers one way of better understanding ourselves and how we respond to what life throws at us. Even though my journey into mindfulness has been very closely related to my spiritual journey I am very aware that it doesn't have to be the case for everyone.

The nursing strategy of Oxford Health NHS Foundation Trust, where one of the authors worked, includes the following statement, 'All nurses will understand mindfulness techniques and also utilize teachings that may help their patients and themselves', which is wonderful and courageous, but I do wonder about the working out of it. Even if it were possible on a practical level, can we actually build mindfulness into strategy or is it a bit more complex than that? If there are people saying, 'this is not for me,' and others asking why mindfulness in particular, why not another therapy, then can it be imposed? My experience is that mindfulness works, and is most beneficial, when you have a group of willing people, not a group of people who have been told to do it. Any negative media coverage about mindfulness is usually in the context of people who have been 'sent' on mindfulness courses and have not found it helpful. Mindfulness does feel inclusive and beneficial for so many people and in so many different contexts but it is not for all.

Of course, I'm torn because I am passionate about mindfulness and am so thankful for the difference it has made to my life and those I have practised with. I am also aware that if compassion is one of our aspirations in care, we need to find practical ways of ensuring it is happening. Mindfulness is a compassionate practice, but it is only 'one way' of nurturing compassion.

Within the health care setting, mindfulness can be engaged with on different levels. People can go down the whole Buddhist or spiritual route, or they can simply engage at a level that helps them negotiate through life in the here and now. I feel the really important thing is that mindfulness remains a choice. For those who want to incorporate a more mindful approach to nursing or spiritual care or psychological work, then we need to ensure that there are opportunities to learn how to do that, but I feel there is a delicate balance to be had, because of where mindfulness comes from.

This is the approach we are taking in our Trust. Opportunities to practise or learn more about mindfulness are things people can choose to be part of. What is lovely is that a more mindful approach to how we support and enable those in our care is naturally and gently spreading.

A nurse from one of our community teams came on a 'Mindfulness in the Workplace Course' that I run jointly with our staff support service. Experiencing and beginning to practise mindfulness has had a big impact on her working life. Her colleagues have seen a change in how she interacts with people and how she responds to situations and have asked us to run the course for the whole team. The way this has happened seems to capture the essence of mindfulness. It is experiential, it is embodied. It can be taught but can't be imposed.

A nurse's experience of being a patient

Gavin Garman

In 2010, I was at a retreat at the University of Nottingham. On the first evening, we gathered in the main hall for a short bit of chanting by the monks and nuns and a talk from Thay. At the end of the session, I went and found my shoes amongst the many left in the corridor to the hall. I found them difficult to put on and thought that I must be very tired. As I walked quietly to my student study bedroom, I kept catching my foot on the pavement. On reaching the hall of residence, I repeatedly dropped my door key before finally opening the door. I felt that something was wrong but couldn't think what it was. I lay in bed paying attention to the wrongness of the way I felt. At one in the morning, I phoned a friend who was also at the retreat and asked for help. She drove me to the local accident and emergency department.

I had had a stroke and spent the next week in hospital. Overall, I was not well looked after. I was left waiting in Accident and Emergency for over four hours before I saw a doctor, despite slowly losing the function of my right arm and leg and my mouth drooping to one side. I felt as if none of the nurses I met knew anything about me. My friend who had brought me in and stayed with me was rudely told to leave. I looked in the notes left at the end of my bed and found entries every four hours recording that I was not in pain and had not opened my bowels. At no point had anybody asked me about either. It was literally a tick-box exercise.

One evening I was told I was to be 'nil by mouth' from midnight. I asked why. The nurse said I was going to have a procedure in the morning. 'What procedure?' I asked. She didn't know. I asked how she expected me to give informed consent if I didn't even know what the procedure was.

She said that they sorted that all out when I got down there. I told her I wasn't happy with that. Later she came back to say it was a CT scan. 'Who asked for me to have that?' I said. 'Neurology,' she replied. I had not met anyone from Neurology.

When I began to get my senses back and started to use words like 'clinical governance' and ask who the director of nursing was, I found I received more information. A consultant neurologist came to my bedside. I told him I would like to make notes of what he said but when he started to talk, I found that I could not write with my newly incompetent right hand. I happened to have a voice recorder with me and asked him if I could record our conversation. He allowed it and gave very clearly thought-out advice, spelling out the names of who was responsible for my care (not himself).

One afternoon, a different consultant stopped at my bedside and began to discuss my condition with a junior colleague standing next to him. Hearing something he said, I attempted to ask him a question. He held up his hand and told me he was talking to his colleague, not me.

I did find out the director of nursing's name and wrote her a long letter, not a complaint, describing my experiences in their hospital. They launched several investigations and apologized for every point I had made, including endangering my life by not following their own stroke protocol in Accident and Emergency. Most amusingly, the consultant at the end of my bed had discussed the incident with the medical director and accepted that he was arrogant.

A year later I found myself in a London cardiac hospital, equally suddenly, unexpected and frightening. There, I felt wonderfully cared for. Every step was explained to me. The nurses were great. One of them even gave me a Hospital Anxiety and Depression scale. I scored well.

I hear and read the words 'compassion' and 'kindness' very often now. It is very positive that they have become familiar words that clinicians are not embarrassed to use. The Chief Nursing Officer (Commissioning Board Chief Nursing Officer and DH Chief Nursing Adviser 2012) defined the six Cs of nursing as care, compassion, competence, courage, communication and commitment. It's hard to argue with that. As NHS nursing managers we were dutifully expected to produce action plans that would demonstrate how our workforce put the six Cs into action. I found myself disagreeing whenever compassion was action planned. The actions that were put forward – for example, increasing one-to-one supervision or senior nurses working alongside 'front-line' staff more – could, I argued, as readily be uncompassionate as compassionate. Not that I had the answer, except to suggest that it is in the way that we listen and talk to people that compassion can be demonstrated.

I find mindful practices a help every day at work. On arriving at work in my car, I turn off the engine and my heavy metal music is cut off. I sit for a few breaths, reminding myself why I chose nursing as a career and why I am at work that day. I turn away from thoughts of all the other places that it might be nicer to be that day, before opening the door and walking, counting breaths in and out with each step to wherever it is that I am going.

Have you experienced that moment of irritation when you can hear the person you are talking to on the phone typing on their keyboard and you know you do not have their full attention? Would interactions by phone be different if when our phone rings we stop what we are doing, take a slow breath in and out, smile, then lift the receiver (or press the screen of our mobile) and say hello? I think so.

In a meeting, on a sunny day, it is hard not to think of how nice it would be to be elsewhere, anywhere but stuck in the room you are in. But however dry the meeting, you are there for a reason, to represent your team or your patients, so you should pay attention and contribute what you can. In some of the meetings I attend it can be very difficult to see the chain connecting the discussion to a benefit experienced somewhere by a service user or staff member. But if we look deeply, it should be there. If it is not, then we should challenge the way that meeting is run.

At a retreat in Plum Village,[1] we were divided into 'Dharma families' for daily discussions. I became a little disillusioned at my group. I had not expected so many of the participants to take the opportunity to discuss their marital problems, fears and unhappiness. It was practice that only one member of the group spoke at a time. The others would sit and listen until they had finished, which they would signal by putting their hands together and bowing. The next person who wished to speak would then bow to indicate that they had something to say. After a particularly grim and depressing contribution from an unhappy spouse, I took my bow and had what I would describe as a mindful rant. I said that the reason I was drawn to Thay's teachings was that they were full of joy, but that too often at the retreat, I failed to see people realizing the joy of being there. When we meditate, Thay advises that we have a half smile on our faces, but the people I passed meditating in the grounds seemed all too often to be frowning fiercely. Before we eat in silence we should smile and bow

1. Plum Village, near Bordeaux in southwest France, is the largest international practice centre in the Plum Village tradition, and the first monastic community founded by Zen Master Thich Nhat Hanh (Thay) in the West (see http://plumvillage.org/about/thich-nhat-hanh).

at each other, but the groups always looked so preoccupied and serious. When the bell sounds during the day, it is an opportunity to stop for three breaths and re-centre ourselves. When the bell sounds, they all looked like they were at a funeral. Thay's talks are full of laughter and funny stories. When I hear Sister Chang Khong sing, it fills me with love. So there, I said, or words to that effect.

I cannot remember exactly what was said or happened next but a short while later the group got up and began to dance around our tree in a conga line, all whooping and singing. I did not join in but stood back watching with a Dutch man from the group. After we had watched for a while he leant over and said to me, 'I think you hit a nerve.'

Many patients experiencing psychosis become fixated over religious ideas when unwell and in the past I have found it best (easiest?) not to get drawn into discussing their strongly held, sometimes delusional views. However, that carries the risk of failing to engage with what may be the patient's own search for a spiritual meaning to life, if expressed in a language affected by their illness.

Thich Nhat Hanh, in a lecture I attended, once stated that there are already enough Buddhists in the world and he saw no need to try to create more. Buddhism teaches that one of the delusions that prevents us from attaining happiness is attachment. Attachment to our possessions, to other people or to our beliefs. The thought that having more money, more possessions or the love of one person will make us happy is the source of much misery in the world. Equally, we should not be attached to our views, including the Buddhist views about attachment. Or the medical, scientific view of mental illness. Believing that we have discovered a great truth can lead to the desire to convert those around us to that world view. We can create barriers dividing us from those who do not share our views, which may ultimately lead us to turn against and harm others, unwittingly or deliberately.

Mindfulness and meditation enable us to step back from our thoughts and see them for what they are, only thoughts. They support our therapeutic goal of being non-judgemental of our patients, of separating who they are from what they may have said or done. Although I believe that psychosis does exist, that anti-psychotic drugs can help people, and that medication may quiet a patient's voices, at the same time experiencing serious illness often leads to spiritual reflection and a quest for meaning in life. Psycho-spiritual care is sensitive to that dimension in our patients. To provide such care sensitively, we need to have paid attention to our own development and practice.

Mindfulness enables us to consider spiritual questions without rules or expectations. Familiarizing clinical staff with its practices may facilitate improvements in care by letting in discussion and consideration of the spiritual aspects of care. Considering a patient's spiritual needs has long been a tenet of holistic psychiatric care. That includes enabling patients to practise their beliefs, honour their festivals and eat as their faith requires. Spiritually sensitive care is not necessarily in place once we provide a multi-faith room. It happens in the way that we treat people every day, listening to what they wish to tell us and nurturing compassion in our relationship with them.

Mindfulness encourages us to focus on the detail, of breathing, of paying attention to the texture and taste whilst we eat a raisin, something usually done in an instant with no attention, or of how we listen to and care for others.

A chaplain's experience of mindfulness practice

Emma Louis

I lead a multi-faith spiritual care team in an NHS mental health Trust. When we meet as a team we spend the first few moments together doing a short mindfulness practice. It feels different than just having 'a bit of quiet together', which is often the way those from different spiritual traditions end up sharing time together. In mindfulness we have found some practical common ground.

So, what do we do? We become aware of how we are as we arrive in that moment, notice what we are experiencing, and check in with where our attention is and what our mind is up to. We notice what feelings might be around, become aware of how our body is, aware of our breath… We let that lead us into our reflective time together. Mindfulness provides a language and practice we can all participate in. It's not instead of prayer or trying to be prayer. It is a way of us being together without diminishing anything we might stand for or value as individuals in our diversity, and strengthens what we share in being human.

Mindfulness is not about doing more things; it's about doing things differently. People sometimes say that they don't have time to do mindfulness. A nurse may say they don't feel they get a moment to breathe, let alone try to spend 30 minutes sitting meditating. In nursing, or any other profession, we can be more mindful in the things we are already doing. Mindfulness in this way is very practical and can be 'used' anywhere, any time and in any place.

Mindfulness in itself is not a religion or a spirituality, but you can approach the practice of any religion mindfully. Mindfulness in itself is not psycho-spiritual care, but taking a mindful approach can create the conditions for psycho-spiritual care to happen.

Working in a mindful way with other people can bring compassion, deep attentive listening, awareness, calmness, affirmation, acceptance and the opportunity for a really meaningful encounter to happen. Mindfulness is about the quality of a relationship. Mindfulness is not about doing something to someone, it is about how you are with someone.

If we are asking ourselves when we are with someone what do we notice, what is our experience, where is our attention, it can help us be mindful of our responses or to have more choice about our responses to those we encounter. It is a way of working, not an end in itself.

Being mindful in whatever we do is not about the pursuit of a mysterious 'other' or 'beyond' or 'transcendence' – words often used to describe what spirituality or psycho-spiritual care is about. It is about the 'here' and 'now' and 'this'. Enlightenment and spiritual care can be found many times each day, when we stop to listen or to share a drink of tea.

References

Chadwick, P. (2014) Mindfulness for psychosis. *British Journal of Psychiatry*, 204, 333–334.

Commissioning Board Chief Nursing Officer and DH Chief Nursing Adviser (2012) *Compassion in Practice: Nursing, Midwifery and Care Staff. Our Vision and Strategy.* London: Department of Health.

Hanh, T.N. (1991a) *The Miracle of Mindfulness.* London: Rider.

Hanh, T.N. (1991b) *Peace Is Every Step.* New York: Bantam Books.

Kabat-Zinn, J. (1990) *Full Catastrophe Living: How to Cope with Stress, Pain and Illness Using Mindfulness Meditation.* London: Piatkus.

Kabat-Zinn, J. (1994) *Wherever You Go, There You Are: Mindfulness Meditation in Everyday Life.* New York: Hyperion.

Segal, Z.V., Williams, J.M.G. and Teasdale, J.D. (2002) *Mindfulness-Based Cognitive Therapy for Depression.* New York: Guilford Press.

9

Searching for Identity in Uncertain Professional Territory

Psycho-spirituality as Discourse for Non-Religious Spiritual Care

Steve Nolan

As a measure of my ignorance, when I first used the word 'psycho-spiritual' in an article for a professional journal (Nolan 2006) I thought I had coined a new term. My over-active sense of achievement was chastened when I realized that others had thought my original thought before me. The term had, in fact, been used by Roberto Assagioli at least 40 years earlier (Assagioli 1965) and had been emerging into wider consciousness since the early 1980s. In 1984, Barnard proposed 'psycho-spiritual' as a replacement for 'psycho-social', which he saw as a confused and confusing term, used indiscriminately to refer 'to almost any non-biophysical aspect of illness' (Barnard 1984, p.74). Since then, the term 'psycho-spiritual' has generated its own sense of confusion, associated as it now is with an array of ideas: the 'superconscious' (Assagioli 1965); a sense of self (Nosek and Hughes 2001); 'working with clients' spirituality in a psychotherapeutic encounter' (West 2004, p.6); various therapies (Tyrrell 1993); health outcomes (Schreiber 2011); and even gender (Sell 2001).

The term came to be used within chaplaincy care a full ten years before I wrote my article. For me, Richard Grey's (1996) use of the term is significant, in part because he used it in the context of palliative care, but more so because he suggested the term could help redefine hospice mission and identity. I found this political redefinition significant because, as a palliative care chaplain, it mirrored my need to redefine my personal and professional sense of mission and identity.

My move into chaplaincy followed what had increasingly been an unfulfilling period of Church ministry. Lacking any prior health care experience, the move was a gamble, and I now appreciate the naïvety of my assumption that the transition would be easily navigated – pastoral care is pastoral care, is it not? In some respects, the transition was a homecoming, and I began to flourish in an environment where colleagues were supportive and respectful of my professional training and experience. But the more I grew acquainted with my new environment, the more I was confronted by the intellectual and cultural gap that existed between the familiarity of the Church from which I had felt alienated and the strangeness of the health care setting into which I now felt welcomed, and the more my identity as a 'minister' was challenged by the demand to become a 'spiritual care specialist'. This challenge was as disconcerting as it was stimulating, because it challenged a role that I consider a vocation. 'Vocation' is itself a loaded term, but from whichever source it is understood to come (God or one's unconscious), I see vocation as an intimate binding of my sense of identity with my work (who I am, bound up in, and to, what I do). The challenge, then, was to rethink my sense of who I was becoming now that I was no longer who I thought I had been; and key to rethinking my identity was rethinking my philosophy of ministry.

I now realize that the impetus for rethinking my identity was a question about the professional territory I was beginning to occupy. The obvious and probably expected position is that a chaplain occupies the territory of the religious professional. Historically, chaplains have been drawn from the Church; latterly, the recruitment pool has widened to include suitably qualified/experienced people of other faiths – and even more recently to include Humanists. But the perception remains that chaplains are primarily concerned with religious beliefs and practices. This perception is earthed in the fact that, when the National Health Service was formed in 1948, the state Church was proactive in negotiating the role and funding of chaplains (Swift 2009). This historic association of chaplains with religion is strong, so here was my answer: as a chaplain I was a religious professional. Yet the world has changed since 1948, a time when Norman Autton could describe a chaplain's ministry as primarily sacramental, the chaplain acting 'as a steward of the mysteries of God…administering the sacraments both in the hospital chapel and on the wards' (Autton 1966, p.14). To be fair, Autton by no means limited chaplaincy care to the administration of sacraments, but he did typify a view of chaplaincy that was religiously oriented. Yet Autton's emphasis on religiously focused ministry is less appropriate today. Of course, contemporary chaplains continue to fulfil religious duties, but they also regard their clinical work as likely to include active listening, crisis intervention, discussing care plans, consulting on ethical issues and facilitating life reviews (Massey et al. 2015). The fact that a contemporary chaplain spends a relatively small proportion of her time offering what might be considered to be traditional religious care and a larger proportion offering care that might equally well be offered by a social worker, occupational therapist or counsellor makes the question about professional territory, and the related question of identity, salient (and, as an aside, it makes engaging with the criticisms directed by the National Secular Society an imperative for chaplains).

A radical rethink

Contemporary chaplaincy care is offered in a context that is secular. It is important to understand that this context is *non*-religious not *anti*-religious; in other words, it is a context that does not privilege one religion or set of beliefs above any other, but neither does it exclude religion. A secular context acknowledges the important role belief (religious or otherwise) plays in people's lives and supports an individual's right to hold and practise their belief, to the extent that they do so ethically. In a secular context, all beliefs are respected and provided for equally. Chaplaincy care must, therefore, offer spiritual care equally to all people, regardless of their belief. This much is axiomatic, and it quickly became clear to me that, to be relevant within this context and to be of any use to the sizable proportion of patients who do not identify as religious, I needed to develop (for myself at least) an understanding of non-religious spiritual care. (Here I need to underline that for me, *non*-religious does not mean *anti*-religious. I see religion fulfilling an important role, and I would argue that it has ongoing value both culturally and for individuals. For me, religion names a community of practice that is oriented to the Sacred (however that is defined) and founded on a (sacred) narrative (typically a set of texts) that offers a particular interpretation of the meaning of life and provides guidance on how it should be lived. In my view, non-religious spiritual care should not privilege religion, nor should it start from a religious perspective or define or constrain spiritual care by religion.)

The majority of research on spirituality in health care was either work published by medical or nursing researchers, who were non-specialists in religious or spirituality studies and whose lack of appropriate academic training meant their work was often philosophically naïve, or it was studies undertaken in the United States, where the practice of religion is culturally very different from that of Europe and where spirituality is often just another word for religion. Either of these factors worked against an adequate understanding of non-religious spiritual care, which I considered needed to be informed by religious studies (including philosophy and theology) and to be culturally contextual.

My starting assumption was that, to have integrity, I needed to understand non-religious spiritual care in a way that would resonate with my own experience and, if it were to have teaching potential and be meaningful across a spectrum of belief, it would need to be empirically congruent with the experience of others. In terms of religious studies, this meant that rather than starting from above, with theology and the kinds of faith statements that privilege religion, I needed to start from below and adopt a Christian human(ist) perspective. Consequently, I needed to think phenomenologically, from lived experience, rather than in the abstract. To me, this is important because I wanted to park speculative questions about mind–body dualism: whether or not humans have an eternal soul; whether the soul is the same as or distinct from the mind; how the soul may be related to mind, spirit and body; whether the soul lives on after death; and the possibilities of transmigration to some form of eternal disembodied existence or reincarnation to yet further forms of life on earth. Since the time of Socrates, these questions have troubled the most able philosophers, and after 25 centuries philosophy remains unable to provide definitive answers. The fact is that questions about the nature of the soul are religious questions that need not inform an understanding of non-religious spiritual care, except insofar as they become a practical issue of that care.

At this point, I was helped by finding a little-known and little-used but robustly researched definition of spirituality, which was both humanistic and phenomenological. I found this succinct definition especially useful because, unlike most of the definitions I was reading, it did not tie spirituality to the search for meaning and purpose, but to experience and relationship: 'Spirituality is a way of being and experiencing that comes through awareness of a transcendent dimension and that is characterized by certain identifiable values in regard to self, others, nature, life, and whatever one considers to be the Ultimate' (Elkins et al. 1988, p.10).

I had never been happy with the endless recycling of the assertion that meaning making is the essential component of spirituality. This is an unsubstantiated claim that somewhat ironically is authorized in the evidence supplied for NICE guidance on cancer services (2004). 'The concept of spirituality outlined in the recommendations concurs with recent interpretations of the term, identified as "the search for meaning" which can include religion but equally can refer to existential concerns in a broader sense' (Gysels and Higginson 2004, p.174; see also Walter 1997). I found this connection problematic. Not only does it depend on an understanding of 'existential', which is itself a highly contested term, to interpret 'spirituality', the connection is too reductive (Dyson, Cobb and Forman 1997). For me, it also misses the point that questions of meaning and purpose are more appropriate to the domain of theology (d'Aquili and Newberg 1999, p.8) and/or philosophy (Walters 2010) than they are to spirituality. For me, a vitally important point about spirituality is that it is experiential and relational, which is the essence of the definition proposed by Elkins et al. (1988). Another key idea in their definition, which again is rarely considered, is that of transcendence. For Elkins et al., an individual's 'awareness of a transcendent dimension' might be in terms of 'the traditional view of a personal God', but equally, their awareness might be in terms of an openness to 'the "more" – that what is "seen" is not all there is' (p.10).

Approaching this phenomenologically, rather than as an abstract theological concept, the sense that I am 'more' than just flesh and bone, that what you see of me is 'not all there is', the sense that somehow I have significance and that I matter, is a common sense: it is the cry of the refugee who says, 'We are humans! Why do they treat us as animals?' The nature of this 'more' may be the stuff of speculation, but that we share this sense is unquestionable, and it is the sensing that is important because it has real-world cash value in my beliefs and behaviours. Things that are sensed are often intangible, difficult to quantify or evidence, but the sense that I am 'more' has reality in the everyday: at the supermarket, someone jumps the check-out queue and I am indignant because I sense I am 'more' than just another object and I believe myself to have been disrespected; at the crematorium, I speak well about our friend because I sense his funeral is 'more' than the disposal of a dead body and I believe it is right to honour our friend's memory. The sense that we are 'more' is intuitive; it is the basis for our sense of common justice and it informs our transferences and projections. And the sense that we are 'more' is itself a transcendence, a going beyond: a transcendence, not in the sense that religious worshippers or spiritual practitioners report as their encounter with the Transcendent, the kind of intense, ecstatic going beyond the everyday that results in a state of altered consciousness. Rather, it is a transcendence in the sense that Luckmann (1990) describes as one of the 'little transcendences' of life that favour self-realization, self-expression and personal freedoms; what Elkins et al. (1988) describe as the 'extension of the conscious self' (p.10).

Psycho-spiritual reflections

In taking spirituality to be 'a way of being and experiencing that comes through awareness of a transcendent dimension' as Elkins et al. (1988)

suggest, I wanted to go further and say that the sense that we are 'more' is our sense of spirit and with it our sense that we are 'spiritual'. It is at this point that I began to think in terms of 'psycho-spiritual'. For me, the sense that we are 'more' emerges with and is dependent upon 'awareness of one's self in one's being as a self' (Nolan 2011, p.59), which put otherwise is consciousness: consciousness of ourselves as beings who are conscious of ourselves as beings; beings who are aware of our own being, who know ourselves as creatures who know and who are capable of experiencing our own experience; beings who have the capacity to reflect on our present, reconstruct our past and dream a future that could be utterly other; beings concerned with the 'being-ness' of our own being (Heidegger 1962, p.32) such that we necessarily transcend the limitations of our physicality; beings who live in the knowledge that one day our being will cease to be. I began to see this as the point at which the disciplines of spirituality and psychology, or perhaps more accurately the discourses of soul and spirit, converge or interface (Welwood 2000, p.xvi).

For me, 'psycho-spiritual' was *la bâtardise du mot* (Greek *psyche* – soul; Latin: *spiritus* – spirit) (Lacan 1966) that named the convergence of the discourses of soul and spirit. I also saw in the term a way of laying claim to professional territory and reconfiguring my professional identity. As a newbie chaplain, I had quickly realized that if I was to be defined by religion and religious care, then my professional identity and territory would be severely restricted, both in terms of the number of people who would seek my ministrations and in terms of my input into the multi-disciplinary team. But at the same time, I noted that by adding the prefix psycho- to describe their work (psycho-social), social workers had extended their professional territory to include psychological and emotional support. I also noted that this work had originally been the responsibility of the Church, which social workers had taken over as a secularized form of pastoral care (Payne 2005). It did not seem unreasonable to me to appropriate the prefix and talk about *psycho*-spiritual care as a way of reclaiming that territory (a move that irritated certain social work colleagues!).

Equally, the ambiguity of *psyche*, a word originally meaning 'soul' but in contemporary use closely associated with 'mind', offered a way to connect chaplaincy care with both the priestly arts, known traditionally as 'the cure of the soul' (Latin: *cura animarum*), and modern psychological 'science of the mind'. Most significantly, 'psycho-spiritual' named the territory on which I thought non-religious spiritual care could be grounded, and on which I could rethink my professional identity.

My academic background and training disposed me to think that non-religious spiritual care should not be occupied with esoteric speculation about the nature and reality of 'soul' or 'spirit'. As a postgraduate, I had studied religion and contemporary continental philosophy under the late Professor Grace Jantzen, a feminist philosopher of religion. She introduced me to the French post-structuralists Michel Foucault and Jacques Derrida and supervised my doctoral thesis on the French Freudian psychoanalyst Jacques Lacan, and her non-realist view of religious language has shaped my own thinking. For me, non-religious spiritual care starts from the premise that we sense ourselves to be 'more' and (informed by non-realism) it regards our talk about 'soul' or 'spirit' as approximations, heuristic attempts to speak about what it means to be 'more' and the ways we experience our being 'more'; but it also recognizes that our talk of 'soul' or 'spirit' is always already frustrated by the limitations of language and culture.

From this essentially Kantian perspective, I take constructs of 'the person', however rudimentary or sophisticated, to be heuristic and metaphorical and, although I accept an individual's construct as their description of reality as they inhabit it, I resist temptations to harden or reify metaphors into facts, which would be to confuse language with things in the real world that exist as independent ontological entities. (In my view, psycho-spirituality has little to gain from conjecture about the nature of the soul as higher consciousness, however beguiling that might be.) For me, the sense that we are 'more' is rooted in human evolution, possibly in biology (Hardy 1979), probably in neurophysiology (Newberg, d'Aquili and Rause 2001; Hay 2007), and as such it cuts across boundaries that have historically divided religion from science. As such, the sense that we are 'more' offers a shared terrain on which not only religion and science, but also theists and atheists might find some kind of rapprochement (Walters 2010). For me, psycho-spirituality does not name an independent ontological entity or phenomenon; rather it is the coming together of the discourses of mind and spirit into a single discourse that can speak more completely about human experience. To attempt a definition, I would say: *Informed by a non-realist perspective, psycho-spirituality is a discourse of the human condition that integrates historically divided discourses of 'soul' (psyche) and 'spirit' (spiritus) in a way that has 'cash-value' in non-religious spiritual care.*

An important realization that I took from non-realism is that this perspective dissolves categories such as psychology and spirituality. From a non-realist perspective, there is no *thing* that can be called 'psychology'; psychology is not more than a discourse on the human condition developed by the scientific community and based around scientific method. Equally, there is no *thing* that can be called 'spirituality', which although developed originally within religious communities and based on religious experience has become complexified by nursing discourse and the emergence of humanistic spirituality (Nolan and Holloway 2014, pp.71–74). The point is that the categories of psychology and spirituality are convenience categories, created arbitrarily for the purpose of analysing and describing the human condition, in ways that lend themselves to the exercise of power: those who describe reality, control reality. It makes little sense to talk about a person's psychological needs as distinct from their spiritual needs, since they are essentially the same: *human* needs described by different, and at times competing, discourses. As a discourse rooted in non-realism, psycho-spirituality deconstructs itself as a discourse with a claim to power and integrates the discourses of psychology (*psyche*) and spirituality (*spiritus*). In this way, psycho-spirituality maps with the kind of therapeutic *I–Thou* relationship Buber (1958) describes, where (drawing on the discourse of psychology that addresses the other as an object – *It*) *I* as counsellor-therapist am aware of the other's particularity as an *It*, but at the same time (drawing on the discourse of spirituality that addresses the other as a subject – *Thou*) *I* connect with the universal in the other as *Thou*, thereby undoing something of what Buber calls 'The melancholy of our fate' (Buber 1958, p.39).

Non-religious spiritual care: An example of psycho-spiritual care in practice

Here it would be helpful to offer an example from my own practice of non-religious spiritual care informed by psycho-spiritual discourse. I have chosen the following example because, although it is ostensibly religious, it did not privilege a religious perspective but worked with the person's inhabited reality. For this reason, I maintain it as an example of non-religious spiritual care.

Liz

Liz contacted me some time after her son, Pete, had taken his life. Having separated from his partner, who then became very difficult about allowing access to their son, Nathan, Pete had moved back to live with his mother. The breakup of his family unit was reprising his childhood experience of abandonment by his father, and several years of struggle for access took a profound toll on Pete. One Sunday afternoon he told his mother he was tired and would lie down until tea. When she went to his room to wake him, she found him dead on the bedroom floor; he had taken an overdose. Liz was traumatized and broken by Pete's suicide, and in the weeks after his cremation, she daily visited the place his ashes were spread, laying fresh flowers and spending hours talking to him. Several months after

Pete's death, Liz was referred to me by a colleague. Liz knew I was both a chaplain and a counsellor-therapist, and we began weekly meetings, which lasted for nine sessions.

During our first meetings, Liz went over the details that led up to Pete's suicide and the trauma itself: what she saw as the manipulative attitude and calculated, callous behaviour of his former partner; the commitment and support she and her other children offered Pete in the years prior to his death; Pete's behaviour on the day he killed himself and how she found him; and her bewildered incongruity about why he would abandon the little boy in whom he clearly delighted. Liz struggled to comprehend the reason for Pete's death – his partner had seemed finally to be softening and the situation looked as if it might have been about to improve; she also needed to understand why she was finding things so difficult – should she not be feeling better by now? Discussing Liz in supervision, I felt the work with her was mainly about being supportive, allowing her to say what she needed to say and normalizing her experience, helping her to gain a sense of perspective about what had happened to her and her family. As the work developed, I also offered her a tentative interpretation of Pete's suicide, suggesting that he had so wanted to be the father to his son that he himself had never had, but that his former partner was making it impossible; that the pain of his frustration had become unbearable and the prospect of a thaw in her attitude too unpredictable, raising his hopes only to be crushed once again. I suggested Pete may have seen death as a release from his torment. Liz found comfort in this interpretation.

Around this point, a Christian friend of Liz's suggested she come to church with her. Church had not previously been a feature of Liz's life, but she had what could be described as a 'cultural belief': she believed in God, heaven and hell, and the stories of Jesus; she considered herself a Christian and respected the institution, attending services to mark births, deaths and marriages and the occasional Christmas. Her friend's evangelical church proved to be welcoming, and Liz quickly found new friends and was introduced to Bible reading and prayer meetings. I was concerned about the kind of support Liz might receive from her well-meaning friends, whether she would be treated as someone in need of being 'saved'; but although she spoke about her struggles to understand the Bible, she seemed to find benefit from the church such that she soon felt she no longer needed to see me. We agreed to finish, but left open the possibility of further sessions if she felt she needed them.

I thought Liz and I had finished, but after some weeks she called to arrange a meeting. When she arrived, she seemed less burdened.

The anniversary of Pete's death was approaching and she showed me a beautiful album she had had made as a gift for Nathan. She told me how he was speaking openly about his daddy's death. Then she spoke about her church, how she had visited the minister's wife, who had told Liz that she loved her husband and children very much, but that she loved the Lord more. Liz was troubled by this and found it almost impossible to comprehend. She understood that she should love the Lord a lot, but more than her family? Really? Was that right?

Evangelicalism is part of my spiritual history. As a young man, I left my parents' Roman Catholicism and joined an independent evangelical, 'Bapti-costal' church, attended an evangelical Bible college and worked in independent evangelical churches. I have an understanding of evangelical culture and values and a sense of the sentiment expressed by the minister's wife. But I no longer see the world as an evangelical; evangelicalism ceased some time ago to make sense of my reality. However, I recognized that Liz was adopting the world view of her new friends, that it was meeting a need for her and that I needed to respond with integrity but in a way that would be supportive. So I explained that Jesus had indeed said that we should love God above family, that he had said if we put our mother or father, or our wife and children before God, then we would not be fit for the Kingdom (Luke 14.26), but that he had used many different ways to communicate his message: stories, parables, metaphors and, in this case, hyperbole, an exaggeration to make a point. I gave a couple of everyday examples and another example from Jesus: 'If your right hand causes you to stumble, cut it off and throw it away. It is better for you to lose one part of your body than for your whole body to go into hell' (Matthew 5.30). I explained that this wasn't to be taken literally.

Liz continued speaking about her visit and in passing voiced a question about whether Pete would be in heaven. I heard this as more than idle musing, so I brought her back to her question.

'Is that a question in your mind?'

[Thoughtfully] 'Yes…yes I think it is. Will he be with the Lord?'

'What do you think?'

'I think that maybe…when he was due to take his life…that he might have prayed and he might have asked the Lord to let him be at peace, to put an end to his pain. So I do think he is at peace…but I do wonder. Will he be in heaven? Will he? What do you think?'

Her direct question put me in a sensitive position. Liz was clearly finding strength from her new community of faith and in her developing relationship with the Lord, and I wanted to be supportive, despite myself feeling distanced from that world. But equally Liz was finding it a challenge to adopt the specifics of the beliefs to which she was expected to subscribe. My instinct was to debate those beliefs, but I considered this would be unhelpful; Liz's nascent faith is not sophisticated and her education has been disadvantaged. Therefore, I thought it important to work with her reality.

Commentary

Working with Liz, I was conscious that my experience in bereavement support has been generic rather than specific with regard to suicide. Nonetheless, it is informed by my training as an integrative counsellor-therapist, and I drew on insights from psychotherapy and bereavement theory (*psyche* discourse), adopting a person-centred approach that facilitated her to talk openly about her experience and feelings. This was broadly congruent with evidence-based thinking about suicide bereavement (Jordan 2001; Hawton and Simkin 2003), which suggests that people bereaved by suicide find meaning making around the death more difficult than people bereaved by natural or accidental death (Jordan 2001, p.92). Sitting with Liz during our sessions together, her struggle to comprehend why Pete had killed himself was palpable and it was necessary for her to have time to explore his reasoning; the interpretation I offered Liz was a form of 'psychoeducation' (Jordan 2001, p.99). But perhaps of equal benefit was the fact that Liz did not feel she or Pete were being judged. Bereavement by suicide can leave people feeling 'more isolated and stigmatized than other mourners and may in fact be viewed more negatively by others in their social network' (Jordan 2001, p.93). For this reason, Liz's relationship with her church friends could be significant, since this welcoming community may become a replacement for her existing social network, which she may perceive to be negatively judgemental, a perception Dunn and Morrish-Vidners term 'self-stigmatization' (1987–88, p.177).

Understanding the potential for Liz in joining this church, my concern stemmed from my own direct experience of evangelical churches. I was unable to explore with Liz what motivated her to attend the church, whether it was her discovery that she was loved by God or whether the warmth of their welcome sparked her desire to belong to their community. I was concerned that, in their willingness to embrace a new convert, they might subtly pressure Liz to conform to their beliefs. For this reason, when she expressed her struggle, first, to accommodate the conflict of her values with her friend's belief that she should love her Lord more than her family, and, second, to understand the broader and more threatening idea that the Lord might not welcome Pete into heaven because he had ended his own life, I felt I needed to work with her need to relate to others and to God (*spiritus* discourse).

It is not my normal style to be so directive or didactic, but Liz's questions were direct and urgent, and it seemed appropriate that I should address them directly. Religion was becoming increasingly important for Liz and the content of her speech was ostensibly religious; as a chaplain, a religious professional, it may have seemed natural to have treated her questions *prima facia* as religious. But a less superficial reading sees that in expressing her desire to belong to a community (the Church) and to find God (the Lord) she was simultaneously expressing profound anxieties about death, isolation and meaning. I took Liz's questions to be just as much existential as religious. Not that I thought Liz was *displacing* her anxieties about death onto Church and God, but rather that, according to 'the laws of metaphor and metonymy' (Lacan 1992, p.61), her speech condensed two sets of concerns: one about Church and God, the other about death, isolation and meaning.

For this reason, I answered her direct question – 'Will he be in heaven?' – explaining that no one can judge the heart of another person; we can never tell what is really going on for them, so we have to leave that to God. I then pointed her to Jesus' teaching about the love of God, and said that God loved Pete and understood how painful things were for him and that being a God of love, I felt sure God would have a place for her son. In this way, I tried to work non-religiously with Liz and her reality: aiming to integrate insights gained from psychotherapy training, which offered me some objective understanding of her (as *It*), with insights gained from empathizing with her over time, which enabled me to connect subjectively with her (as *Thou*). Ultimately, I was trying to foster her healing in and through our relationship.

How has an understanding of psycho-spirituality helped me redefine my personal and professional sense of mission and identity?

Making the transition from church to hospice, I needed a way to integrate the realities of what I had been with what I was becoming: the religious, spiritual world of the Church, in which I had been nurtured and trained as a minister, with the scientific, clinical world of health care, in which I was becoming a spiritual care specialist. I also needed to find an approach that was *non*-religious (rather than *anti*-religious), that would enable me to work with anybody, not just people who identified as in some way 'religious'. In other words, I needed to reconstruct both my professional identity and professional territory in a way that integrated rather than rejected what I had been and the way I had practised.

Seeing my work as psycho-spiritual care allows me to integrate the language and concepts of psychotherapy with that of my religious, sacramental role, and to see myself as caring holistically for the soul/mind (*psyche*) and spirit (*spiritus*) regardless of a person's belief. West (2004) has used the word 'psycho-spiritual' to talk about 'working with clients' spirituality in a psychotherapeutic encounter' (p.6). My perspective might be characterized as working psychotherapeutically in a spiritual encounter, but I would prefer to dissolve both categories and see what I do as working holistically in a human encounter.

A Response

Judy Davies

I've been asked to offer a personal response to Steve Nolan's chapter, with reference to its impact on me, the thoughts and feelings it evokes, and its implications for my practice and for health care chaplaincy. At first, I confess that I struggled with the task, as the language of this erudite paper did not seem easily translatable to my daily work. But as I read and re-read it, themes emerged that were important to me, and with which I think health care chaplains need to engage.

My deepest instinct is to begin where Steve's paper ends, after his disquisition on *psyche* and *spiritus* in relation to psycho-spiritual care. Steve's final sentence reads '…I would prefer to dissolve both categories and see what I do as working *holistically* in a *human* encounter'. This is where I want to cheer. After more than 20 years in health care chaplaincy I am as passionate about the work itself as when I first began. However, I have grown weary of definitions and redefinitions of spirituality and spiritual care, and of labouring over spiritual needs assessment tools, which feel like endlessly revisiting old ground.

This instinctive response has a history, and I identify with much of Steve's story which resonates with my own. Like him, I came into chaplaincy from Church-based ministry and quickly felt that I was coming home. Moving from the acute sector to palliative care only intensified the feeling. Here was an environment where holistic care was taken seriously, and where I was welcomed into a multi-disciplinary team with the expectation that I would have something to contribute in the realm of spirituality and spiritual care. But as a Christian minister I was entering a very different world. I found, like Steve, that much of my daily work was with people who didn't have any connection to a faith community, and whose first words to me were often, 'Thank you, I'm not religious.'

Yet this was where I instinctively felt I belonged. Early on, I remember feeling stung by a hostile question from a Methodist colleague: 'When are you going to come back into the *real work*?' So how was *this* real? And how could I be real, and true to my vocation, within it? It became important to engage with these questions, first for my own self-understanding, but also to be able explain my role to others, whether colleagues, people using our services and their families, or a plethora of external voices – the Church which had given me permission to work in this field, those making decisions in health care about funding or staffing, or those questioning the need for chaplains at all.

So I needed to think about what it meant to offer what Steve calls '*non-religious* spiritual care'; and in one way or another I've been thinking about it ever since. Steve's article speaks to me of a path that I have travelled, looking for helpful signposts, for a very long time. Along the way, I have lost count of the number of workshops and seminars I have attended, discussing competing definitions of spirituality, and I have come to feel that searching for *the* definition is a dead-end. The late Rabbi Hugo Gryn said, 'Spirituality is like a bird: hold it too tightly and it chokes; hold it too loosely and it flies away' (Westminster Local Education Authority 1993, p.23). I find myself wanting to say, not so much 'this is it', as 'these are the places where we might want to look'. So I respond warmly to Steve's preferred understanding of spirituality (quoting Elkins et al. 1988) as fundamentally rooted in being and relationship; but I wouldn't want to exclude questions of meaning and purpose, which will often become part of a broader conversation about spiritual issues. What speaks to me most powerfully is the notion of transcendence, of there being 'something more'; and this, I believe, is where we find common ground as human beings. I encounter this every day, from the patient whose pain recedes while he is sitting out in the hospice garden watching the birds to the aromatherapist massaging a person's hand, where both seem so linked by a profound, relaxed attentiveness that they resemble a Renaissance annunciation painting. It links for me with a word that has profound Christian connotations – the notion of sacrament, where the stuff of ordinary life is transformed and becomes a means of invisible grace.

Clearly, the chaplain is not the only person who senses or communicates this 'something more', but perhaps one of our functions is to represent it. Recently, I was stopped in the corridor by a senior nurse who had walked the ward for a whole morning, not making eye contact, wearing a tabard that said, 'Do not disturb: nurse on drug round'. She said, 'I'm glad you're here. You're a visible reminder of the things that can't be measured.'

All health care professionals can feel at times that they are swimming against the tide in the face of a health care system obsessed with measurement. (I recall a dispiriting period when all staff members had to record daily how many minutes were spent on the different aspects of their work. The categories were supplied for us, and in desperation I ended up classifying a funeral as a 'patient-facing activity'.) Chaplains, in their work with patients, relatives and staff, have a particular role in demonstrating the worth of things that are difficult to measure. I'm quite happy to call this 'psycho-spiritual' care. It's a helpful term which holds together, as Steve eloquently describes, the *psyche* (soul/mind) and *spiritus* (spirit) and can provide an integrative model for non-religious and religious care. And while it isn't the sole preserve of the chaplain, there is something distinctive about the chaplain's contribution that is worth noting.

In my hospice I'm the only person aside from the medical and nursing staff who sees people without referral; but I always see them with permission. We provide an opt-out so that patients can decide that they would prefer not to see me. This means I'm at the mercy of the admitting nurse and how they choose to describe me, but I would prefer that to making an assumption that people want my services (or would do if they understood what I was offering). At my first chaplains' conference, a keynote speaker offered the thought that 'Chaplaincy is the ministry of being able to be told to piss off.'

So chaplains are dependent on the hospitality that patients, or family members, afford them, and if we are welcomed, or tolerated, what we have to offer is ourselves. We don't come armed with a set of interventions, drugs, equipment, even a bedpan. What we bring is (as Steve has argued in a previous article, Nolan 2006, p.19) 'the nakedness of our own being'.

The extent to which we have worked with our own 'psycho-spirituality' has a direct bearing on the extent to which we can be truly present and attentive to others. In such encounters, I frequently feel that the boundaries between non-religious and religious care are porous.

I include here a fragment from my conversation with Dave, a hospice patient whom I had previously met several times, and who had originally agreed to see me on the basis that we wouldn't talk about religion.

Dave: 'There has to be something more than this.'

'More than…?'

'This pain, this being sick all the time…'

'I wonder – how do you see the "something more"…?'

'Dunno really – but I'd like it to be peaceful…'

Long pause

'…It feels hypocritical to ask, but would you say a prayer for me?'

So I said a prayer for Dave. I include this fragment, because it exemplifies for me how sometimes 'non-religious' spiritual care shades into something else. That's how I feel about Steve's description of a pastoral encounter with Liz. It is offered as an example of non-religious spiritual care. However, his responses to her anguished questions about her son feel to me like priestly ministry. Maybe all I am saying is that I feel uncomfortable with drawing lines between psychological, spiritual and religious aspects of care, and prefer to 'work *holistically* in a *human* encounter'.

My final thought is that Steve's paper presents a challenge to health care chaplaincy, and I trust that reflection upon our own mission and identity will also sharpen our thinking on how we make the case for psycho-spiritual care. Chaplains, with some notable exceptions, have been notoriously slow (and I include myself in this) to engage with research, to be able to say, 'This is the difference we can make; here is evidence of how patients can benefit from our presence and activity.' Anecdotes about how we're there for everyone will, I fear, not be enough. And if we cannot demonstrate the worth of psycho-spiritual care – if we cannot argue for and in some measure represent the 'something more' – then how will we, in a pressurized, cash-strapped health care environment, ensure that such care survives in any meaningful way?

A Response

Steve Nolan

There are resonances between Judy's experience and mine, in particular, the way our relationship to the churches that authorize us informs what we do. Judy describes moving into chaplaincy as like 'coming home', despite the fact that much of her daily work 'was with people who didn't have any connection to a faith community'. The hostility of her Methodist colleague concerning 'the *real work*' tells the story.

Describing the complexity of health care chaplains' identity, Cobb locates chaplains at the centre of three overlapping communities: health care, disciplinary and faith. He notes that standard practice is for chaplains to be 'authorized and licensed' by their faith community, empowering them 'to act as its representative within the health care setting' (Cobb 2004, p.13). This representative role is made explicit by the UK Board of Healthcare Chaplains (2014), where being in 'good standing with their faith community or belief group' is a condition of registration. The difficulty, as Swift notes, is that there is a high probability many chaplains 'feel disenchanted with the leadership and structures of the Church' (Swift 2009, p.151; cf. also Hancocks, Sherbourne and Swift 2008). Swift identifies several reasons for disenchantment, including issues of sexual politics and theological disenfranchisement. While it is unclear what 'in good standing' means, it is unlikely to intend clergy who feel disenchanted or marginalized. It is equally unlikely to intend clergy who theologically challenge their faith community, although if we take the implications of psycho-spiritual or non-religious spiritual care seriously, that challenge is inescapable.

Health care chaplains understand our care is to be person-centred and aimed at addressing the spiritual needs of all health care services users, regardless of belief. This is no small challenge. In the early days of the NHS, when the majority of the population identified as 'Christian', spiritual needs were likely to be interpreted in terms of religion, and met straightforwardly without compromising the integrity of the (normatively) Anglican chaplain. But the faith landscape has changed since 1948, and the percentage of the UK population who identify as non-religious is now around 50 per cent. Specific faith affiliation has also altered dramatically, with only four in ten now identifying as Christian, a decline that coincides with increased diversity among those who profess religious faith (Commission on Religion and Belief in Public Life 2015, p.7). The context of the '*real work*' of health care chaplains is simultaneously secular *and* multi-faith and complicated by the demands of overlapping communities, which compete for our loyalty without necessarily supporting our work adequately.

Within the complexities of this context, alongside the pressing need to develop an evidence base for our work (Nolan 2015a, 2015b), health care chaplains need a coherent and consistent philosophy of care that can make sense in our environment without compromising our integrity by taking recourse in the principle of 'pastoral expediency'. It remains to be seen whether psycho-spirituality can provide that philosophy. But if it doesn't, something very much like it will be needed to understand, relate to and attempt to address the spiritual needs of religious *and* non-religious people.

References

Assagioli, R. (1965) *Psychosynthesis: Individual and Social (Some Suggested Lines of Research)*. Available at www.aeon.ch/fileadmin/user_upload/Daten/Downloads/01_Psychosynthese/03_Spezifische_Themen/ps-individual-and-social.pdf, accessed on 10 June 2016.

Autton, N. (1966) *The Hospital Ministry*. Church's Ministry Series 6. Westminster: Church Information Office.

Barnard, D. (1984) Illness as a crisis of meaning: Psycho-spiritual agendas in health care. *Pastoral Psychology*, 33(2), 74–82.

Buber, M. (1958) *I and Thou*. Translated by R.G. Smith. Edinburgh: T&T Clark.

Cobb, M. (2004) The location and identity of chaplains: A contextual model. *Scottish Journal of Health Care Chaplaincy*, 7(2), 10–15.

Commission on Religion and Belief in Public Life (2015) *Living with Difference: Community, Diversity and the Common Good*. Cambridge: The Woolf Institute. Available at https://corablivingwithdifference.files.wordpress.com/2015/12/living-with-difference-online.pdf, accessed on 10 June 2016.

d'Aquili, E. and Newberg, A.B. (1999) *The Mystical Mind: Probing the Biology of Religious Experience*. Minneapolis, MN: Fortress.

Dunn, R.G. and Morrish-Vidners, D. (1987–88) The psychological and social experience of suicide survivors. *Omega*, 18(3), 175–215.

Dyson, J., Cobb, M. and Forman, D. (1997) The meaning of spirituality: A literature review. *Journal of Advanced Nursing*, 26, 1183–1188.

Elkins, D.N., Hedstrom, L.J., Hughes, L.L., Leaf, J.A. and Saunders, C. (1988) Toward a humanistic-phenomenological spirituality: Definition, description and measurement. *Journal of Humanistic Psychology*, 28(4), 5–18.

Grey, R. (1996) The psychospiritual care matrix: A new paradigm for hospice care giving. *American Journal of Hospice and Palliative Medicine*, 13(4), 19–25.

Gysels, M. and Higginson, I.J. (2004) *Guidance on Cancer Services. Improving Supportive and Palliative Care for Adults with Cancer: Research Evidence.* London: National Institute for Clinical Excellence and King's College London.

Hancocks, G., Sherbourne, J. and Swift, C. (2008) 'Are they refugees?' Why Church of England male clergy enter health care chaplaincy. *Practical Theology,* 1(2), 163–179.

Hardy, A. (1979) *The Spiritual Nature of Man.* Oxford: Clarendon.

Hawton, K. and Simkin, S. (2003) Helping people bereaved by suicide. *Bereavement Care,* 22(3), 41–42.

Hay, D. (2007) *Why Spirituality is Difficult for Westerners.* Exeter: Societas Imprint Academic.

Heidegger, M. (1962) *Being and Time.* Oxford: Blackwell.

Jordan, J.R. (2001) Is suicide bereavement different? A reassessment of the literature. *Suicide and Life-Threatening Behavior,* 31(1), 91.

Lacan, J (1966). Subversion du sujet et dialectique du désir dans l'inconscient freudien. In J. Lacan, *Écrits.* Paris: Éditions du Seuil.

Lacan, J. (1992) *The Seminar of Jacques Lacan: Book VII. The Ethics of Psychoanalysis.* New York: Norton.

Luckmann, T. (1990) Shrinking transcendence, expanding religion. *Sociology of Religion,* 51(2), 127–138.

Massey, K., Barnes, M.J.D., Villines, D., Goldstein, J.D., Pierson, A.L.H., Scherer, C., Vander Laan, B. and Summerfelt, W.T. (2015) What do I do? Developing a taxonomy of chaplaincy activities and interventions for spiritual care in intensive care unit palliative care. *BMC Palliative Care,* 14(10). Available at www.ncbi.nlm.nih.gov/pmc/articles/PMC4397872/pdf/12904_2015_Article_8.pdf, accessed on 10 June 2016.

Newberg, A.B., d'Aquili, E. and Rause, V. (2001) *Why God Won't Go Away: Brain Science and the Biology of Belief.* New York: Ballantine Books.

NICE (2004) *Guidance on Cancer Services: Improving Supportive and Palliative Care for Adults with Cancer.* London: National Institute for Clinical Excellence.

Nolan, S. (2006) Psychospiritual care: A paradigm (shift) of care for the spirit in a non-religious context. *Journal of Heath Care Chaplaincy,* 7(1), 12–22.

Nolan, S. (2011) Psychospiritual care: New content for old concepts – towards a new paradigm for non-religious spiritual care. *Journal for the Study of Spirituality,* 1(1), 50–64.

Nolan, S. (2015a) Making Spiritual Care Visible: The Developing Agenda and Methodologies for Research in Spiritual Care. In J. Pye, P. Sedgwick and A. Todd (eds) *Critical Care: Delivering Spiritual Care in Health Care Contexts.* London: Jessica Kingsley Publishers.

Nolan, S. (2015b) Health care chaplains responding to change: Embracing outcomes or reaffirming relationships? *Health and Social Care Chaplaincy,* 3(2), 93–109.

Nolan, S. and Holloway, M. (2014) *A–Z of Spirituality.* Professional Keywords Series. Basingstoke: Palgrave.

Nosek, M.A. and Hughes, R.B. (2001) Psychospiritual aspects of sense of self in women with physical disabilities. *Journal of Rehabilitation,* 67(1), 20–25.

Payne, M. (2005) *Modern Social Work Theory* (3rd edition). Basingstoke: Palgrave Macmillan.

Schreiber, J.A. (2011) Image of God: Effect on coping and psychospiritual outcomes in early breast cancer survivors. *Oncology Nursing Forum,* 38(3), 293–301.

Sell, I. (2001) Not man, not woman: Psychospiritual characteristics of a Western third gender. *Journal of Transpersonal Psychology,* 33(1), 16–36.

Swift, C. (2009) *Hospital Chaplaincy in the Twenty-First Century: The Crisis of Spiritual Care on the NHS.* Farnham: Ashgate.

Tyrrell, B.J. (1993) Christotherapy: An Approach to Facilitating Psychospiritual Healing and Growth. In R.J. Wicks, R.D. Parsons and D. Capps (eds.) *Clinical Handbook of Pastoral Counseling, Vol. 1* (expanded edition). Mahwah, NJ: Paulist Press.

UK Board of Healthcare Chaplains (2014) *Code of Conduct for Healthcare Chaplains.* Available at www.ukbhc.org.uk/chaplains/professional_conduct, accessed on 10 June 2016.

Walter, T. (1997) The ideology and organisation of spiritual care: Three approaches. *Palliative Medicine*, 11(1), 21–30.

Walters, K. (2010) *Atheism: A Guide for the Perplexed.* New York: Continuum.

Welwood, J. (2000) *Toward a Psychology of Awakening: Buddhism, Psychotherapy, and the Path of Personal and Spiritual Transformation.* Boston, MA: Shambhala Publications.

West, W. (2004) *Spiritual Issues in Therapy: Relating Experience to Practice.* Basingstoke: Palgrave.

Westminster Local Education Authority (1993) *Things of the Spirit.* Westminster: LEA Publications.

Conclusion

As an exploration of psycho-spiritual care, this book has rooted what it has to say in the lived experience of patients and health care staff. The research outlined in Chapters 1 to 4 and the subsequent symposium papers and responses in Chapters 5 to 9 have provided a conduit for that lived experience to be heard, explored and further understood. As a direct consequence of this exploration and in order to continue to develop the concept of psycho-spiritual care, I conclude by proposing an approach to care that I call Radical Presence. In discussing and presenting this approach both formally and informally to health care practitioners and therapists, I have been delighted and surprised by the number of people who want to talk more about what psycho-spiritual care means to them. A broad range of health care practitioners have also expressed a desire for further discussion, training and self-understanding. This developing interest has given added impetus to the establishment of the Oxford Centre for Spirituality and Wellbeing (OCSW). In this conclusion, I therefore intend to briefly focus on the development of psycho-spiritual care as Radical Presence.

Radical Presence is the integration of contemporary spirituality with practical theological or pastoral insights and an applied model of Person-Centred counselling and psychotherapy. It is 'radical' in the sense of returning to the origin of the concepts of both the psyche and the spiritual. 'Psyche' is from the Greek word for 'breath' or 'soul'. Hence psychotherapy is literally healing of the 'soul', the art of 'healing' being the original meaning of the Greek word from which 'therapy' derives. The word 'spiritual' is derived from the Latin word *spiritus*, which has been interpreted as relating to non-physical aspects of personhood, in particular to a person's 'spirit' or 'soul'. The integration of meanings of both 'psyche' and 'spiritual' as psychologically informed spiritual care or psycho-spiritual care forms the foundation stone upon which Radical Presence may be built.

Radical Presence is 'presence' rooted in the relational stance that is foundational to Buber's primary word 'I–Thou' (cf. Chapter 2, section 'The implications for developing psycho-spiritual care in health care practice'). Yontef (1993) cited by Finlay and Evans states that, 'fully present people share meaning with each other...[including] despair, love, spirituality,

anger, joy, humor, sensuality… The therapist is present as a person'
(2013, p.4). Presence is a way of being with someone that demands
authenticity and patience. It is more a quality of relationship than a set of
skills; a quality of self or a way of being that is brought to each therapeutic
encounter. Bugenthal (1987) describes three components of presence.
These are being open and available to all parts of the 'clients'' experience,
being open to one's own experience and being open to responding
congruently from the immediacy of that experience. Presence is therefore
a way of compassionate relating that involves the whole person, physical,
emotional, spiritual and social.

Within the Person-Centred approach the majority of a therapist's
congruent responding takes the form of being fully present with a client
(Mearns and Thorne 1999). Presence as a consistent quality on the part of
the therapist is central to Person-Centred counselling and psychotherapy.
In his later writing, Rogers describes how transcendent awareness is a
prerequisite for understanding the 'unity of the cosmic system including
man [sic]' (1980, p.352). He postulates that this awareness is most likely to
take place if the therapist as 'spiritual seeker' (p.352) attends to the quality
of presence in each and every encounter with a client. Thorne develops
Rogers' emphasis on the cosmic unity of the universe to suggest that if
the therapist is to be open to transcendent awareness then they should do
'all that they can to be at home in the "cosmic unity" where the visible
and invisible worlds meet' (2012, p.210). It is this meeting of inner spirit
with inner spirit and the consequent experience of being part of something
larger that is also a characteristic of Radical Presence.

Thorne goes on to describe how Rogers' understanding of 'being in the
moment' develops into a quality of relationship:

> where a level of intimacy and intensity is reached that he [sic] feels
> his simple presence is healing…at such times there comes a meeting
> of inner spirit with inner spirit and the experience of being part of
> something larger. (2012, p.221)

Thorne also describes a 'quality of tenderness' (2012, p.32) that includes the
following attributes: 'It communicates through its responsive vulnerability
that suffering and healing are interwoven…it demonstrates a preparedness
and an ability to move between the worlds of the physical, the emotional,
the cognitive and the mystical without strain' (2012, p.35).

These elements of tenderness create an understanding of presence
that together with the possibility of 'presence as healing' contribute to
an understanding of Radical Presence as integrating Person-Centred
approaches with pastoral care and practical theology (cf. Chapter 1, section

'Pastoral care and counselling and psychotherapy and the community of faith' for a definition of practical theology).

It is important to state that Radical Presence is not dependent upon Christian understandings of personhood and care. However, for those of us who do come from a faith tradition it is worth noting that as the leading Person-Centred therapist and practical theologian, Schmid, argues, the Person-Centred approach and Christian practical theology are mutually challenging approaches that in practice share much in common. He suggests that they 'share the phenomenological contemporary stance, both approaches aiming at "becoming who you are", they both have a belief in a constructive principle instead of a dichotomy or dualism of "good" and "evil"' (2006, p.37). It is equally true that both the Person-Centred approach and pastoral care require person-to-person relationships. In this context, the theological approach evidenced in my research data incorporates an understanding of the Divine as relational, as a process of becoming in creation. Within the Christian tradition, the essence of being human is the relationship of God with humanity; what makes humans human is the response to that call into a relationship. In this sense, pastoral care as Radical Presence in the practice of a chaplain who is also a therapist is also about supporting patients and staff as they seek an understanding of this relationship, a relationship that both individually and socially embraces the whole of life and culture, including health and wellbeing. Similarly, while not making any explicit reference to the Divine, Rogers' (1980) understanding of the person incorporates personal autonomy and solidarity in relationship. Person-Centred personality and relationship theory understands personalization as a process of becoming independent *and* of developing relationships. My research suggests that for chaplains and others within multi-disciplinary teams who are also therapists, this close relationship between spiritual care and the Person-Centred approach can act as a resource for the development of the concept of Radical Presence as outlined above.

In summary, psycho-spiritual care as Radical Presence includes the following:

- an unconditional hospitality that is rooted in personal experience and empathic understanding

- the willingness to enter liminal places: 'holding' the risk of chaos and disintegration together with the possibility of change and transition

- psychologically informed spiritual and pastoral care that is orientated towards establishing I–Thou (Buber 1970) relationships

- a form of presence that is integrative and holistic, bringing together spiritual, pastoral, psychological and theological insights and qualities into relationships with patients and staff

- creation of the right conditions for growth (Rogers) so that recovery (healing and wholeness) may begin to take place.

The fact that some within the nursing, medical and therapy professions have recently been advocating the need to incorporate spiritual care within their practice also indicates that training is sorely needed if the gap between theory and practice is to be bridged. The experience of both developing and leading workshops and seminars together with the feedback from participants further suggests that there is considerable scope for the development of opportunities for personal learning and professional development. In a series of day workshops held over three consecutive years (2014–16) participants particularly expressed their desire to develop their own practice and understanding of the relationship between counselling and psychotherapy and spiritual care.

The comparatively recent upsurge in interest in spirituality and health care is further evidence of the interest in less mechanistic, prescriptive and pathologized approaches to practice. There is an urgent need to develop an evidence-based psycho-spiritual approach to health care where spiritual care is integral to person-centred care and where health care staff are resourced, both personally and professionally, to develop that care. In 2016 OCSW[1] was established to help meet this need and in doing so to support the bridging of the gap between theory and practice. OCSW seeks to:

- build a culture of care where people can feel safe to disclose their spiritual needs in confidence with the knowledge that health care providers will make every attempt to understand their beliefs, accommodate their values and facilitate their spiritual practice

- move from the bio-psycho-social model of care to a holistic model that recognizes people as whole persons with interrelated emotional, social, physical *and* spiritual needs

- address the question of what a holistic model of care would look like for patients and staff.

---

1. If you are interested in this work or would like to contribute to its development, further information can be found on the OCSW website at www.oxinahr.com/our-centres-and-groups/oxford-centre-for-spirituality-well-being-ocsw.

This book has argued that contemporary psycho-spiritual care is central to the future development of health care practice and that it has its own integrity within the daily attention to holistic patient care. It has also called for the ongoing development of research, education, training and support for the integration of psychologically informed spiritual care. The authors of Chapters 5 to 9 have illustrated a variety of approaches to psycho-spiritual care within their own practice and have shown just how important it is to integrate all aspects of care for the benefit of patients, carers *and* health care staff. It is clear that the generation of knowledge about the relationship between spiritual care and therapeutic practice within multi-disciplinary contexts is vital if the bridge between theory and practice is to continue to be bridged. This book is a contribution to that knowledge, and the reflections and ideas within it will, I hope, be further refined and developed over the coming years.

References

Buber, M. (1970) *I and Thou*. Translated by W. Kaufmann. New York: Charles Scribner's.

Bugenthal, J. (1987) *The Art of the Psychotherapist: How to Develop the Skills that Take Psychotherapy Beyond Science*. New York: Norton.

Finlay, L. and Evans, K. (2013) An Invitation to Engage in Relational-Centred Phenomenological Research. In P. Brownell and J. Melnick (eds) *The Challenge of Establishing a Research Tradition for Gestalt Therapy: The Research Conference 2013*. Charleston, SC: Create Space Publications.

Mearns, D. and Thorne, B. (1999) *Person-Centred Counselling in Action* (2nd edition). London: Sage.

Rogers, C. (1980) *A Way of Being*. Boston, MA: Houghton Mifflin.

Schmid, P. (2006) *In the Beginning there Is Community: Implications and Challenges of the Belief in a Triune God and a Person-Centred Approach*. Norwich Centre Occasional Publication. Norwich: Norwich Centre for Personal and Professional Development.

Thorne, B. (2012) *Counselling and Spiritual Accompaniment: Bridging Faith and Person-Centred Therapy*. Chichester: Wiley-Blackwell

Yontef, G. (1993) *Awareness, Dialogue and Process: Essays on Gestalt Therapy*. New York: The Gestalt Journal Press.

Subject Index

Author Index